Chile in Their Hearts

Chile in Their Hearts

THE UNTOLD STORY OF TWO AMERICANS
WHO WENT MISSING AFTER THE COUP

John Dinges

UNIVERSITY OF CALIFORNIA PRESS

University of California Press
Oakland, California

© 2025 by John Dinges

All rights reserved.

Cataloging-in-Publication data is on file at the Library of Congress.

ISBN 978-0-520-41318-4 (cloth)
ISBN 978-0-520-41319-1 (pbk.)
ISBN 978-0-520-41320-7 (ebook)

GPSR Authorized Representative: Easy Access System Europe,
Mustamäe tee 50, 10621 Tallinn, Estonia, gpsr.requests@easproject.com

34 33 32 31 30 29 28 27 26 25
10 9 8 7 6 5 4 3 2 1

To the Americans, from the North and the South, who came to Chile hoping for a better world. Our lives were forever changed.

Contents

		Introduction: Chile's Allure	1
PART I.		ROADS TO THE REVOLUTION	
	1.	Charlie and Joyce	13
	2.	Frank	24
	3.	Living the "Chilean Process"	36
	4.	New York	49
	5.	The Coup	56
	6.	Valparaiso	66
	7.	Vicuña Mackenna	71
PART II.		THE SEARCH	
	8.	Missing	81
	9.	The Embassy	95
	10.	Investigations	105
	11.	Distract and Deceive	110
	12.	Mr. Horman Goes to Chile	117
	13.	Disappeared in Plain Sight	127

PART III. UNRAVELING THE TRUTH

 14. The Making of "The Man Who Knew Too Much"   143

 15. How and Why   155

 16. Scenario for a Movie   167

 17. A Trial in Chile   179

PART IV. CONCLUSIONS

 18. The U.S. Role   195

 19. Leads Not Followed   205

Acknowledging a Legacy   219

Sources and Methods   223

Notes   239

Index   275

Photo essay follows page 126

Introduction

CHILE'S ALLURE

Chile was very much a crossroads for progressives from all over the world. It was a magnet.

MISHY LESSER, who arrived as a 19-year-old student in 1971

The North Americans who arrived in Chile in the early 1970s loved that the new Socialist president was committed to revolution and democracy. Salvador Allende had come to power in an indisputably fair election, lending him international credibility and confounding a hostile U.S. government. Hundreds of Americans came to experience the revolution. They described themselves as progressives and were inspired by Allende's plan to defeat poverty and restructure an unfair economy. In the excitement of the times, they didn't think they were in danger. After all, they had U.S. passports.

Among the arrivals were Charles Horman, a freelance journalist, and Frank Teruggi, a student, who made their ways to Chile separately in 1972, embarking on a grand adventure. Living there soon evolved into a serious political commitment. Then, in the first days of a violent military coup, they were picked up, executed, and their bodies thrown in the street. This is their story.

In the late '60s and early '70s, thousands of young people flocked to Chile, many of them as political refugees from countries such as Bolivia, Brazil and Uruguay, where dictators or rightwing governments had defeated leftist uprisings. Often fleeing imprisonment and torture, they were welcomed in Allende's Chile: given a haven, status as refugees and a new hope. Some of the Bolivians and Uruguayans had fought in guerrilla struggles in their own countries, inspired by Cuba and Che Guevara more than by Chile. They also supported Allende, but were skeptical of his democratic model, adhering to the Marxist premise that real revolution could be achieved only through armed struggle.

From 1970 to 1973 Chile radiated energy and light like the shining city on a hill of the Bible, visible from afar and irresistible to seekers of many stripes. Large numbers of Europeans arrived; there were even a few Vietnamese and Japanese. The international allies of the *proceso* were a diverse group, but tilted toward the intellectual: students, academics and professionals intending to lend their skills; journalists and political activists wondering if Chile's seeds of change would take root elsewhere in the region. Everyone seemed to have a project, at the core of which was to observe and to contribute. Being in Chile was to experience the most exciting political experiment in Latin America of the time, certainly since Fidel Castro's victory in Cuba in 1959.

The confluence of foreigners in solidarity with Chile was a singular moment with few precedents. They numbered at least 20,000. Later, after the outrage and bloodshed of the coup, it was easy to see an apt parallel in the International Brigades that fought to defend Spain's Republic during the Spanish Civil War. The fighters included 2,300 Americans organized in the legendary Abraham Lincoln Brigade. "Chile was the Spanish Civil War for our generation," said Dr. Patricia Fagen, a research fellow in a Santiago think tank. "People were invited to participate; it was very exciting. And for many of us, our lives were transformed by our time in Chile, and by the coup."[1]

In retrospect, Chile could easily be seen as another pitched battle of socialism vs. a new version of fascism. That experience had transformed Pablo Neruda, whose 1936 poem *Spain in Our Hearts* captured the horror of the outbreak of war in terms easily translated to Chile's coup:

> One morning everything was burning
> and one morning the fires
> were shooting out of the earth
> devouring what existed,
> and ever since then fire,

and gunpowder ever since,
and since then blood.
. . .
You will ask: why does your poetry
not speak to us of sleep, of the leaves,
of the great volcanoes of your native land?
Come and see the blood in the streets,
come and see
the blood in the streets,
come and see the blood
in the streets![2]

Neruda worked for years to raise money for Spain and brought hundreds of refugees to Chile after the war. He was a fierce supporter of the Popular Unity and an icon of its movement to reinvigorate cultural life, especially the reading of books and poetry. He died under still unresolved circumstances soon after the coup. His death and those of Horman and Teruggi were only a few days apart.

· · · · ·

South America in the 1970s, not unlike 1930s Europe, was one of the theaters of Great Power competition. The principal conflict during this era was the war in Vietnam, where the United States and the Soviet Union backed opposing armies in a deadly civil war that killed more than 58,000 U.S. soldiers and more than a million Vietnamese. After Allende's surprise electoral victory, Chile also was very much on the Cold War agenda of U.S. president Richard Nixon. His national security adviser Henry Kissinger, who was orchestrating U.S. strategy in Vietnam, considered Allende and his coalition of Communist and leftist parties even more dangerous to U.S. interests than the flareups of leftist guerrilla activity in other Latin American countries. Not only had Chile become an opening to Soviet and Cuban influence, but Kissinger feared the model of socialism and democracy would spread.

Most of the Americans who arrived in solidarity with Chile had been participants in the movement against the U.S. war in Vietnam, and their newfound political allegiance to the Chilean experiment further widened the political divide from their own government. They had brought from the United States a political vision forged in the civil rights and antiwar movements on U.S. campuses. To the extent they defined their politics, they tended to call themselves "radicals," or members of the New Left. Marxism and Communism were part of the conversation but not an alignment. They viewed the Nixon administration with anger as the Vietnam War dragged on despite years of protests. The year Allende was elected, 1970, was one of the darkest and most violent in the United States. A wave of protest bombings engulfed the country, including three in Des Moines, Iowa, where I was working as a journalist.[3] Protests exploded on more than 800 campuses after the U.S. launched an invasion of Cambodia. National Guard troops opened fire on protesters at Kent State University in Ohio. Four White students were killed there and several Black students elsewhere.[4] This followed official violence in Chicago, including the police raid in December 1969 on the apartment of Black Panther leader Fred Hampton, who was killed in his bed.

Elections in small South American countries are not usually big news in the United States, but this one seemed to be different. A story on Allende's victory ran high on the front page of the September 5, 1970, edition of the *Des Moines Tribune*. "Marxist Victor" was in the headline. Salvador Allende and his Popular Unity coalition had won a narrow plurality, and Allende was expected to be confirmed as president in a runoff vote in Chile's Congress.

Kissinger quickly signaled U.S. government hostility. In a briefing in Chicago with a group of Midwest newspaper reporters, he warned of grim consequences should Allende be confirmed. It would mean nothing less than a "Communist government" in a major Latin American country. "We should not delude ourselves," he said. "An Allende takeover in Chile would ... present massive problems for us, and for democratic forces and for pro-United States forces in Latin America and indeed to the whole Western Hemisphere."[5]

Kissinger's public comments did not do justice to the furious activity against Chile playing out behind the scenes in the White House. In secret meetings that came to light years later, Nixon and Kissinger ordered the CIA to prevent Allende from being inaugurated, using a "military solution" if necessary. When that failed, the U.S. government embarked on a

INTRODUCTION 5

well-financed covert campaign to ensure Allende's government could not succeed.[6]

U.S. military and CIA operatives maintained liaisons as military plotters against Allende gained strength, but avoided direct involvement. The CIA poured millions of dollars into opposition parties and their leading newspaper, *El Mercurio*, to support a propaganda campaign. On September 11, 1973, the Army commander General Augusto Pinochet, considered loyal up to that point, launched one of the bloodiest coups in Latin American history. The Air Force bombed the presidential palace, La Moneda, and troops sweeping into factory areas and squatter camps overwhelmed leftist resistance. By the end of the day, Allende was dead, the popular movement was destroyed and bodies began to appear in the Mapocho river running through Santiago.

The killings of Horman and Teruggi, which happened just days after, helped crystallize alarm about human rights violations in Chile. For the U.S. government, the coup was seen as a victory, and the killings as an unavoidable cost, as U.S. policy turned away from democracies to instead support the military regimes that came to rule most of South America.[7]

· · · · ·

The slain Americans were only two among the thousands of victims of the repression unleashed by Chile's new military regime. But their cases had outsize impact in the United States and focused attention on the U.S. government's enthusiastic defense of the regime even as bullet-riddled bodies lined the corridors of the Santiago morgue. A book on Horman's case and a 1983 movie, *Missing*, directed by Costa-Gavras, portrayed him as apolitical but "the man who knew too much," who had stumbled on information about direct U.S. involvement in the coup. The accounts endorsed the theory that U.S. Embassy officials approved of his killing and may have even caused his detention by the Chilean military.

We will see how this theory gained ample plausibility in the light of other U.S. efforts to subvert the Chilean experiment, but that it ultimately rested on the fabricated statements of a Chilean agent who later retracted his charges. Congressional investigations revealed a long playlist of CIA covert actions in the destabilization of Allende's leftist experiment.

Suspicion of U.S. complicity in the destruction of Chile's democracy was high. That U.S. collaboration with a brutal dictatorship extended to the targeted murder of an American citizen did not seem beyond the pale. Teruggi's killing, while separate and bearing no evident connection to Horman's, was conjoined in the popular perception to the charge that U.S. officials bore responsibility.

Support for the theory was understandable in the context of the coup. The elusive proof, it was said, was to be found in secret Embassy documents the U.S. government refused to release or declassified only partially. The dispute played out in two civil trials. In a 1979 lawsuit, the Horman family accused Henry Kissinger and a dozen other U.S. officials of involvement in Charles's death. Then, in the wake of the *Missing* movie—one of the most popular films of the year—the former U.S. ambassador to Chile and other former embassy officials brought a libel suit claiming that the book and movie had defamed them. Both suits ended with no resolution.

I began to investigate the case in the early 2000s. Tens of thousands of new U.S. documents about Chile's dictatorship had been declassified in a mass release, including a collection specifically tied to the Horman and Teruggi killings. At least some of the documents were widely quoted as appearing to support the accusation of U.S. involvement. I had long thought the movie's theory of the case was highly probable, and I set out to find the evidence to prove it. My motivation was partly personal. I had lived in Chile at the time of the coup, and for five years thereafter. I was a journalist, but I shared the enthusiasm for the Chilean experiment and was part of the informal community of pro-Allende foreigners. I was one of the few Americans to stay on after the coup. I got a job teaching English at the Catholic University and eventually landed jobs as a "stringer"—a regular freelancer—for *Time* magazine and the *Washington Post*, among other outlets. At first writing with a pseudonym for protection, I set out to document the regime's hidden world of prisons, disappearances and torture.

I knew many of the Americans in Chile, and was familiar with the publication *FIN*, put out by the group that included Horman and Teruggi. I had met Horman only once, in Mexico, but did not meet him again in Chile. I was friendly with Teruggi because we shared a class at the Catholic University. On September 10, the day before the coup, I saw Teruggi in the university courtyard, and we chatted about the rising tension, but were optimistic Allende could survive it. In the terrifying days and weeks after the coup, I learned that Frank had been executed and Charlie was missing. Chilean police had already twice raided my own house, where I lived with a group of foreigners and Chileans.

Those years were the most violent of the 17-year dictatorship. I reported extensively from Chile on the 1976 assassination in Washington, DC, of Orlando Letelier, Allende's former foreign minister and ambassador to the United States. An American women, Ronni Moffitt, riding with her husband in Letelier's car, was also killed—the third alleged American victim of the Chilean dictatorship. Having returned to Washington in 1978, I worked at the *Post* and wrote a book, with Letelier's colleague Saul Landau, about the car bombing and the ensuing FBI investigation.[8]

When *Missing* appeared, Landau and I wrote a review. We noted that the movie should not be confused with documentary truth: "Yet it does convey a powerful, and essentially accurate, image of the Chilean tragedy and of U.S. involvement. For those who were in Chile during the coup, the film is like a series of devastating flashbacks to real life, to real terror."[9]

I was writing from my personal experience in Chile, which was still fresh. When I embarked on investigating Horman and Teruggi's cases 20 years later, I hoped and expected that I would put to rest the most critical question: did the U.S. government participate in or approve the murder of two American citizens by its ally the Chilean military? I fully expected to prove the hypothesis in the affirmative. A vast array of new U.S. documents on Chile were declassified in 1999 and 2000, and some seemed to provide promising leads on the Horman-Teruggi cases. One State Department memo in particular has been frequently quoted in books and articles in support of the charge of U.S. involvement.[10] "There is some circumstantial evidence to suggest," the so-called Fimbres memo said, that "U.S. intelligence may have played an unfortunate part in Horman's death." Another set of documents showed that the FBI had conducted an investigation of Frank Teruggi's involvement with an antiwar group in Germany.[11]

Not only were the new U.S. documents available as a starting point, but a Chilean judge had opened a formal murder case investigating both Horman's and Teruggi's deaths. The verdict in 2016 also seemed to ratify the accusations against U.S. officials. I obtained exclusive access to the court's official record, including 17 volumes of evidence and filings. This book is based on a careful reading of that voluminous documentation and more than 100 interviews of the Chileans and Americans involved, including U.S. officials.

The evidence I found led me to conclusions I had not expected, especially about the U.S. role. The facts that came to light contradicted major elements of the widely-accepted view of Horman as the "man who knew too much" and who was killed with U.S. approval. A careful examination of U.S. documents and Chilean court records failed to show any U.S. involvement in the deaths of the two Americans. Far from exonerating the U.S. government, however, the evidence demonstrates definitively that the U.S. Embassy and State Department shielded the Pinochet regime by hiding the truth, conducting a sham investigation, and sanctioning Chile's official coverup of the murders.

I also endeavored to explore the rich personal stories of Charles Horman and Frank Teruggi and the ideological journeys they embarked on in Chile. The film *Missing* misleadingly portrayed Horman as apolitical, and coverage of the case of the two slain Americans largely overlooked Frank Teruggi. My investigation was focused on their political associations and actions that might be related to their death. In short: who were these two young Americans, how were they killed, and why?

This is the first full account of the personal and political journeys of Frank Teruggi and Charles Horman, two Americans from very different backgrounds whose curiosity and commitment led them to Chile. Their intended short sojourns lengthened into almost two years for Teruggi and 15 months for Horman as they came to love the country and its people and to immerse themselves in the history-making political drama in Chile. Their reaction to that drama, their decisions, their friendships, and their evolving careers converged in the tragedy of their deaths, and provide clues about what happened.

．　．　．　．　．

Why should we relitigate these events that occurred a half century ago? The short answer is that history deserves the truth, especially regarding key moments in U.S. government actions that paved the way for anti-

Communist dictatorships and changed the lives of millions of people. From a moral and historical point of view, the United States bears indisputable responsibility for enabling the Pinochet dictatorship and supporting it regardless of the massive human rights crimes it committed. Yet an argument from outrage should not mislead us into an assumption of U.S. officials' guilt in the executions of the two leftist Americans. In a serious investigation, a dispositive showing of evidence is necessary to resolve the key questions one way or the other. That is the challenge I have taken up in this book.

It would be preferable if the U.S. government would allow alleged crimes and abuses involving U.S. officials to be fully investigated by officially sanctioned bodies, such as a truth and reconciliation commission similar to those created by South Africa, Chile and Argentina. I am not alone in advocating for such an impartial examination, even after so many years. In fact, the United States has never convened such an official investigation of U.S. actions in the dark period of the 1970s and 1980s in South and Central America. Nor did the Department of Justice ever assign the FBI to conduct any investigation of the deaths of Horman and Teruggi, despite the assigning of such resources in other cases of Americans killed abroad.[12] Consequently, journalistic investigations such as this book and the work of other private researchers are virtually the only path to establish an accurate account of what happened. A journalistic investigation like this one may lack the unlimited resources and authority to compel testimony deployed by official probes, but it is able to arrive at a much more accurate picture of what happened than was previously available.

It is my conviction that demonstrably erroneous portrayals of past events should not be allowed to stand because they fit a political narrative. And they should be corrected as soon as possible in order to avoid their repetition in otherwise credible literature. A good number of books and articles in the voluminous literature on Chile mention the Horman and Teruggi cases, often repeating some version of the theory that Horman was killed with U.S. involvement because he "knew too much." Newspaper, magazine and broadcast stories are even more likely to repeat the erroneous portrayals. It must be said that the U.S. government's 24-year delay in declassifying key information allowed evidence to grow cold, memories to fade and witnesses to die. The Chilean perpetrators named in this book could have been brought to trial in the 1990s when Chile's democracy was restored. Nevertheless, the conclusions presented here, based on the best practices of investigative journalism, offer the measure of justice that revealing the truth can bring, even if convictions and punishment will not be possible.

Because those conclusions require a reevaluation of what we thought we knew about this famous case, it is doubly important to be transparent about my methods and meticulously document my findings. All major statements of fact are documented, and detailed sourcing is described in footnotes and endnotes. A description of the documentation used, a review of existing literature on the Horman-Teruggi case, a list of interviews and an explanation of my investigative methods is provided in "Sources and Methods" at the end of the book.

PART I Roads to the Revolution

I really was upset by the way Charlie was portrayed in the movie. They didn't have the courage to portray him as he really was.

RICHARD PEARCE, Charles Horman's filmmaker friend

Down here everyone acts just like Marx and Lenin said they would. . . . Everyone is politicized along class lines and follows the whole script just like they'd been rehearsing since 1848.

CHARLES HORMAN in a letter from Chile, 1973

In Chile we either build socialism or there will be a military dictatorship.

FRANK TERUGGI in a letter to his family, 1973

1 Charlie and Joyce

Charles Edmund Horman had just turned 30, a little older than the others who had gathered in Chile and already with a taste of professional life. He was born in Manhattan to a well-off family that mostly voted Republican. He grew up in comfort but pursued a career in journalism and film that increasingly positioned him on the side of the poor and underprivileged. His early path led seamlessly from the Upper East Side, to preparatory school at Phillips Exeter, to Harvard University. He had a "somewhat gentle manner," a friend said, but behind the shy exterior abided a probing, restless intellect that toggled between observation and activism. He was about five feet ten, always very slim and erect and had an easy smile under his dark eyes and sandy hair, which he wore long after his stint in the military. He got top grades, joined the drama club, was active in the Christian Science organization on the Harvard campus, and won a prize for creative writing. He also liked to hang out in pool halls and had a reputation as a run-the-table billiards ace.[1]

"Charlie" to his friends, he alternated between ivory-tower reflections and an activist pursuit of adventure and risks. His Harvard years, 1960–1964, spanned the explosion in White consciousness in support of the Civil Rights Movement. Newspapers covered the fearsome journeys of

13

Freedom Riders defying segregation in the Jim Crow South. The images of burning buses and battered faces of protesters awakened consciences on university campuses in the North. During summer break in August of 1963, Horman found himself in Plaquemines Parish, Louisiana, a Mississippi River community just south of New Orleans. He was in the vanguard of a movement of White students to help register Black voters.

There had been a protest in the town the day before, he wrote: "The jails were full and the state troopers were loading them into school buses and taking them to the fair ground just outside of town. The streets were full of troopers. Most of them were on horses, clopping down the sidewalk with white riot helmets and cattle prods. I had never seen police use cattle prods before."

Charlie and his friend Frank, a Black Louisianan, ducked into a bar for beers. Charlie played pool with some local farmers and won a few bucks, he said, recounting the incident later. The two then took their beers out into the street to look around; they were quickly stopped by troopers and taken to jail.

"Well, we got one local boy and a northern feller here," the sheriff said. "You boys picked a funny time to come through town." He reminded them that drinking in the streets was illegal in his town. A deputy demanded to know what degree Charlie was aiming for in college, since he wasn't in the Army. "I think he's aiming for the third degree," the sheriff said, using a slang term for brutal police interrogation. "The deputies laughed. Then they took us back into the corridor which led to the jail and beat us for an hour," he wrote. When they were released they got in their car and drove north. They met other activists doing similar work in Albany, Georgia, also the scene of a recent repression of civil rights workers. From there the group drove to Washington, DC, where they joined hundreds of thousands of people in what was then the largest civil rights protest in history, the March on Washington on August 28.[2]

Horman's writing about the incident is almost jocular, downplaying the police violence that was often lethal in the Jim Crow era. The following summer hundreds of middle-class volunteers converged on the Deep South to train in nonviolent tactics in a more massive voter registration project. Three young volunteers, two White and one Black, were stopped on June 21, 1964, by police outside Philadelphia, Mississippi, and disappeared. Their brutalized bodies were found weeks later.

Horman graduated summa cum laude from Harvard, with Phi Beta Kappa honors. U.S. involvement in the Vietnam War was in its early stages, but all young men were subject to being drafted into military service. To fulfill the draft obligation Horman served for six months in the Air National Guard. It was light duty in an era before the massive call-ups of draftees to serve in the Vietnam War, which would claim more than 58,000 American lives in addition to over 1 million Vietnamese before it ended. The civil rights struggle, not yet the war, was the cause inspiring a rapidly growing movement of progressive young people, especially on college campuses.

On his release from the Guard Horman chanced into a life-changing opportunity that took him to a real job in journalism on the opposite coast. He was recruited, along with a small group of Ivy League grads, to join the expanding and freewheeling staff of King Broadcasting, an early television powerhouse with stations in Seattle, Spokane and Portland. King's owner, Stimson Bullitt, was a blueblood millionaire with a contrarian streak that translated into programming that was often antiestablishment and increasingly antiwar. Bullitt was building a team of talented young men to do socially provocative documentaries. One of these, *The Redwoods*, directed by Mark Harris, had already won an Oscar. For Charlie Horman it was a gateway to real writing, real investigation and good prospects for a career in the booming new industry of broadcast journalism.[3]

Harris, who had graduated from Harvard a year ahead of Charlie, became a friend and mentor, along with Don Lenzer, Richard Pearce and Trevor Greenwood, all experienced filmmakers whose friendship would frame Horman's professional life in coming years. Horman was brought on as a writer for the half-hour documentary *Napalm*, directed by Lenzer and Greenwood. It was the story of people in a California city protesting the presence of a plant producing napalm for the Vietnam War. He worked on another documentary on the Black community in Portland. Sometimes the documentaries were too gritty, too political for some of the stations to put on the air. "The project never made money for King, but it launched a lot of careers," according to Harris.

Harris remembers Horman as an observer, almost shy, staying on the margins of the action. "He was not a revolutionary, you can see that in his writing. There was definitely a naivete about him. I think he saw going to Chile was a way to find himself," Harris commented.[4] In mid-1967, a year the country was roiling in protests and urban rioting, Horman left Portland, the first of the King TV group to go back to New York. The circle of friends, all left-wing but rising in filmmaking, kept in touch with Horman in the fluid East Coast–West Coast media world. The television documentary work qualified him for a job at WNET, New York's educational station, which in the days before the creation of PBS was public television's principal source of national programming. It lasted only a year.

He kept up a prolific correspondence with friends, often expressing his yearning for reading and his passion to discuss what he had read. In a tangent in a discourse about politics, he tells a friend he just wants "a nice ivory tower" where he can read and write letters. To Lenzer he writes, "I'm rediscovering fiction. So I've been rereading some of the classics like *Slaughterhouse 5*, *The Brothers Karamazov*, Freud, the Bible, and Karl Marx." He writes that he spent a long night looking for a quote from Tolstoy. It fit his mood: "We imagine that as soon as we are thrown out of our customary ruts all is over, but it is only then that the new and good begins. While there is life there is happiness. There is a great deal, a great deal before us."[5]

He had moved in with his parents in their apartment on East 76th St. and quickly reconnected with a young woman he had met during a summer trip to France soon after graduation from Harvard. Joyce Hamren had graduated from the University of Minnesota and was working in New York. He invited her to the apartment to meet his parents, Edmund and Elizabeth. In June 1968, Joyce and Charlie married. There was a church wedding in her hometown of Owatonna, just south of Minneapolis, where her father owned the Superfair grocery store. They took a nice apartment on West 75th St. back in Manhattan. Joyce had become a computer programmer and systems analyst, a good job that positioned her on the cusp of new technology and a promising career. The young couple seemed settled, but Horman, as always, was restive.

Like many of his contemporaries, Horman was becoming deeply angry about the Vietnam War and the polarized Civil Rights Movement. In the year of his marriage the country seemed to be falling apart. Martin Luther King, Jr., and Bobby Kennedy had been assassinated. Horman traveled to

Chicago in August to protest at the chaotic Democratic National Convention. In his private writing, he describes running from the police, taking shelter in a house and watching through a window as police beat a man senseless over the roof of a car. Some weeks later he freelanced a piece for *The Nation*, giving his eyewitness account of the fighting between police and demonstrators. He attests to the events as a journalist, not necessarily as a participant, although clearly his sympathies were with the protesters.

"Because I was there, I know the attack was unprovoked," he writes about the infamous moment when police charged demonstrators in Chicago's Grant Park. At another confrontation, he vividly describes a scene of mayhem.

> I rushed to the side behind the police barricade where the crowd was jammed so tight it was impossible to move anything but my head.... I heard the plate-glass windows in the Hilton [Hotel] begin to creak. Then they shattered and someone cried out in pain.... A girl in front of me was clubbed. Blood sprayed over her blond hair and green V-neck sweater. She fell down and I couldn't see her anymore.[6]

The Chicago convention polarized not only the country but the antiwar movement itself. More and more activists saw the police attacks as reason to abandon the nonviolent tactics of the past and turn to the rhetoric of Marxist revolution. It was around this time, according to later revelations, that the FBI began systematic surveillance of "New Left" organizations. President Johnson, repudiated by many in his own party, ordered FBI Director J. Edgar Hoover to spy on leftists at home and abroad in an ultimately unsuccessful attempt to prove the antiwar movement was the creature of foreign actors, in particular the Soviet Union. Communist Party members had been under surveillance for decades, but now student and antiwar leaders became targets of the FBI's COINTELPRO and a CIA surveillance operation code-named CHAOS.[7] Many of those who went to Chile mentioned the Chicago rioting as one of the dark moments that caused them to look outside the country for a path to a more just society.

Horman's political evolution was still more liberal than radical. He had chosen a career as a writer and, if anything, wanted to effect change from within. "Charlie had an acute moral compass," said Don Lenzer, his filmmaker friend who had also moved back to New York. "I am reminded how searching he was, how curious he was. He vacillated a lot, but his focus was on doing meaningful things that will make people's lives better." He wrote frequently for publications like *The Nation*, the liberal Catholic publication *Commonweal* and the *Christian Science Monitor*, a national newspaper that despite its religious name was a respected voice on national and foreign affairs. But freelancing on political and cultural topics was poorly paid, so Horman looked again for a staff job. Between his father's conservative bona fides and his Harvard degree, he was able to be hired at the unquestionably establishment *Innovation*, an organ read in high-end finance and business circles. Horman was lefty enough, however, to see his new job as a project to move a conventional publication in a progressive direction. In a letter, he jokingly described it as his effort "to fuck up a small business magazine ... and why I failed so completely." In the letter he describes going to a meeting of the so-called "Media Project"—an effort by the "Movement" activists to organize people with established jobs in the media. In the unsettled spirit of the time, many felt isolated in their work, "deeply sympathetic with the Movement but incapable of finding ways by themselves of merging their working life and their impulse toward social change." There were journalists from major institutions—*Look*, *Life* and the *Wall Street Journal*, among others. Lenzer had been working for an offshoot of the newly formed PBS and had helped organize the Association of Public Television Producers aimed at protecting the congressionally funded network from government censorship. Horman wrote about the effort in a magazine piece. The association consisted of progressive journalists who had been "flying to Appalachia, Mississippi, and the universities to record the discords associated with social change." He noted a certain irony that "the men who filmed organizers have become organizers themselves."[8]

Horman seemed to be describing his own internal dilemma between activism and observation. So was Lenzer, who was fired by his PBS unit. Horman found that organizing journalists was frustrating, because "people in the Media were tremendously frightened of being manipulated or used as mouthpieces by some of the tough radicals." Whatever Horman did at *Innovation* to further his inchoate activist agenda, he does not say. But it was a flop. "We got creamed," he wrote. "It fell apart completely. After the last fight, I just fell out of the movement and I'm not sure how to get back in."[9]

In writings sent to Harris as these events were unfolding, Horman was self-deprecating about his indecision and lack of professional direction: "I suffered ... from the disability of abstract thought, in which events become arguments so quickly that they don't have time to lodge in the gut." The business magazine job was well paid, but when he and Joyce had accumulated some money in the bank they began to plan a new odyssey. It was to be a kind of grand tour of Latin America. Chile was at first just a glimmer in their aspirations, but soon became the main focus. Joyce describes it as a trip in a camper down the Pan American Highway on South America's west coast. She brought her skis. With seasons reversed, Chile's Portillo ski resort in the Andes offered great snow and Olympic-quality slopes in June, July and August, the Southern Hemisphere winter. "Allende had been elected and Charles was very interested in this and in Allende's goal of a peaceful transition to a more socialist democracy. He was looking forward to writing about this extraordinary political development from the inside."[10]

On visits to the West Coast in early 1971, Joyce and Charlie got to know a young Chilean filmmaker. Pablo de la Barra was a grad student at Berkeley and perhaps the first person from the remote country they had encountered. De la Barra told the Hormans about the "revolution in liberty" going on in his home country and planted the idea that they should go to South America to see for themselves. De la Barra would be returning to his country soon and promised to introduce Horman to the vibrant filmmaking scene in Chile, as well as to its revolution.[11]

The journey began in Owatonna. They had quit their jobs in New York and decamped to Joyce's hometown to spend Christmas 1970 with Joyce's family. The general goal was South America, but they weren't in a hurry. They bought a used 1968 Chevy pickup and outfitted it as a camper. There was room for the skis, photographic equipment and lots of books. In late January they packed up and started off going south through Iowa, hitting a blizzard that almost made them turn back. Near Des Moines they got on Interstate 80 and drove west, crossing Wyoming and Nevada and arriving in San Francisco two weeks later. The pace from there was even more leisurely. They bunked with friends for several weeks, then drove the length of California toward Mexico. A month later they had just reached Mexico City, where Charlie wrote to Lenzer:

All of March we sat on the beach in Mazatlán, San Blas, and a few days at Puerto Vallarta. We swam a lot, read, walked, met hundreds of people, both Mexican and American, and watched palm trees sway. We're going to spend a couple of months—if we like it—in Cuernavaca. We want to take Spanish at Ivan Illich's school and I want a library. . . . I don't know whether we'll get to South America this time.[12]

It was a time of "deep peace and great intellectual excitement . . . easily the happiest time of my life." On the road he had been "getting into the classics . . . Marx, Engels, Trotsky, Rosa Luxembourg, some studies on industrial democracy. I've been doing notes on a super-inclusive theory about mass media and social movements." In Cuernavaca they discovered a progressive paradise that was also a staging area for the dozens of American lefties heading for Chile. The language courses, using textbooks developed for training State Department diplomats, were effective and immensely popular. The course fees paid by the young gringos financed the main attraction, the Intercultural Documentation Center, known by its Spanish acronym, CIDOC. The Center had been created by Ivan Illich as a free university and radical think tank. Illich, a freethinking philosopher, priest and social critic, had made CIDOC into a counterculture Mecca. Horman was in his element.

So was I. I had quit my job as a police reporter for the *Des Moines Tribune* with the idea of becoming a foreign correspondent in Chile, easily the most interesting story in Latin America. My plan was to spend a year seriously studying the region at Stanford University, which had a unique master's program in Latin American Studies. I had been to Mexico several times before, but Cuernavaca seemed the ideal environment to improve my Spanish and make contacts. I paid almost nothing for a bunk in an old convent with several dozen men and women, living communally and sharing cooking and cleaning duties. After class, students lounged on the shady grounds of CIDOC's villa to listen to talks by Illich and luminaries ranging from writer Susan Sontag to Brazilian education reformer and visionary Paulo Freire and a variety of lesser-known speakers.[13] The sessions were seldom ideological but always deeply challenging to conventional social and economic systems. It was freethinking in a genuinely democratic sense.

I remember being introduced to Charlie and Joyce and having a brief conversation beside their vehicle about our common destination. They had been there for several months. Cuernavaca was a movable feast. Horman's friend from King TV, Dick Pearce, spent several weeks there before heading to Chile to make a film. Pearce and Horman became fast friends with Milton Jamail, a Mexican American graduate student and sometime professor who was a fixture at CIDOC. Horman described Jamail affectionately to Lenzer as "clearly the heaviest lurk and raunchiest dude who ever blew out of Texas." Several people the Hormans met in Cuernavaca would later become part of their circle of friends in Chile.[14]

One was Mishy Lesser, a 19-year-old student at Friends World College, a progressive Quaker institution that had a program in Cuernavaca. Lesser had been politically active since junior high school in Plainview, New York, and the Kent State killings strengthened her resolve. The killings had become a local story because Jeffrey Miller, one of the students shot on the campus by the National Guard on May 4, 1970, had graduated from a high school in her town. A senior, she spent the final weeks of school in teach-ins and protests over the Vietnam War and the killings. Once in Cuernavaca, Latin America became her classroom, which helped her answer the question: why do so many people in the world hate my country? At CIDOC, she heard an inspiring lecture by a Chilean lawyer about Allende and his Unidad Popular (UP, Popular Unity) government.

"My eyes popped open and all I wanted to do was go to Chile," she said. "As soon as I heard that a socialist had been elected president of Chile through democratic means and that his agenda was one of social justice, I was like, how do I get there?" She found a way. She convinced Jamail, one of her professors, to let her travel with him overland to Chile. Arriving in May 1971, the middle of Allende's first year, she decided to stay, putting down what she called "tentpoles." Her education for the next two years was not in classrooms, but in the exhilaration of Chile's politics "unfolding in the public square and in the streets, and in the communities of the urban poor."

Jamail could only stay a month. He returned bursting with excitement and hope and relayed his experience in Chile to the Hormans. They had been undecided about continuing south, but getting Jamail's eyewitness account sealed the decision. The destination now was definitely Chile—or as Jamail put it, "Their plan was to get to the end of South America."[15]

. . . . .

The Hormans' route was circuitous and their ambivalence persisted, but in good humor. Instead of heading directly from Mexico to Chile, the Hormans returned to San Francisco for several months, staying with their friend Janet Duecy, who would join them in Chile. "Our plans indefinite," Horman wrote to Lenzer in July. They would stay on the West Coast for the summer. "Then in the fall, maybe around November we may have another shot at Chile. We don't know if we'll try it thumbing, shipping or driving. Or at all. . . . Things have to become clear soon, don't they. Sure they do. Right on. That's the spirit." They threw a raucous going-away party for Pablo de la Barra, who had finished his degree in film studies and had ambitious plans to produce a feature movie in Chile.[16]

Horman's hesitation wasn't political. His voracious reading, as recounted in letters, showed his steady evolution to the left. Building on Marx, a constant in his eclectic reading lists, he added Henry Miller, neo-Marxian economist Paul Sweezy, *Ramparts* magazine, Jewish writer Michael Lerner and Isaac Deutscher's biography of Leon Trotsky. He was trying to understand the paroxysms of violence that had enveloped the left in the previous year, the riots on hundreds of campuses, the Kent State killings and the bombings perpetrated by the now-underground SDS Weathermen faction. Putting it all together, he commented to his friend that Trotsky, the grand theoretician of the Russian Revolution, was changing "my whole sense of what a revolution is—and it certainly is more difficult than what I thought and way, way different from what's been going on here [in the United States] for the last couple of years."[17]

Finally, in late November, the Hormans pointed the Chevy truck due south. They crossed the border at Tucson, destination Chile. "We will give your best to Salvador Allende and anyone else we meet in the bush," Horman wrote in his final letter posted from the United States. It was the grand adventure they had embarked on ten months before, and they wanted to enjoy it all. They spent a week on the gorgeous beaches of

Zihuatanejo in Mexico and got a ride on a DC3 for an excursion to the jungle ruins of the Maya city of Tikal in Guatemala. They swam in Lake Atitlán, a magical place. It is said the Mayas—before they were conquered by the Spaniards—would row out in boats and throw gold figurines over the side, returning their riches to the gods.

Predictably, the truck broke down in Panama. They sold it, then flew to Colombia to avoid the impassable Darién Gap. Traveling overland again, they took buses through Ecuador and Peru. Weeks passed. They hiked in the high Andes to visit the majestic Inca city of Machu Pichu, at 2,400 meters (7,875 feet) overlooking the immense Amazon basin. Charlie turned 30 years old in Lima. His reading had expanded to Spanish translations of "schlock novels" such as *Valley of the Dolls*. He spoke Spanish well enough now to exchange stories with the truck drivers they occasional hitchhiked with.

In early June, they crossed the border into Chile, at the city of Arica at the northern edge of the Atacama Desert. On June 19, he writes: "How incredible! After several years of thinking, willing, rushing, philosophizing, and theosophizing we're in Santiago, Chile. I think we'll be staying here a while. Sometime between 3 months and ten years, depending on conditions."[18] The trip that began in Minnesota in a Chevy pickup camper had finally ended 18 months later with a long bus ride through the world's driest desert. Chile was now their new home.

2   Frank

Frank Teruggi's path to Chile was more direct, and he exhibited little of Horman's tendency toward second thoughts. His reasons for wanting to see the revolution were unabashedly ideological, even as the ideas that drove him were a confluence of Catholic as well as Marxist doctrines.[19]

Teruggi was also younger, barely 22 when he arrived. He hadn't waited to finish college before he headed for Chile. Born in 1949, he was raised by working-class parents determined to give him the higher education they did not have. His roots were Italian American and midwestern. He grew up in the Chicago suburb of Des Plaines, Illinois, where factory workers owned their own houses and sent their kids to Catholic school. His father, Frank Sr., was a typesetter whose dedication to the International Typographical Union was only slightly less fervent than his devotion to his family and the Catholic Church. His mother Johanna, "Jennie," did not go to high school and had worked factory jobs. His grandfathers on both sides immigrated in the early 1900s and worked in coal mines. Frank was close to his younger brother John and especially to his sister, Janis, with whom he maintained a vibrant correspondence on politics.

His Catholic education began in a tuition-free parish school followed by a scholarship to attend the academically rigorous Notre Dame High

School for Boys in a neighboring town. The nuns and priests pushed books and Catholic values, and imbued him with the instinct to always side with the underdog. Slender, and about five foot six, he eschewed athletics in favor of brainier pursuits like building his own ham radio shortwave radio set. At Notre Dame, he excelled in sciences and graduated with honors. It was there he was exposed to the radical side of his religion and learned about Chile. Notre Dame was run by the Fathers of the Holy Cross, a missionary and teaching order that—in addition to founding the University of Notre Dame—had been sending priests to Chile since the 1940s to staff an elite boys' school in Santiago, St. George's College.[20] But perhaps more important for his future in Chile, the priests talked about new ideas emerging from the Second Vatican Council, which challenged Catholics to have a "preferential option for the poor." Bishops in Latin America had begun to speak out and organize on behalf of the oppressed in the region, and Chile's Church was among the most progressive. The radical trend was soon given the name "liberation theology" and its advocates used terminology that reflected the critiques of capitalism and class oppression found in Marxism. "I think that was the beginning of his interest in Latin America," his sister said.[21]

The religious instincts he acquired in his family and early education led to more radical political activities in college. His grades and interest in science got him a full scholarship at California Institute of Technology, CalTech, reputed to be the "MIT of the West." He entered college in 1967, just as a nationwide antiwar movement was spreading from campus to campus. Teruggi was a founder of the CalTech chapter of Students for a Democratic Society (SDS). With other students from his religious studies course, he picketed the appearance of Dow Chemical recruiters on campus and was pictured in an article in the *Pasadena Star-News*.[22] But CalTech was not a good fit for Teruggi's growing interest in politics and social justice.

Over the summer, he joined an antiwar group back home in Des Plaines called Rapid Transit Guerrilla Communications. He marched for Hiroshima Day, with gruesome makeup depicting himself as a nuclear bomb victim. He was in the streets protesting during the Democratic National Convention in Chicago, then shortly after was arrested during a "guerrilla theater" performance against police brutality. Transferring in the fall to the University of California, Santa Barbara, he roomed off campus with an economics graduate student, Michael Couzens, who remembered him as an avid listener and an intense questioner: "He was especially interested in topics from my background in economics, and in social sciences generally. This was an intense period, immediately after the assassination of Martin Luther King, Jr., and Robert Kennedy, and many students were passionate in opposition to the Viet Nam War. Frank and I talked about everything—about elections, organizing, protesting, models of economic development—and above all how to stop the war."[23]

Couzens influenced Teruggi to pursue economics as a major, and he changed schools once again, enrolling at UC Berkeley in the fall of 1969. There he began volunteering at the leftist magazine *NACLA Report on the Americas*. That year, NACLA writers had begun to shine special focus on political change in Chile and the rise of Salvador Allende. In the wake of President Richard Nixon's election, it was also among the first publications to document U.S. government opposition to Allende and to leftist movements in Latin America. Another major story covered in NACLA was Uruguay and the Tupamaros Movement for National Liberation, whose militants styled themselves as Robin Hood guerrillas who minimized violence while robbing banks and turning the booty over to the poor.

Impatient to see the revolutions for himself, Frank finished his third year of college and returned to Chicago to earn money for a trip to Latin America. He got a union job at the Post Office and a place to live in a Hispanic neighborhood where he could practice his Spanish. He worked hard, read political literature on his own and doubled down on activism. His reading ranged from peace studies to liberation theology to forays into serious Marxism.

Frank worked in a new organization called CAGLA, the Chicago Area Group on Latin America, supported by the United Methodist seminary. With a new political friend, Roger Burbach, he helped organize meetings in Chicago and Colorado of antiwar Peace Corps volunteers who had returned from their service abroad and wanted to support Third World social movements. Frank attended as the CAGLA representative. Another friend was Shepherd Bliss, a seminarian who would also go to Chile. "Frank was a brother to me," Bliss said. "He had a great mind and was always helping people, which was why he wanted to travel to Chile. He was very interested in the process going on in that country, where [we thought] they were carrying out work with peasants and workers according to the ideas of Pope John XXIII and the Second Vatican Council."

Some of the organizing targeted draftees in the Army. Andy Scott Berman, a radicalized former volunteer, planned to joined the Army to continue antiwar activities from within. He met Frank at the Committee of Returned Volunteers office in Chicago and told him of his plan to join the Army and organize resistance. It was a connection that would have a major impact. "In early 1971, I left CRV and enlisted in the US Army, for the purpose of pursuing antiwar activities from within," he said. "There was a fair amount of spontaneous, sporadic, antiwar activity going on in the military at the time, and it looked like it just might be the key to actually ending the damn war. So in my youthful bravado, I decided to try 'organizing inside.'"

Bliss was from a famous military family and was also a veteran. Recently released from the Army, he recounted that his own disillusionment with the military began when he met young antiwar activists at coffee houses outside his base at Ft. Riley, Kansas. "They fed us better food than the military, and there were girls there our age. So, I mean, there was a real innocence." A similar antiwar coffeehouse for soldiers was operating in Chicago, he said.

It was an increasingly effective tactic. In early 1972 Berman, who had been commissioned a lieutenant, was stationed at a U.S. base near Heidelberg, Germany, and quickly made contact with people in the resistance movement. He called Max Watts, a Austrian gadfly of several adopted nationalities who had created a kind of underground railroad for GI would-be deserters. Watts, Berman said, had organized "an eclectic collection of antiwar folks, American, German and other nationalities, soldiers and civilians, students and wanderers." They helped AWOL soldiers get to France, and gave them housing and legal assistance. One of the names for the activity was RITA—Resistance in the Armed Forces. Their newsletter was called *FighT bAck*. The soldiers got the joke: the letters FTA were Army slang for "Fuck the Army."

Berman kept in touch by letter after Teruggi traveled to Chile, and sent copies of the RITA newsletters to his new address in Santiago. Activist students in Germany were also interested in the Allende experiment, and

Berman passed on Teruggi's address to several people. "To the best of my knowledge, Frank was living and working quite openly in Allende's Chile, so I would not have treated his address as a secret."[24]

What Teruggi did not know and Berman did not find out until years later was that U.S. Army intelligence was closely monitoring RITA activity, with the assistance of German intelligence, the Bundesnachrichtendienst. The BND was tapping the phones and opening the mail of Berman and his colleagues. As a result, the FBI opened an investigation in July 1972 with the ominous heading "Frank Teruggi, SM Sub," which was FBI code for "Security Matter Subversive," indicating Teruggi was suspected of connections to possible subversive activity. The term at the time encompassed a wide range of activity, including antiwar and civil rights activity.[25] Agents in Chicago reported on Teruggi's connection to CAGLA and a related group, the North American Anti-Imperialist Coalition (NAAIC). The documents of that FBI investigation contain Teruggi's address in Chile and were kept secret for 26 years after Teruggi's murder.[26]

By the end of 1971, Teruggi had saved over $1,000 from his jobs, just enough, he thought, to get to Chile and maintain himself while he completed one or two more semesters in economics. The biggest expense was the airline ticket, so he bought the cheapest one possible: Miami to Bogotá, Colombia. With minimal baggage and a few books in a backpack, he hitchhiked from Chicago to Miami. Arriving in Bogotá, he took buses to complete the journey through Ecuador and Peru, finally crossing the border into Chile and arriving in Santiago on January 14, 1972.

He quickly wrote an ebullient collective letter to ten of his CAGLA friends: "Arrived 7:30 am this morning. Now 1:30 pm after lunch sitting in hotel on the Alameda [Chile's main avenue] . . . listening to real jazz on Chilean radio—John Coltrane's love supreme FM loafing along at the speed of life (PRAISE GOD!)."[27]

Teruggi's friend from Chicago, Shepherd Bliss, had traveled to Chile several months earlier and was staying with Holy Cross priests while he researched Chile as a case study in nonviolent tactics. Bliss had headed back home only two weeks before, but had given Teruggi a short list of other contacts in Chile. Teruggi called Mishy Lesser, who was happy to help him get settled. Money was not much of a problem, he told his sister, because the black market exchange rate for the dollar made things incredibly cheap.

Lesser, an early arrival, had an apartment on Lastarria Street in central Santiago near the Catholic University and offered to let Teruggi stay there with other roommates for a while. More and more foreigners were arriving, she said. "Chile was very much a crossroads for progressives from all over the world. It was a magnet for young people and activist academics and, you know, historians and politicians and of course, exiles who were being drawn to Chile because of the hopefulness and also as the place of refuge."[28]

．　．　．　．　．

After a few days in his friend's apartment, Teruggi headed south for his next adventure. January was summer in the southern hemisphere, and in Allende's Chile that meant *trabajo voluntario*—joining the voluntary work brigades in the countryside to support the UP's agrarian reform program that had already put land in the hands of hundreds of thousands of peasant workers, in direct ownership or cooperatives.

Frank quickly hooked up with the student organization Frente de Estudiantes Revolucionarios (FER, Revolutionary Students Front). By the end of January he was on a large farm, called a *fundo*, near the southern town of Nancagua. The farm was still privately owned but had been targeted for expropriation. Frank's group of about a dozen students and several Brazilian exiles helped with some of the farm work but saw their primary role as recruiting workers for the peasant workers campaign.

"We're here at the invitation of the Revolutionary Campesino Movement (MCR)," he wrote to his sister Janis. "Our job is alphabetization (literacy training), teaching math, conducting political education classes, giving basic instruction on self-defense and military training. Our goal is to create new chapters of MCR in the month and a half we're here."

The MCR plan was to lobby the government to expropriate the farm, and if that didn't happen, he wrote, "We're helping the campesinos prepare to seize the *fundos* themselves." Part of the routine was for each member to stand guard. "We post a guard outside at night and have a gun or two just in case," he wrote, adding that one of his shifts was at 3:00 a.m.

A photo shows a joyous Frank, his fist in the air, standing in front of the farm gate, his arm around the shoulders of Brazilian Carlos Beust. Also in the picture is Jorge Alberto Basso, the encampment's "comandante," and Basso's girlfriend Paulina Vidal. All became close friends and political comrades. All were members of the far left political party the Movimiento Izquierda Revolucionaria (MIR, Movement of the Revolutionary Left).[29]

Teruggi was immersing himself in the mass mobilization of farmers and workers unleashed by Allende's Popular Unity coalition, in power for just over a year at that point. The new government's programs and promises were attracting mass support and in the early months all seemed to be on the right track. Allende left no doubt about his commitment to democracy. Though he had long called himself a Marxist, now in power he bent the ideology to show there would be no dictatorship of the proletariat, but—on the contrary—that Chile's strong social and political institutions would be brought to bear to introduce a "socialist path" to development. In his inaugural address, he paraphrased Friedrich Engels to, in effect, refute the Leninist doctrine that only violence could bring revolution. "Peaceful evolution" is possible, he said, "where the representatives of the people have all the power and in accordance with the constitution, . . . when they have the majority of the nation behind them."[30]

Allende lacked that majority in Chile's parliament, and had been elected with a fragile plurality of 36.2 percent of the vote. But in nationwide municipal elections in April 1971, Popular Unity candidates and parties significantly increased their vote to a plurality of just under 50 percent (49.7 percent, to the opposition's 48 percent). Allende's earliest actions were bold and met with broad political support. Congress unanimously approved a constitutional amendment to nationalize Chile's largely U.S.-owned copper industry, with promised compensation. Copper mining was Chile's largest industry by far, and accounted for 70 percent of earnings from international trade. Allende called the dollars from copper "the wages of Chile," and said they would be invested for the first time toward the national welfare.

Allende mostly named Communists and Socialists to lead the most powerful ministries, but reserved the key economics ministry for a respected independent, Pedro Vuskovic, who was a former officer of the UN Economic Commission for Latin America. Vuskovic designed and implemented a plan to convert large manufacturing enterprises to state control, using provisions of laws from the 1930s. The Development Corporation, using credit from the Central Bank, made attractive offers to buy up controlling shares of several of the largest banks, and gained control of other banks through regulatory intervention.

The boldest and most effective part of the plan was a variety of government measures to immediately put money in people's pockets. Wages were "readjusted" upward by 40 percent to compensate for inflation. Pensions and social security payments soared to three times the rate of inflation. And the government fast-tracked programs to build 100,000 low-cost houses. The measures amounted to a gigantic boost to consumption, to which Chilean factories responded with increasing production and employment.[31] In the first year of the Popular Unity, domestic production rose by 8 percent, unemployment fell to a record low of 3.8 percent, and even Chile's chronic inflation fell by 14 percentage points compared to the previous year.[32]

It seemed an undeniable win-win for both government and people, according to the authors of a respected history: "[The government] greatly increased social spending, and made a determined effort to redistribute wealth to the lower-paid and the poor. As a consequence of higher wages and new initiatives in health and nutrition, many poorer Chileans, perhaps for the first time in their lives, ate well and clothed themselves somewhat better than before."[33]

The government's agrarian reform program was much more controversial, because it provided for the expropriation of the largest farms, the *latifundios*, which were owned by Chile's conservative landed elite. All farms in excess of about 200 acres, according to a technical measure taking productivity into account, were subject to the law. The legal framework for the expropriations was a law passed during the previous government of Christian Democrat president Eduardo Frei. The countryside of southern Chile, such as the area where Teruggi went as a volunteer, however, had become an arena of conflict and lawlessness, in which de facto occupations, called *tomas* by farm workers and their political supporters, became the accepted practice, legitimized in most cases after the fact by the government.

· · · · ·

This was the situation into which Teruggi and his friends, all of whom were associated to one degree or another with MIR, had inserted themselves. MIR was founded in 1965 in emulation of Cuba's success and the ongoing guerrilla campaigns of Ernesto "Che" Guevara. Like Guevara, it advocated a strategy of armed struggle to bring socialist revolution. Prior to Allende's victory, MIR had carried out a series of bank robberies and other violent actions, but it suspended such extralegal activities and positioned itself to the far left of Allende's Popular Unity as a kind of "loyal opposition" collaborator. MIR criticized the "bourgeois reformism" of the UP programs while initiating its own campaign to organize farm workers and the urban poor. Andrés Pascal Allende, one of its top leaders, was Allende's nephew.

Like many foreigners, including many of the Americans, Teruggi easily gravitated to MIR, whose sister organizations FER, the students' front, and FTR, the Front for Revolutionary Workers, welcomed participation by foreigners. Official membership in MIR, which maintained an aura of semi-clandestinity, was off limits to all but a few, mostly Latin American, foreigners and exiles who had participated in allied militant groups in other countries.

· · · · ·

After a summer of voluntary work, Frank enrolled in economics courses at the University of Chile for the fall semester beginning in March. He also arranged to do a kind of internship at CESO, the prestigious think tank on Republic Street led by Andre Gunder Frank and Teotonio Dos Santos, two intellectual giants in the field of neo-Marxist economic development theory. Frank was a rigorous student and was happy to have the opportunity to write summaries of books and prepare bibliographies for the eminent researchers. He hoped to accumulate credits to transfer to Berkeley to finish his degree.

He also deepened his political connections. He was active in the FER and took part in protest actions. Ramon Barceló, a fellow student, spoke highly of him: "He was a very *simpatico* guy, not typical of the society of the times, since he always wore jeans and sandals. He was very informal in the way he dressed, but it was remarkable how rigorous and meticulous he was. He took notes on everything he heard and observed." In the second semester, Frank attended a course at the Catholic University with Franz Hinkelammert, a German theologian and economist who critiqued capitalism from the point of view of liberation theology.

His letters display a mind absorbing ideas and facts at an intense pace. Reading voraciously, he accumulated books—collections of Marx, Lenin and the Italian philosopher Antonio Gramsci, which he found for unbelievably cheap prices at the book fairs and flea markets that abounded in Allende's Chile. He marveled in his letters that Chile was a "real" revolution with a worker class that was competing for political and economic power. The movement in the United States and its rhetoric was beginning to taste like weak tea.

"I'm with revolutionaries from all over the continent and learning theory and practice in a way that is probably not available anywhere in the States," he wrote on the day before May Day—celebrated with great fanfare in Chile as International Workers Day. He was beginning to question the coherence of the American left:

> In retrospect, I didn't know as much about the U.S. as I thought I did. At first, when people asked me about the panthers, or the weathermen, or Angela Davis I was proud to have a chance to give my rap. But now I'm shutting up a bit, reading like crazy and trying to find out what's really happening. I had my head full of facts and some good ideas about imperialism and what the pigs were up to; but what were we up to? My head was full of crazy slogans, contradictory tactics, vague feelings, and lots of desire to SMASH THE STATE.[34]

His reading of Lenin was helpful. The Marxist leader had captured the complex dynamics of class struggle and managing the pace of social revolution—a major issue in the Chilean left. "He knew what to do," in a sly allusion to Lenin's seminal work "What Is to Be Done" on the need for a dominant revolutionary party.

Through his friend Mishy Lesser, Teruggi had widened his circle of like-minded Americans. He joined a group that had come together to talk revolutionary politics and try to contribute to the Chilean process. They created a newsletter called *FIN—Fuente de Información Norteamericana* (North American News Source), which he described as "a little like

Liberation News Service in Spanish." The idea was to compile news about the antiwar movement and U.S. foreign policy and distribute a slim mimeographed newsletter to the ubiquitous kiosks in Santiago. One of the first issues had a profile of Angela Davis, a prominent Communist and one of the most famous antiwar activists in the United States.

Steven Volk, a Columbia University student researching his PhD thesis in Chile, and his wife Dinah were important members of the editorial team.* The group wanted Chileans to know that there was also a vibrant leftist and antiwar movement in the United States, but they were careful not to present the United States as any kind of a model. A later *FIN* document described the project as "a small group of progressive young North Americans drawn to Chile to witness, study and live *el proceso chileno*, [and] to inform Chileans about how the U.S. government and corporations were using their power to suppress popular movements in Chile and around the world." In January 1973, the group organized an antiwar protest outside the U.S. Embassy near the presidential palace, and Frank, carrying a banner, and Mishy Lesser were pictured in *El Mercurio*.[35]

But the *FIN* team was not so serious as to not also have a good time. Parties were a regular part of the routine, gathering large groups of leftist Americans, Chileans and exiles from other Latin American countries at the large houses and apartments rented by the Americans. On Thanksgiving Day, there was a memorable feast at Teruggi's house, with roast turkey and pumpkin pie to feed more than 20 guests. As the weather warmed, Americans and Chilean friends gathered for a swimming party— bathing suits optional—at a well-appointed house with a large pool, located in the Andean foothills just outside Santiago.

Foreigners, especially the Latin American refugees, had become a visible presence in Santiago. Allende's government set aside apartments in a new high-rise complex called the San Borja Towers, on the broad Alameda Avenue, for the many political exiles, and some of the Americans were

---

* The early editorial team of *FIN* also included Ruth Needleman, Judith Brister, Mishy Lesser, Jill Hamberg, David Hathaway and Kyle Steenland. The Hormans joined the team in late 1972. A good number of other Americans were associated with *FIN* as well. According to Steve Volk, they included Kathy Fitzgerald, Charlotte Ryan, Jon Lepie, Jack Spence, Susan Rabinovitz, Stephanie Campbell and Leslie Krebs. Seventeen people attended the group's online reunion in 2020. Some of *FIN*'s articles were published in Chilean newspapers.

able to rent apartments there as well. Just across the street was the modernistic convention center called the UNCTAD building, recently constructed for a meeting of the United Nations Conference on Trade and Development. After the international conference, the building had been transformed into a cultural center, with cafés and performance spaces in addition to its vast ballrooms and aulas. The UNCTAD cafés and restaurants became the congenial social center for the growing numbers of expatriates who had settled in Chile in solidarity with the Allende government. It was a place to meet, be seen, find dates, network, look for jobs and change money on the black market. For the expats, Chile had become a comfortable world, seemingly full of opportunity and hope.

There was reason for optimism, even joy, as the foreign arrivals deepened their engagement with Allende's Chile.

3 Living the "Chilean Process"

Arriving in June 1972, Charles and Joyce were ecstatic about their new home. He found the people to be physically beautiful and politically fascinating. No one was apolitical. The multiple newspapers—which Horman's new Spanish ability allowed him to voraciously devour—did not even feign journalistic neutrality. He liked the energy of the city. People walk as fast as they do in New York, he commented to Lenzer. "There isn't an apolitical person here—well, maybe two or three. Everyone has something concrete to win or lose in the next few years depending on how things turn out. . . . The people are very beautiful, physically and spiritually. Physically a fine mix of Araucanian Indian, Spanish, Irish, German. The food is fucking far out. Abalones, fantastic fish soups full of oysters, shrimp, fish of all sorts. The wine is great."[36]

They quickly connected with old and new friends. Janet Duecy, with whom they had stayed in Berkeley, was also in Chile, and they met up with several Swedes "who are working in the propaganda ministry." With Duecy and her friend Bob Brown, a math teacher, they had found a house to rent on Paul Harris Street in the Las Condes district, on the eastern flank of the city with views toward the foothills of the Andes. The house had plenty of room, and like Teruggi's, became the abode for a multinational cast of characters, but with a somewhat artistic bent. Lluis Mestres, not yet 20, was a graphic designer recently arrived from Barcelona, and he had brought his friend Jaromir, a Czech artist, to the house.

Janet was also a friend of Pablo de la Barra, the filmmaker the Hormans had met the year before in Berkeley. Now in Chile busy making films, Pablo was a frequent visitor, engaging in long conversations about politics and film with Charlie. In graduate school at Berkeley, he had developed a treatment for a feature on the lives of MIR militants and had created a production company. He also had a working arrangement with Chile's most important film producer and distributor, Chile Films. He was able to raise some money, including from Janet, and planned to start shooting before too long.

Chile's dynamic filmmaking scene became the center of their activities. The French-Greek producer-director Costa-Gavras, who had attained fame with his political thriller *Z* about Greece's dictatorship, was in Chile making a new film about the Tupamaros in Uruguay and the real-life story of their kidnapping of a U.S. police official. Horman reported to Lenzer that Joyce and Janet had been cast as extras in a scene representing U.S. embassy wives. "Estimated on-screen time 12 seconds.... It's really fun. It's the sort of scene that could be cut, I guess, really easily." Horman said he tried out but didn't get a part. "I was too young and way too scraggly for anything they had in mind."[37]

They both wanted to find work in Chile. It wasn't just for money. The couple's nest egg was far from exhausted more than a year after leaving their full-time jobs in New York. They had arrived in Chile with about $5,000 in savings and things were cheap. Joyce found a job in the government-owned Forestry Institute writing computer programs to track production statistics. The job was more to keep her career skills up to date and to find a productive role in Chile than for money. But it lasted only a few months, until the end of the year.[38]

Both Joyce and Charlie eventually jumped into film projects as well. He was also writing poetry. Joyce's heart was with her new project. Enlisting the artistic talents of Lluis and Jaromir, she began work on a film intended to be produced with animated cartoons. It was based on a children's story Charlie had typed on his portable typewriter during the long bus rides from Panama to Chile. *The Sunshine Grabber* was an enchanting tale of a family living in an igloo covered with snow. The two children meet a monster called the Sunshine Grabber, who transports them to a warm place where there are mangos and flowers and big red bugs. Joyce and Lluis made drawings and illustrations, and Pablo de la Barra provided paints and other materials and helped with technical aspects. In synopsis, Horman called his story "an allegory, but it also has an implicitly social message stated in color, music and dance. The message is primarily for people who experience rigidity, authoritarianism and boredom in their working lives."[39]

Charlie was mainly interested in trying to set up freelance assignments about Chile for newspapers like the *Christian Science Monitor*, but told Lenzer he wasn't having much luck. He had little hesitation researching stories before getting an assignment, however. He had latched onto a promising investigative project about the murder in 1970 of a famous general in the chaotic weeks after Allende's election. A right-wing squad had killed General Rene Schneider, the constitutionalist chief of the Army, who was seen as standing in the way of a plot to prevent Allende from taking office. In September 1972 the local press was full of new developments in the case, which was being investigated by a military court. More than a dozen suspects had been charged, including retired General Roberto Viaux and General Camilo Valenzuela. Valenzuela, who led teams of civilians to carry out the kidnapping, will appear later in our story providing false information about Horman's death. The government publishing house Quimantú quickly brought out a book about the court hearings that was in all the kiosks. It contained the indictment, investigative accounts, transcripts and photos of dozens of suspects. The lurid evidence included the blood-stained page of notes General Schneider was writing at the moment of the attack. Chile was also abuzz with new revelations published in the United States about collaboration between the ITT corporation and the CIA to prevent Allende from coming to power. The "ITT Papers," leaked to journalist Jack Anderson, reinforced already strong suspicions in Chile that the CIA was at work to subvert the Allende government. That the CIA was indeed financing and providing weapons for the plot was not yet known at the time, but would be revealed in a U.S. congressional report in 1975.[40]

In a letter to his mentor Lenzer, Horman said he thought he could get a long article or a book out of the research.

> I've been reading the trial transcripts and talking to people about the Viaux case—an attempted coup against Allende when he was first elected before he took office, in which the head of the army was murdered. The details of the case are incredible. Very much like *Z* in the kinds of people involved. Small fascist groups, the sons of the rich, the generals, even Christian Democrats. For now I'm happy reading about it, but later, if I keep finding out interesting stuff, I may do a long, long piece on it almost novelistically getting into the details of their meetings and network.[41]

Z was a 1969 mystery thriller about a political assassination in Greece, and Horman would soon meet its director, Costa-Gavras. He was also interested in the political discussions of a group of Americans, including some of those who worked on the *FIN* newsletter. He had gotten to know them and liked them. "The people in the group are Northamerican, very nice, leftists," he wrote. "They're very serious. Everyone gets together once a week and talks about *State and Revolution* [a book by Vladimir Lenin], or Mao, or whatever. I can dig it."[42]

Toward the end of the year, he got a break that would pull him back into the world of filmmaking. Walter Locke, another curious American from Boston, had been in Santiago for a few months, renting a room and studying Spanish. He had recently received an inheritance and wanted to use it to a produce a film that would tell an American audience the story of Chile and the experiment of building socialism in a democracy "without bullets." He teamed up with Jorge Reyes, a Peruvian director, and was looking for a writer. Journalist Leslie Krebs introduced them to Charlie Horman, whom she knew from the *FIN* circle.

Horman was immediately intrigued. Locke and Reyes wanted to develop a shooting script and begin as soon as possible. They were passionate about the idea, and Horman threw himself into research and writing. Locke paid him a monthly stipend in local currency. "He got hooked," Locke said. The first script was sprawling and ambitious—a history of Chile's struggle against imperialism. It included historical scenes from the sixteenth and nineteenth centuries, and the beginnings of the workers' movement in the Iquique massacre of nitrate miners in 1911. Horman showed his draft script to friends for suggestions. Economist Warwick Armstrong, who worked in a UN agency in Santiago, said it made sense. "It was a defense of the Allende government, of how imperialism had wrecked the economy and so on. I found it sound for the most part—if you consider the bias. It was a documentary and from the left-wing point of view. It was logical, and it carried a message. They [the producers] were committed to the defense of the UP." Steve Volk, a student of development history, suggested a way to portray the threat of U.S. imperialism using the "dependency theory" concepts of Andre Gunder Frank, then in vogue. Based on the suggestions, "Charlie completely rewrote the script," Locke said. "He was a real professional."[43]

Reyes, in his forties with two full-length features under his belt, was an idealistic professional who supplemented his income as a street vendor. Like Horman, he had come to Chile because of Allende. The film, eventually called *Avenue of the Americas*, was high concept, he recalled: "With Charlie Horman as script writer, we had a common vision of a film about the second independence of Latin America, beginning in Chile.... The Popular Unity of Chile represented the beginning of the struggle for the second and definitive independence of America."[44]

Reyes worked on a shooting schedule and hired Brazilian exile Migueliño Costas as sound engineer and Peter Overbeck, a veteran cameraman and MIR sympathizer who had grown up in Germany. Locke said the crew worked "in and out of Chile Films," which was generous in supporting independent productions, especially those with a strong political angle. Reyes, the director, had other film projects in development at Chile Films.

Locke hired a taxi and driver for a month and, bringing a 16 mm Éclair camera, the crew headed south in early March 1973 to film scenes of the agrarian reform near Temuco, then to the far north to the nitrate mines of Iquique and the gigantic open-pit copper mine at Chuquicamata. Chile Films provided contemporary newscast footage from the government's Channel 9. By the end of April, Locke and Reyes figured they had most of what they needed and—providentially, it turned out—Locke packed up the 10 hours of film and headed back to the United States.

Horman's involvement in projects at Chile Films* and his connections to Pablo de la Barra thrust him, perhaps unwittingly, into association with people and situations that attracted controversy, especially after the coup. The management of the state-owned film company was politicized, like almost every aspect of public life in Chile. Leadership jobs, film projects and financial support were meted out according to party connections, mainly by quotas to the Socialist and Communist parties.[45] Allende had named a high-profile and polarizing Socialist, Eduardo "Coco" Paredes, to head the company. It wasn't an obvious choice. Paredes had been the head of the police investigative agency PICH and was hated on the right, whose leaders considered him the chief of Allende's political police.[46]

· · · · ·

Teruggi also was deepening his involvement in Chilean politics. His choice of friends and roommates tended to place him on the far left edge of activists working on behalf of the Chilean process. He had rented a good-sized house at 2575 Hernán Cortés St. in the middle-class Ñuñoa neighborhood. The house went through a changing roster of occupants that grew to eight by mid-1973. Another American, David Hathaway, moved in with his Chilean girlfriend Olga Muñoz. Paulo Santos Lopes, a Brazilian exile Frank had gotten to know through the summer voluntary brigade, moved in. Carlos Beust, also from the volunteer work group, was a frequent visitor.

Everyone in the house was a committed leftist, but politics came front and center when Olga, a militant in MIR, invited fellow Miristas Fernando

---

* Horman never worked directly for Chile Films, according to de la Barra and Reyes. In an email exchange with Trabucco, Reyes said: "I think that with Chile Films there is a confusion. The only ones who worked in Chile Films were Peter Overbeck and Migueliño Costas. It could be, I mean it could be, that when we worked with Charlie on the script for *Avenida de las Américas*, on more than one occasion I was at Chile Films and he came to meet me, but I was not an employee, I was going to use the editing table as a favor, thanks to colleagues like Carlos Piaggio. It is evident that because of political affinity, when the production was put together, I hired Peter and Migueliño and rented the camera (for four weeks) to Darío Pulgar."

Alarcón and Maria Virginia Hernández Croqueville to move into the garage, which was set up as their bedroom. Alarcón described himself as a "professional revolutionary," had trained in Cuba and was part of MIR's clandestine military arm the Fuerza Central (Central Force). Completing the household was a Uruguayan couple, José "El Peláo" and "Leda," who were given the largest bedroom rent free. They were Tupamaro exiles known only by their nicknames. El Peláo (which translates roughly as "Baldy") had lost most of his eyesight in a bomb explosion in Uruguay and had been one of the thousands of political prisoners rounded up in the Uruguayan government campaign to defeat the Tupamaro movement.

Hernán Cortés 2575 became known as "una casa MIRista"—a MIR house.[47] It was an informal gathering place for MIR militants from various units. Alarcón remembers fondly that Frank introduced him to the unfamiliar concept of combining breakfast and lunch as "brunch," which became a regular late morning event on weekends. Olga, who had an official job with the MIR Central Committee, had sponsored David Hathaway's application to join MIR. He was accepted as a *simpatizante* (sympathizer)—an official status indicating active collaboration prior to full membership. It was especially rare for MIR to accept a North American but Hathaway was an exception because of his relationship with Olga, a trusted figure in MIR.

Frank himself identified most closely with the leftist faction of the Socialist Party—Allende's party—as well as with MIR. Dual MIR-Socialist militancy was common and reflected MIR's influence inside Allende's UP. The most militant Socialist faction was called the Elenos for their connection to the Bolivian ELN, the National Liberation Army, which had fought with Che Guevara at the time of his death. The Elenos were a driving force organizing the workers' defense units in the Cordones Industriales, the industrial belts of occupied factories surrounding Santiago. Teruggi had been most active in the FER, the student front, and applied for formal membership in MIR, but the party did not act on his application. He had begun using the political name "Alejandro" during his voluntary work with the farm workers. Adopting a political pseudonym was a nearly universal practice among Miristas. Olga went by the name "Francisca" or "Ita," Fernando Alarcón was "Marcelo," and his girlfriend Maria Virginia was "Daniela." The two Brazilians Carlos Beust and Paulo Santos went by

"Augusto" and "Daniel," respectively. Some of the members of the household did not know the others' real names.[48]

. . . . .

As 1973 began, the optimism of the first two years imploded into an ominous atmosphere of crisis, though not yet violence. A transportation strike organized by truck owners and small businessmen had virtually shut down the economy for three weeks the previous October. Allende had been forced to call on top military officers to take key posts in his cabinet to defuse the crises. But the economy irretrievably lost the rosy glow of the first year, as production fell sharply and inflation began to soar. Supermarket shelves no longer had regular stocks of items such as chicken, beef and cooking oil. Toilet paper, called "comfort paper" in Chile, had disappeared, and people on the left proclaimed that the right-wing newspaper *El Mercurio* was the most appropriate substitute.

The Christian Democratic Party, which had provided the votes in Congress to ratify Allende's election just a year before, had now joined in an alliance with the right-wing parties to form a strong and angry opposition coalition. Factories and farms were being occupied by workers far beyond the plans laid out in the UP program. Negotiations between the Christian Democrats and the UP to map out a definitive list of properties subject to legal takeover had broken down, and the opposition was accusing Allende of violating the constitution. Copper prices had plummeted, cutting in half Chile's largest source of export income—a blow to the economy later linked to manipulation by the U.S. government. The first months of the year were devoted to campaigning for congressional elections scheduled for March. The now united opposition, already in the majority, was betting on obtaining enough additional seats to be able to impeach Allende, which required control of two-thirds of the chamber. The elections were peaceful, in keeping with Chile's century-long tradition, but Chile's democracy once again confounded opposition expectations. Allende's parties won 44 percent of the vote, and actually gained several seats in both chambers of the assembly.[49]

I had arrived in Chile during the October strike, on a fellowship from the InterAmerican Press Association. I wrote about voluntary work during the strike, the collapse of Chile's currency and the inability to obtain international loans, in part due to a boycott organized by the U.S. government. My story on the March elections was detailed but pointed to no viable resolution to the bitter divide.

With the political stalemate, a peaceful solution seemed out of reach. The opposition's goal had escalated to the demand to end Allende's presidency in advance of presidential elections, scheduled for 1976. Talk turned to violence and the specter of civil war. The polarization was symbolized by a mile-long ditch for a new subway splitting the city down the middle of La Alameda. Pop-up demonstrations and counter-demonstrations by militants from both the right and left now devolved into street fights, rock-throwing and the occasional gunshot. Allende warned that "dark hours" lay ahead.

The possibility of a military coup went from rumor to reality on June 29. A tank regiment rolled into downtown Santiago and its leader demanded that Allende resign. The ditch hampered the tanks' ability to maneuver and the uprising was quickly overpowered by loyalist Army units mustered by General Carlos Prats, the commander of the Army. The coup leaders surrendered, but 22 people had been killed, mostly civilians caught in shooting around the Defense Ministry.

At my house in Ñuñoa, I heard what was happening on the radio. I grabbed my camera and headed downtown. A block from the Ministry I tried to take a photo of an enormous pool of blood on the sidewalk, but a soldier aimed his rifle at me and I backed off. On the other side of the Alameda, on Agustinas Street a short distance from the presidential palace, known as La Moneda, I saw another large bloodstain covered by newspapers. I learned this was the spot where a rebel officer firing from the bed of a truck had killed a Swedish-Argentine journalist, who captured his own death on film. Frank Teruggi also headed to the center of the action, arriving in the central city while shooting was still going on. A bullet or shrapnel grazed his foot, and he had to be treated at a hospital. He was one of 50 people wounded.

The coup attempt was called the Tancazo. Up to that day violence had been scattered and mostly nonlethal. No one, however, thought the abortive tank offensive would be the end of the attack on the UP. Allende went on the radio several times to call on workers to defend the government. With the uprising under control, he pointed to the continuing threat. "I call on the people to take over all the industries and enterprises . . . to act with prudence with whatever material they have at hand." He said he was confident the armed forces would remain loyal, but warned, "If the coup comes, the people will have weapons."[50] Later in the day, from a balcony of the presidential palace, he amplified the proclamation with a somewhat ambiguous call for workers in Santiago to "organize and create people's power, but not against the government or independent from it, ... to advance in the revolutionary process."[51]

Allende's proclamation was a call to arms taken up by the Elenos faction of the Socialist Party, the Communist-dominated workers' confederation the CUT, and the MIR. The three organizations began to plan—and talk publicly—about organizing armed resistance to defend the workers' movement. Allende had adopted their slogan *Poder Popular* (People's Power), which the most radical factions had been promoting since the election impasse. The epicenters were the worker-controlled factories, organized into a dozen Cordones. Immediately after the Tancazo, the CUT and its allies occupied 244 additional factories, for a total of more than 500 worker-controlled factories. The Cordones had been set up during the October truckers' strike the previous year as a coordinated way to keep production going. Outside controllers (*interventores*) named by the government ran the factories in coordination with union and party leaders. Now the expanded Cordones had a new task: defense of the workers' movement and resistance, armed if necessary, against any future coup attempts by the military and the right.

In several long letters that were to be the last his family received, Frank discussed the situation in Chile following the attempted coup and his own safety. People were talking about the prospect of "civil war," but he didn't think it was imminent. He assured his parents he would be OK:

> My personal position here is one of relative safety: I've been around long enough to know the ropes and know how to keep out of trouble. We live in a section of Santiago where there is little possibility of serious trouble, and finally, as a foreigner, I should have little trouble leaving the country if the situation should ever get so bad that it would be necessary. I think that from the struggle here I'm learning a lot about the real advances that socialism can bring, and about the realities of capitalism. Since I have some skills, I am going to stay down here a few months more and try to contribute in whatever way I can.

Probably I will begin writing some news stories for the US leftist press about Chile. With a few friends, I have just finished writing a pamphlet for distribution in the US about the situation in Chile. I will send you a copy in my next letter. In addition, some friends are setting up a research center on the US imperialism here in Santiago and I may get a job working there for a few months.[52]

Teruggi teamed up with Steve Volk, Mishy Lesser and other *FIN* members to write a long analytical article, for publication in the United States, on the increasingly perilous situation in Chile. At almost 10,000 words, the piece documented U.S. efforts to undermine Chile's economy, in addition to describing the coup attempt. The political situation for Allende was grim:

> For the first time, significant segments of the opposition advocate nothing short of a military takeover by the nation's "constitutionalist" armed forces.
>
> Confronted by this blatant rejection of the legal structures within which the UP set out to move toward socialism, workers throughout the country have occupied their places of work and have vowed to defend them to the end. In short, dialogue has all but ceased, the nation's institutional framework is tottering, and there now seems little to save Chile from open and widespread conflict.[53]

Teruggi had been planning to leave Chile and return home overland to arrive in time for the fall semester in California. But his wound during the Tancazo and the day-to-day drama of the political battle put his plans on hold. He had signed up for a French class, and on Mondays had Hinkelammert's lectures on liberation theology at the Catholic University. In August he wrote that some Americans were leaving Chile, so the previously active social scene had devolved into a series of going-away parties. "Since there were neither classes nor riots nor political projects to work on, I spent the day working in the garden and re-reading Trotsky's HISTORY OF THE RUSSIAN REVOLUTION. I'm one of the very lucky gringos because I have a house (and therefore garden, front & backyard, etc.)." Teruggi had been in Chile going on a year and nine months. He had learned a lot. He was putting off his departure, waiting to find out how things were going to turn out. He was far from alone in seeing the Allende experiment at a crossroads: "In Chile we either build socialism or there will be fascism and a military dictatorship."⁵⁴

. . . . .

Having finished the film with Locke and Reyes, Horman was looking for new projects, observing the political dynamics, and—as usual—thinking and reading.

He sent a copy of the *FIN* newsletter to Lenzer at the time of the March elections. *FIN* was going well and articles were being published in major newspapers. He enclosed a piece in Spanish he had written about the Nixon administration for the government-run newspaper *La Nacion*. His comments to Lenzer on Chilean politics showed his bemusement. "The MIR and the left-wing of the UP have been active the past few weeks, trying to push the government off center. They've seized streets, supply centers, government offices, and a whole town for a day or so. Maybe there will be a revolution. I hope it doesn't come till I get over my cold."⁵⁵

Likewise in an earlier letter. He said he was involved in a "Marxist-Leninist study group"—a reference to the discussions conducted by Teruggi and some of the *FIN* members but attended by other Americans. "Down here everyone acts just like Marx and Lenin said they would. Every time I get a letter from the States, it all seems fuzzy, frustrating, and weird—The kind of situation that would give Lenin ulcers. But down here everyone is politicized along class lines and follows the whole script just like they'd been rehearsing since 1848."⁵⁶

His jocular tone aside, he also said he was "much involved in Leninism and in being <u>serious</u> about revolution." The underlining is his. His first direct contact with workers was a stint of volunteer work during the October strike in a factory making screws, the expropriated American Screw Company.⁵⁷ In the weeks following the Tancazo, according to his friend Warwick Armstrong, Horman had deepened his commitment to the workers' movement. Armstrong, a New Zealander official working at the UN economics office CEPAL, said he last saw Horman in July when he was helping a group of "pro-Allende construction unions" stand guard at night to protect a low-income housing project in an upper-class neighborhood near Cuarto Centenario Avenue in eastern Santiago. It was feared that right-wingers would sabotage the buildings before the poor people could move in. "Many were armed, but not Horman," according to one account.[58]

The dramatic events of the winter months did not dim the Hormans' determination to stay on in Chile. But Janet Duecy would soon return to the United States for health reasons, and others had moved on from the convivial group house. With only Lluis Mestres, the Spanish designer, in addition to the Hormans, the house on Paul Harris Street had become too big and expensive. The new place, found through an *El Mercurio* for-rent ad, could not have been more different from their comfortable Las Condes neighborhood. It was on Vicuña Mackenna Avenue, right in the heart of the factory district that was the largest and most militant of the Cordones. Mestres, still making drawings for the animated film, planned to make the move with them.

The rent was much cheaper, but money—especially in Chile's black market dollar economy—was not a big issue. The location could be an opportunity, perhaps, for Charlie to finally immerse himself in the authentic working-class experience that had always eluded him. In a letter to Lenzer he returned to the theme of his "outsider" status, which had dogged him since his arrival. And he wondered if with all his thinking and reading he was really able to accomplish anything important. "Revolution is a great spectator sport, but there are limits on how much a gringo can get in on it. A few have; but for most, including me, there are definite barriers of culture, language, and being associated through birth with the enemy."[59]

It wouldn't be long before he and Lenzer could talk it all over in person.

4   New York

Horman had been away for almost two years, and August seemed a good time to trade Chile's winter for late summer in New York City. Charlie wanted to see his parents, especially his mother, whose eyesight was failing. They had been pressing him to visit. He looked forward to seeing Lenzer and other friends from his professional life. Joyce decided not to make the trip. She and Lluis were immersed in the *Sunshine Grabber* animation project and wanted to keep working. He told Mestres his main purpose was to raise money for the projects in Chile.[60] Sometime in this period, most likely after the Tancazo and Allende's call to arms, Horman had decided the trip would also be his concrete contribution to the defense of Chile. He intended to ask his friends for money to buy weapons.

Ed and Elizabeth Horman met their son at Kennedy airport on August 1. Within a few days he called Terry Simon, a close friend of his and Joyce's from their days living in the same Upper West Side apartment building. He invited her to dinner at his parents', and she accompanied him on other activities. Charles talked passionately about the situation in Chile to everyone who would listen. To friends who feared for his safety in an unstable, increasingly violent country, he was firm in his determination to return to Chile. Terry was caught up in his perorations about the workers' movement and Allende's programs to help the poor and the peasants. She had some vacation coming from her job at an education magazine. At Horman's suggestion, she decided she would return with him to Chile to see Joyce and visit the country that so fascinated them.[61]

During his month in New York, Charles Horman asked four friends to donate money for political work in Chile. Three of those friends, Don Lenzer, Richard Pearce and Jerry Cotts, said he was raising money for weapons that could be used in the defense of the workers' movement in Chile.

Don Lenzer was Horman's best friend, and they had exchanged many letters during Horman's odyssey in the years since they worked together in the King TV team on the West Coast. He was perhaps the most politicized of the group. He was well known and respected in film circles as a cinematographer, with credits on several Oscar-winning documentaries, including *Woodstock* and *Maya Lin*.

Lenzer was again living in New York and the two friends met at least three times during Horman's visit. The subject of helping in the defense of Chile was broached during a long walk in Central Park, which ended at Columbus Circle. Lenzer was disconcerted about the request and said he would have to think about it. They got together again in the West Village, sitting for several hours on a pier on the Hudson River. They spoke of many other things—Don's recent marriage, Charlie's uncertainty about his career path and his desire to make a difference in life (a recurring topic). Horman recounted his new life in Chile and the crisis facing the Allende experiment. Lenzer was slightly older than Horman and more accomplished professionally, but he had always considered himself more to the left, more radical politically, than Horman, who had been a liberal, far from a radical, when they had worked together. In their letters, he had witnessed Horman's evolution, and now what Horman was telling and asking him was shocking. He was amazed and somewhat skeptical that Horman would have the kind of contacts for the kind of request he was making. "Charlie asked me if I would contribute any money to what I understood was his efforts to raise money for arms that he would on his return to Chile give to groups that would defend the revolution against a coup. My recollection is that they were organized workers who were supporters of Allende, but who were more radical, and who believed in arming the people to defend the revolution."

The Charlie he knew was a cultural person, more of a cool observer than an activist. A leftist, yes, but hardly a person who would have "these kinds of contacts and be involved in this way." But he trusted his friend and he believed him, even though it didn't seem plausible.

He pressed Horman for details. Who had asked him to do this? Who were the groups, were they legitimate bona fide contacts or just a random person? Horman was evasive. "The questions didn't elicit responses that were in any way satisfying," Lenzer said.

They broached the same topic a few days later, and Lenzer gave a qualified "yes" to Horman's request. He recalls it was again at Columbus Circle.

> I told them that I didn't feel comfortable about giving him any money for the purpose that he was asking. But that I would give him some money that he could use for him and Joyce to be able to get out of Chile if they needed to. I can clearly say I knew that he would use the money for any reason he wanted to. This was a matter, I guess, of assuaging my own conscience.

He doesn't remember the exact amount he gave Horman—something on the order of the cost of two airfares, which at the time would have been around $600. When he learned Horman had been killed, he immediately thought it might have to do with the fundraising. It all seemed absurd and his knowledge of it only added to the sadness he felt about his friend's untimely death. "There's still, even now, an enormous amount of mystery, surrounding this whole thing, which I haven't resolved."[62]

Horman's next call was to Dick Pearce, another old friend from the job with King TV. Pearce had been with the Hormans in Mexico taking CIDOC language classes, then traveled to Chile for several months to film the radicalized poor people who had squatted in the Nueva La Havana encampment in Santiago.[63] Returning to New York, he worked as associate producer and cameraman on the Hollywood documentary *Hearts and Minds*, one of the most radical and controversial films ever produced about the Vietnam War. The film would win an Oscar for best documentary, even though the studio that commissioned it, Columbia Pictures, disowned the project.

He described his August 1973 meeting with Horman: "We had lunch. He asked me for money to help arm the Cordones Industriales around Santiago against the threat of a right-wing military coup. I have a very clear memory." Pearce was not taken aback by the request. He was familiar with the term Cordones—the belts of worker-controlled factories. His experience making films in Chile had given him a good sense of the workers' movement and the escalating radicalism. Nor was he surprised at his friend's talk of impending violence. "It all made complete sense. I had been in Chile myself. Even in 1971 I felt the tremors of something dark happening. . . . [Horman] said the Cordones were going to be the battleground in the coming conflict. He said arming the Cordones was what was needed." Pearce wondered if his friend might be exaggerating, but he was sure Horman wouldn't raise money under false pretenses. "No question he believed what he was doing was right and that it had to be done. . . . To say the Chilean workers should be able to defend the factories against the impending military coup seemed kind of self-evident."

Thinking back 50 years, Pearce has forgotten how much he gave Horman. "I *definitely* gave Charlie money at that lunch. If I had to guess, I'd say it was no more than a couple of hundred bucks, but I just can't remember the exact amount." Whatever the number, he was impressed by Horman's commitment and his apparent direct involvement in the dramatic political events in Chile. Knowing Horman, he also thought there might be an element of "self-dramatization." He continued: "Charlie was definitely self-aware. He knew what it sounded like when he told me he was raising money to buy guns. He knew he was bringing to the table a world that I could only imagine."

Pearce said he decided to come forth with the story so many years later because he was disturbed by the distorted portrait of his friend in the *Missing* movie and in much of what had been written about the case. "I really was upset by the way Charlie was portrayed in the movie. They didn't have the courage to portray Charlie as he really was," he said. "Making him out to be a naïve victim enraged me. Charlie was described as a cartoonist, a kind of Henry James figure—an American innocent abroad. That was tough for me to swallow. I knew Charlie well. He would have hated that idea." Horman was Harvard, but also a regular guy who liked to talk about how he made money as a pool hustler. And he was political, a movement person who came of age in the '60s. "This is what our generation was like. In a sense we all *were* naïve. Charlie had gone to Chile to be part of the first democratically elected socialist revolution in history. He had gone there to make history. Talk of revolution was everywhere. It was in the very air you breathed. Charlie loved the unique political environment of Chile."[64]

Jerry Cotts, perhaps the least political of Horman's friends, had been best man in the Hormans' wedding in Owatonna, Minnesota. They had worked as a writer-camera team for a while at WNET, the public television station. He remembers seeing Horman before the coup and asking about the "good things" he was doing in Chile. "Dredging up memories," he thinks Horman did ask him for money, but he didn't approve of such radical political activities. "If I gave him $50 or $100, I might have, but I don't remember. It wouldn't have been much more than that."

He said he thinks back on the incident as like a scene from a movie.

> If you were to write a novel or make a movie, but a very sensitive, smart movie, that would be a critical moment because that's so unlike Charlie. But I can also imagine him sort of working his way intellectually up to doing [it] and developing the courage. Yeah, you know, that takes some balls. I think, to openly go around asking people for money to buy guns for a South American revolution. Yeah. So I think, I think that was his one shot at doing something really practical.[65]

There was at least one more request. Simon Blattner, a real estate investor, had met the Hormans in Cuernavaca in 1971. He and his wife Barbara Thorp drove down to Mexico from San Francisco and stayed for six weeks, attending Spanish classes at CIDOC and seeing the sights. They lived in the Humboldt house, named for the German polymath and explorer Alexander von Humboldt, who had nicknamed Cuernavaca the "city of eternal spring" during his visit there in the nineteenth century. When Charlie got in touch with him again in August 1973, Blattner said, he invited him to spend the weekend with him and Barbara at their beach house in Clinton, Connecticut. Horman arrived with Terry Simon.

"He was looking for money, he was raising money," for some kind of political work that was unclear to Blattner. He said he gave Horman some money but doesn't remember how much. "Not more than $1,000," he said. "I didn't have a lot of dough, but he was asking and I wanted to help a friend. . . . We had a lot to talk about. Charlie's politics were much leftier than mine. We talked about the situation in Chile. I thought it was dangerous and I tried to talk him into staying in the U.S."

"He was fomenting political action, trying to bring about a democratic Chile," but Blattner had no idea of the specifics. He said they had a good time that weekend, swimming and drinking beer. When he learned Horman was killed, he said, he thought "for sure" it might have had something to do with his political activity and fundraising. "I begged them to stay in New York, but they were determined to go. All Charles had to do was pick up the phone and tell Joyce to come home, but he wanted to go back to Chile," Blattner told another writer. "It was as though he didn't want to miss the final act of the drama that was unfolding."[66]

Horman also called Walter Locke. He wanted to know what had happened to the precious footage for their film on Chile's struggle against imperialism. Locke, in Boston, remembers Charlie called him from Manhattan in late August and said he was calling from a pay phone. "He said he was being very cautious. He sounded a little ominous, from the way he was talking."

Locke told him he had been successful in getting the 10 hours of undeveloped film out of Chile—"I had to grease some palms."

"How's the project going? Have you made any progress?" Horman asked. The situation in Chile was serious and people in the United States needed to understand what was at stake.

"I say, nothing has happened." Locke told him he had taken a job to save money to develop the film. The cans of film were still in his apartment. Horman was very earnest about getting the film done, Locke said. Funding for the film was very much on Locke's mind, but Horman didn't talk about money. He just urged Locke to get going as soon as possible.[67]

· · · · ·

Horman's decision to take action in the defense of Chile's revolution was something he shared only with a few close friends. The episode shows a dimension of Charles Horman that was completely absent from the film *Missing* and the 1978 book written about the case. It casts Horman as a man of courage, willing to take risks in the cause of defending the constitutional government and the workers' movement of Chile against the gathering threat of military overthrow. His action brings to mind, though on a much smaller scale, the example of the Americans in the Abraham Lincoln Brigade, who took up arms to defend the Spanish socialist republic against fascism in the 1930s.

Charlie arrived back in Santiago with Terry Simon on the first day of September. He was in a good mood, said his housemate Lluis Mestres. "When Charles arrived with Terry from the United States he was pleased, because apparently his economic efforts had gone well."[68] Years later, Joyce said she did not know about the fundraising for weapons, but he may have hinted about those activities. "Charles mentioned to me upon his return from New York that he had also raised funds for friends, which I now believe may have been for worker defense."[69]

But Horman, while happy to be back, quickly became aware that optimism and good feeling were in scarce supply in the Chile to which he was returning.

5 The Coup

Instability and violence had increased in Chile, and the remaining doors to a political solution were closing. There had been another assassination, the third since Allende had been elected. Gunmen linked to the right shot Navy officer Arturo Araya Peeters on the balcony of his home. Araya was serving as Allende's aide-de-camp and was a vital source of information about that military branch. Plotting to overthrow Allende was already underway and later it would come to light that the Navy, with headquarters in the Valparaiso port, was at its center. Second-level officers in the Army and the Air Force were participating in the coup planning, but the top commanders, notably General Prats of the Army, seemed to remain loyal to the constitutional order.

In early August Prats convinced the other military chiefs to join Allende's cabinet when a new truckers' strike threatened to paralyze the economy, already wracked by food shortages and 300 percent inflation. But the military support lasted less than two weeks. Under pressure from his generals, Prats resigned on August 21. The demise of the Allende government seemed unavoidable. Only the manner was unknown. The new head of the Army was General Augusto Pinochet, who had appeared close to Prats and was trusted by Allende.

On the left, the MIR and the new secretary general of the Socialist Party, Carlos Altamirano, were openly organizing resistance in the Cordones factories and other government-controlled institutions. Workers at INDUMET, a tool and die factory taken over by the government, had begun manufacturing automatic rifles, patterned on the Swedish Karl Gustav assault rifle, and were adapting factory equipment to make armored vehicles. Militants at Chile Films, among other entities, carried out military drills with mock weapons and at least a few real ones.[70]

But Allende's strategy was to keep his generals loyal, and close. He agreed to put the military in charge of enforcing the arms control law to search for illegal weapons. Few arms caches were found, but there had been violent confrontations. In a raid of the SUMAR textile factory near Vicuña Mackenna the workers resisted the military incursion and shots were exchanged. Both the MIR and the crypto-fascist group Patria y Libertad (Fatherland and Liberty) declared that some of their most active militants were going underground. In the final weeks, Patria y Libertad was responsible for more than 200 terrorist explosions that destroyed electric towers and an oil pipeline. The group's leader Roberto Thieme later revealed the attacks were secretly coordinated with Navy officers working to undermine the Allende government.[71] Despite the escalating violence, loss of life was still relatively rare.

The Teruggi household in the quiet neighborhood of Ñuñoa was assuming a role in the MIR preparations, according to Fernando Alarcón, one of the housemates. Alarcón worked full-time for MIR, which tended to see the crumbling of the Allende government as a political opportunity that would hasten the revolution. His girlfriend Maria Virginia and Olga Muñoz, David Hathaway's fiancée, were also doing clandestine work for MIR's Political Committee. Alarcón had received a month of military training in Cuba earlier in the year and had returned "urgently" just after the Tancazo. He lived in Teruggi's house, but he met with his cadre of five Central Force militants at a safe house on Avenida Grecia, where their few weapons were stored. MIR had created a network of such safe houses for clandestine activity but also, anticipating a coup, to allow the party to continue operating in resistance.[72]

There were no weapons in Teruggi's house, and as far as is known Frank was not involved in the Central Force activities. Olga and Maria Virginia worked directly for the MIR Political Committee as part of an information unit. Their task was to create forged identity cards, called *cedulas*, and they had a stock of blank identification cards. The phony IDs were needed for MIR militants transitioning into the growing underground network. Alarcón said he kept other MIR documents in the house, including military manuals.

Frank's Brazilian friends Paulo Santos and Carlos Beust were in and out of the house. Both Santos and Beust recall that Frank and Charles Horman had taken photos of military ships in the Valparaiso harbor, which were intended for publication in *Punto Final*, a magazine linked to MIR. Santos said he remembers the photos, which he thought might have put Frank in danger. "I knew about it because I went into his room and saw the pictures. Frank said to me, 'you shouldn't be seeing this.'"[73]

The left's focus on the Navy as a center of subversion was not surprising. It was in the news. On August 11, 43 sailors and officers were arrested and accused of planning a left-wing revolt at the Naval bases at Valparaiso and Talcahuano farther south near the city of Concepcion. The Navy accused leaders of MIR, the Socialist Party and the MAPU party of organizing the infiltration. It was not an invention. In fact, the pro-Allende Naval officers had met with MIR and MAPU leaders and had provided important advance warning about coup plotting inside the Navy. Moreover, U.S. Navy ships were scheduled to arrive in early September to conduct the periodic UNITAS joint Naval maneuvers with Chile.[74]

But in the days just before the coup, Teruggi was preparing not for a coup but for his departure from Chile. He had acquired a formidable collection of Marxist classics and was wrapping them in packages to mail them back to the United States. He had dispatched some of the packages already and was waiting to hear that they had arrived intact back home. David Hathaway and others described Frank as spending a lot of time reading in the house. He was aware in general terms that there were MIR Central Force activities in the house, but knew they were "compartmented" and he should not ask questions.[75]

· · · · ·

Charles Horman and Terry Simon didn't have time to settle in at the house on Paul Harris. Joyce already had taken possession of their new residence at Vicuña Mackenna Avenue 4126, and with her husband at home she rented a truck to complete the move on September 6. The new dwelling was a compact, two-story house that had been a maid's quarters at the rear of the larger house where the owners lived. At the dollar black market rate, the 10,000 escudo rent was less than $25 a month, and they paid in advance through December.[76] The landlords were Dr. Julio Núñez and his wife Ariela Vecchi. She found the couple somewhat "hippie" but otherwise respectable. She remembered they had a good number of visitors, mostly North Americans or Spaniards, but there were no loud parties.[77]

Terry wanted to see some of the sights of Chile during her short visit. Joyce was an avid skier, and she took Terry to spend two days at the Portillo ski resort, high in the Andes, where there was still ample snow on the trails. Charles had three days free, September 7-9, time enough to organize the house, perhaps do some writing[78] and take care of other pending business. In New York he had told friends he was raising money to buy guns for the organized workers of the Cordones Industriales and he intended to turn it over once he was back in Chile. How much money he brought can only be estimated from his friends' inexact memories—between several hundred dollars and two thousand. Now, perhaps unexpectedly, he found himself in the heart of the Vicuña Mackenna Cordón, surrounded by factories controlled by their workers. The free days would have given him the opportunity to make contact with whatever group had asked him to raise the money. But nothing is known about whether he did that.

His wife considers it unlikely he would have gone to any of the factories, saying later: "Since I'm virtually certain that Charles had no direct contact with workers in the Cordones, I believe it's much more likely that any such fundraising was solicited by a person he knew who may have had connections to the Cordones or was part of a political party that was active there, rather than Charles himself having direct contact with workers. That's the most plausible explanation."[79]

Having shown Terry the magnificence of the Andes mountains, Joyce and Charles wanted her to see Chile's glorious Pacific coastline. Terry wrote that she and Charlie traveled "on the evening of Monday, September

10, 1973 . . . to the city of Valparaiso to spend the following day sightseeing." Joyce passed up the trip because she had an appointment in a government office to renew her temporary residency visa.

In Valparaiso, Charlie and Terry saw the sights for a while and had dinner. Then they checked in to the Miramar Hotel, in the adjoining city of Viña del Mar. In contrast to the raucous sailors' bars, bordellos and crowded wharfs of Valparaiso, Viña was an affluent bedroom community with tranquil beaches and sprays of magenta bougainvillea spilling over garden walls. The Miramar was at the time Viña's best appointed beachside hotel, though relatively inexpensive for guests able to pay with dollars. Horman filled out the registration card using his old address, Paul Harris 425 Las Condes. It was almost midnight when they settled in to room 315, with a peaceful view of the lights of the Valparaiso harbor. Terry had only a canvas overnight bag, Charlie an extra shirt. The hotel would be their residence for the next five days.[80]

. . . . .

The military overthrow of Allende, the event that so dramatically and indelibly changed the lives of so many people, began quietly at Naval command headquarters in Valparaiso just after midnight on Tuesday, September 11, 1973. Chilean warships sailing out of port on Monday, ostensibly to join American ships in the UNITAS joint maneuvers, had instead waited just out of sight over the horizon. Then, the order given, they quickly sailed back to port to reinforce other Navy units, and by 7:00 a.m. Chile's second largest city was under martial law. Army regiments around Santiago, responding to orders from General Pinochet, the newly appointed commander in chief, began moving in armored vehicles, tanks and open trucks to seize key installations—among the first targets were television and radio stations—before moving into the center of Santiago. Alerted to the developments, President Allende rushed from his home to La Moneda, the presidential palace on Alameda Avenue, to make what would be his last stand.[81]

Most ordinary Chileans had started their day at work or in classes when they learned what was happening. David Hathaway had already arrived at his job as a lathe operator in the appliance factory MADEMSA. "I was cutting one-inch diameter bolts on the lathe for a maintenance job," he said. Although he had gotten his job through MIR contacts, MADEMSA wasn't politically organized and bosses sent workers home at midmorning.

MIR had been preparing for months for this dreaded day. Standing orders to its members and associated organizations like the Revolutionary Students Front (FER), to which Teruggi belonged, were to gather in their political units and organize actions to defend the government. Teruggi headed toward the Macul Cordón, which was the closest to his house and also along the same street as the Pedagógico campus of the University of Chile. At the campus, he met up with his Brazilian friends Jorge Basso, Carlos Beust and Paulo Santos. They were joined by fellow Miristas Liliana Salazar, Paulina Vidal and Esther "Cuqui" Fuentes, almost the same group that had befriended Frank in the voluntary work brigade on a farm soon after his arrival in Chile. They continued south on Macul Avenue to the area where there were a number of worker controlled factories. Macul was the nearest Cordón to the city, but its factories were among the smallest.

Liliana Salazar knew Teruggi from the School of Economics and was a full-fledged MIR militant, whose organizational unit was GPM5—the Grupo Politico Militar (Political Military Group). The number 5 indicated the GPM was MIR's student organizing arm, which coordinated the non-militant members in the FER. She was following orders, she said. "The order of MIR was to go to the factories, to the Cordones to resist at the side of the workers. We assumed there would be weapons," she continued. Paulo Santos gave a similar account: "They called us, and we went to reinforce the resistance as members of MIR and FER."

They went into a small factory whose workers were associated with MIR. But they were disappointed, Paulina Vidal remembered. "We went with Frank to a factory in the Macul Cordón, and we waited. But there were very few workers present. There were no weapons and no resistance."

The group split up. Carlos Beust went looking for more pockets of resistance. Back at the Pedagógico campus, he joined a group of about 20 students who had been provided with a few weapons from MIR's cache. They had two or three Karl Gustav rifles, some homemade grenades, a few pistols and some dynamite, Beust said. The group decided to capture a nearby neighborhood Carabinero station, where the few policemen on duty put up no resistance and no one was injured. The militants—members of MIR and other parties as well as students with no party affiliation—occupied the station for about four hours. Beust remembers climbing up to the roof and looking out over the city. It was just past noon, and he saw smoke rising from the center of Santiago, a few miles away. Air Force Hawker Hunter fighter planes were strafing and bombing La Moneda, where he knew Allende and members of his armed guard were holding out. It was clearly the beginning of the end, Beust said. Before long a call came from a MIR leader, ordering them to abandon the Carabinero post. Holding on to their small military victory would have invited a massacre when the Army sent troops to retake the outpost.[82]

At my house in Ñuñoa, my housemates and I listened to Allende's heart-wrenching final address on Radio Magallanes, the last station still unoccupied by the military. There was no call to resistance, no promise of weapons. Workers should stay in their factories and avoid provocation. "The people must defend themselves, but they shouldn't sacrifice themselves," he said, then alluded to his own inevitable death and the future. "I will always be next to you. At least my memory will be that of a man of dignity who was loyal to his country. . . . Go forward knowing that, sooner rather than later, the great avenues will open again and free men will walk through them to construct a better society."[83]

It was years later that we learned Allende had committed suicide as Pinochet's troops stormed into La Moneda. Allende instructed his remaining companions to surrender, then, left alone, he sat on a couch in a large room on the upper floor. Taking an AK-47 he had been using in the defense of the building, Allende turned it on himself and fired. His personal physician, Dr. Patricio Guijón, entered the room just at that moment and saw Allende fall back, dead.*

---

* Allende's suicide was disputed for years, especially after a statement from Fidel Castro that the president had died in combat. Isabel Allende Bussi, his daughter, said she was told of her father's suicide by a trusted source soon after it happened, according to her 2023 book *11 de Septiembre: Esa Semana* (Debate, Penguin Random House), 81. In 2017, forensic experts contracted by the Chilean Medical Legal Service released a report concluding there was "absolutely no doubt" Allende committed suicide. "Chilean President Salvador Allende Committed Suicide, Autopsy Confirms," *The Guardian*, July 19, 2017.

. . . . .

We did not know what to think in those dark moments. For weeks, leftist political leaders had been advertising that the defense of the workers' movement would coalesce in the Cordones. Three housemates and I—still unwilling to believe there was no hope—set out on foot. We walked to Vicuña Mackenna Avenue, then several miles south into the heart of the industrial Cordón. There was very little traffic on the usually busy commuter artery. We saw no signs of military control, but occasionally we saw open trucks loaded with nervous-looking soldiers, their rifles pointing upward, driving north toward the center. Each soldier had a white armband with some kind of insignia, which I later learned was a marking to distinguish troops aligned with the coup action from possible military units that remained loyal to Allende. It would turn out that such loyal units were almost nonexistent.

We arrived at the Lucchetti food products factory, which I had visited only a week before to take pictures of a workers' march in support of the Vicuña Mackenna Cordón. A Chilean flag and a large banner calling for the factory to be nationalized were still prominently displayed. Another hand-drawn sign proclaimed "Lucchetti Workers Demand: No! to the Civil War!" But it was obvious nothing was happening. People on the street said the factory was closed, most of the workers had gone home, and that it was stupid and dangerous to be roaming around the neighborhood, where before long the military was sure to arrive in force. As we walked back home we could see a column of black smoke rising from the direction of La Moneda. By early afternoon our group house of three Chileans, two Americans, a Canadian, two Argentines and a Colombian had expanded to accommodate four other Chilean acquaintances who somehow thought our house would be safer than their own.

At Teruggi's house on Hernán Cortés, there was work to be done. Fernando Alarcón had been at the MIR's secret Central Force hideout with his team of five militants. There were a few weapons, but nowhere near what would be needed to put up any real resistance. "We had a few personal weapons and a few rifles. MIR didn't have many weapons. They wanted the Cubans to give them weapons—there were plenty in the [Cuban] Embassy. But out of deference to Allende, the Cubans never distributed the weapons," Alarcón said.

Teruggi's house was kept free of weapons, but there were lots of potentially compromising documents associated with the MIR work carried out by the three Chileans. Alarcón, Maria Virginia and Olga spent most of the day getting rid of anything that could expose them to danger. Alarcón had brought back a set of weapons manuals from Cuba, which were part of his military training. The manuals included instructions for the manufacture of homemade bombs. There were also piles of internal MIR documents from the Political Committee analyzing the political situation.

"Daniela," he said, referring to his fiancé by her MIR name, "was burning documents in the bathtub. We got rid of a big pile of dangerous stuff, like the user manuals for weapons."

When the political cleansing was finished, Fernando and Maria Virginia hunkered down with Frank, David, Olga and the two Uruguayans, as the military-imposed curfew came into force and evening arrived. It would not be lifted for almost two days. Fernando wanted to get out of the house as soon as possible to go to the relative security of the MIR safe house, which had been established just for this purpose. He said he didn't feel safe: "The [Teruggi] house was very hot. It was very well known as a place frequented by members of the [MIR] Central Force. We left as soon as curfew was lifted. We tried to talk Frank and David into getting out, but they stayed. They thought they had the protection of their U.S. citizenship."[84]

Brazilians Santos and Beust spent September 11 moving around Santiago trying to make contact with the resistance that never materialized. "Since there was no resistance, we were left hanging, it was a great disillusionment," Paulo said. They had come to Chile fleeing from the repression in Brazil; now it was dawning on them they were fugitives again. They found shelter in friends' houses for the night. When the curfew was lifted on Thursday they went back to Teruggi's house, asking for help and the location of other North American friends who might be able to hide them.

Teruggi was home, busy packing his things. He was nervous when he saw them and talked to them in the street. "You've got to get away from here," he said. "The house is being watched, go quickly!" He gave them some money.

The Uruguayan couple, José and Leda, were even more vulnerable than the Brazilians. José had been seriously injured in a bomb accident in

Uruguay and was almost blind. He could hide neither his nationality—because of his distinctive accent—nor his Tupamaro militancy. Frank, Steve Volk and other *FIN* members got on the phones with embassies and personal contacts to arrange asylum for their Latin American friends. The North Americans were not immune to the fear, but felt their exile friends were in far greater danger. Sometimes the exiles had to be hidden in the trunks of cars to smuggle them past Carabinero guards who were posted outside embassies after the first few days. Eventually the Brazilians and Uruguayans managed to find protection: Paulo in the Argentine Embassy, crowded with hundreds of refugees, and Carlos in the Cuban commercial office, which had been placed under the auspices of the Swedish Embassy. The Uruguayans got into the embassy of Panama.[85]

It was a time of terror for the foreign exiles. There was continuous gunfire during the night, audible in all parts of the city, even in the upper-class neighborhoods presumably supportive of the coup. By 1973 at least 10,000 to 12,000 people were living in Chile as political refugees, almost all of them from Southern Cone countries.[86] Military announcements on radio and television routinely referred to the exiles as "foreign extremists" who had come to Chile to form a "guerrilla army." An early proclamation ordered all foreigners living in Chile whose papers were not in order to report in person to the Ministry of Defense or to the nearest police station. Political exiles understood the decree to refer to them, even those who had visas. The military issued a chilling warning by radio and television: "We will show no mercy for foreign extremists who have come to kill Chileans. Citizen: Remain alert to find them and denounce them to the nearest military authority."[87]

6 Valparaiso

At their beachside hotel Terry and Charlie woke up to a Chilean world turned upside down. There was less violence in Valparaiso than in Santiago, and in Viña even fewer signs of the military takeover. Stuck in a hotel with people they assessed as upper-class and—worse—affiliated with the U.S. military, their guard went up. During the five days before they were able to return to Santiago, they met five American officers, including Captain Ray Davis, the chief of the U.S. Naval Mission in charge of liaison with the Chilean Navy, and his deputy Lieutenant Colonel Patrick J. Ryan of the Marine Corps. Davis was also chief of the U.S. Military Group (MilGroup) in Chile, which was the U.S. Embassy's office in charge of military sales, aid and training for the host country. Charlie and Terry presented themselves as a couple of stranded tourists and were careful not to betray any hint of their pro-Allende sentiments or the devastation Charlie was experiencing about the demise of the Chilean experiment in which he had invested so much.

According to Captain Davis, Charlie said he was living in Santiago and working in the Chilean film company PROA on a film strip for children—a reference to the *Sunshine Grabber* project. Terry said she was on vacation from her job in New York as a writer for a teenage magazine. Horman's self-description to Davis was understandably somewhat adapted to his audience. Horman worked in film but was not employed by PROA, which was his friend Pablo de la Barra's production company.[88] Horman was guarded, presuming with good reason that the U.S. military personnel he met supported the coup, and he suspected they might even have been directly involved with the actions of the Chilean Navy. U.S. hostility toward Allende was well known, and the United States had a notorious history of military intervention in Latin America. Horman was well-read in past U.S. actions such as the instigation of military coups in Guatemala in 1954 and Brazil in 1964.

Horman and Simon suspected they might have happened onto a nest of U.S. co-conspirators in Chile's coup. The first American Horman and Simon met was Arthur Creter. Horman approached him on the hotel veranda and asked to borrow his newspaper. Creter began to talk freely. He introduced himself as a retired Marine lieutenant currently working as a civilian engineer for the U.S. Naval Base in the Panama Canal Zone. Simon thought she was hearing something important. She reproduced the conversations with Creter and other officers in detailed contemporaneous notes.

[SIMON]   Been here long?
[CRETER]   No, just down here to do a job.
[SIMON]   What kind of job?
[CRETER]   With the Navy.[89]

Terry Simon added to this exchange in an article she wrote for her magazine, *Senior Scholastic*, shortly after returning to the United States. "I was invited here by the military. You see, I work for the U.S. Navy. Now my job is done here and I'm just waiting to get out."[90]

Simon noted that Creter "claims that the coup had been a very smooth operation [and that he] had already talked to Panama by radio." He claimed to know that "around 4:30 in the morning of the 11th the military began mobilizing, and soldiers placed on street corners throughout the country and [quoting him] 'about a half hour later all Chile was under military control.'"[91]

In a conversation with an attractive young woman, Creter seemed to be bragging about inside knowledge of how the coup had happened. Creter's account may have been impressive in the moment, but it was far from accurate, let alone based on exclusive information from Panama. Later documented accounts of the coup events demonstrate that Santiago, for example, was not under military control until well into the afternoon of September 11, and the military was still attacking worker-controlled factories on September 12 and 13. In Valparaiso, the Navy did not declare martial law until 7:00 a.m.

Creter's statement about his work in Chile was later rendered in a *New York Times* article as "We came down to do a job and it's done," and interpreted as proof of U.S. involvement in the military coup.[92] But U.S. Navy officials later specified that Creter was hired by the Navy to come to Chile to work as a "MAP maintenance adviser," and that he was a "shipboard technician" who had nothing to do with the coup. Creter did not deny making the statement, but said its context was his job with the U.S. Navy and that he was not talking about the political situation.[93]

Lieutenant Colonel Pat Ryan met and talked briefly with Horman and Simon on September 11 when he came to the hotel to check on Creter. He saw them every day during their stay and drove them into Valparaiso to check at the Braniff Airways office for possible flights. There were none. They also went with him to the U.S. Naval Mission office and met Lieutenant Commander Roger Frauenfelder, who talked to them at length. He described the U.S. part of the scrubbed UNITAS joint maneuvers, saying the fleet had arrived with two destroyers, two escort ships and a submarine. "Says UNITAS was cancelled, that, ha ha, that was one of the tricky things the Chileans did so that no one would know this was happening," Simon wrote. Frauenfelder said he had been stationed in Chile for two years and in that time "I've become a real support of the [anti-Allende] cause." Frauenfelder pointed out his office window to an elegant four-masted ship in the harbor. He said the deposed mayor of Valparaiso was being held prisoner aboard the vessel. The ship was the *Esmeralda*, a tall ship used for training which became infamous when it emerged that more than 100 political prisoners had been held on board and many reported they were submitted to torture, including electric shock.[94]

Ryan then took them to Chief Paul Epley's house, where the Naval Mission's only radio was located. Simon dictated an airgram to her parents in Waterloo, Iowa, saying she was all right. They had lunch at Ryan's house and met his wife Audrey. He advised them it might still be risky to return to Santiago, but Simon wanted to make sure she was able to get a flight home as soon as the Santiago airport was opened. In that case, Ryan said, he could arrange transportation in a military vehicle back to Santiago. Ryan said his boss, Captain Ray Davis, had arrived that day to check on the Navy Mission and planned to return to Santiago the next day.

Ryan also made comments about the situation in Chile, displaying his fervent anticommunism. He said he had served several tours in Vietnam and blamed Cuba for what was happening in Chile. He said according to his information between 1,500 and 3,000 people had already been killed in Santiago. Such numbers were indeed circulating in U.S. intelligence reports at the time, but they were not correct. The real number was 275 people killed or disappeared as of September 14, when Ryan was speaking.[95] He joked about the pilots' aim in the Hawker Hunter attack on La Moneda. "You'd have to be a real hamburger to miss with a rocket," he said.

Simon's notes reflect her strong suspicions, but she later acknowledged the military men were friendly to her and helpful. On Saturday Ryan picked Horman and Simon up at the hotel and said their ride to Santiago with Captain Davis was all set. He invited them for a farewell lunch at a local restaurant, The Yugoslav Mansion, where they joined an informal gathering of Frauenfelder and his wife and children and Commander Edward Johnson and his wife Corki, whom they were meeting for the first time. Ryan continued to insist it would be safer for them to stay in Viña. Johnson even offered to let them stay in the spare room in his house. But they said they would take the ride with Captain Davis.

The 90-mile drive to Santiago on Saturday, September 15, was tense but uneventful, according to Simon. It was Charles Horman's only meeting with the man later accused of setting up his murder. Davis chatted mostly with Terry, since Charlie chose to ride in the back seat. Davis deflected her questions about the coup. In Davis's account of the ride, he noted that Horman mentioned his work on a children's film. Both his passengers were "well cultured," but he was most impressed by Simon, who he said "asked numerous and good questions." Horman had long hair and a beard but was "neatly groomed." There were few cars in sight as Davis drove them up the steep winding road from the coastal city, past the groves of majestic Chilean palms, and navigated the hills and curves leading to Santiago. Davis dropped them off outside the U.S. Embassy on Agustinas Street about 5:00 p.m.[96]

7 Vicuña Mackenna

Downtown Santiago, in contrast to the placid environment they had left behind on the coast, had the fearsome aspect of an occupied city. The bombed-out La Moneda Palace was just around the corner from the U.S. Embassy, at the far end of the large Constitution Plaza. Soldiers manning gun emplacements guarded the intersections. The smell of explosives still hung in the air. It was already too late to make it home, because of the 6:00 p.m. curfew. Charlie decided to get a room for them in the Hotel Carrera, which overlooked the plaza and the palace.

The next morning Horman called his landlord's house and left word for Joyce, saying he was in Santiago and would be home soon. He had not been able to reach her since going to the coast. After the relative tranquility of five days in Viña, he was reentering the scene of his chosen professional and political activities—his film project with Jorge Reyes and his commitment to the workers in the Cordones.

A lot had happened in the Vicuña Mackenna neighborhood and its Cordón since September 11, almost all of it disastrous for the workers' movement Horman had hoped to support. The area surrounding the Hormans' house was still the scene of ongoing military operations. On

September 11, within walking distance, workers at large factories had waited for weapons that never arrived to defend against the coup.

In 2019 I revisited the Cordón area near the Hormans' house. My guide was an eyewitness and protagonist in the events of September 11: Guillermo Orrego, a Communist union leader at the Standard Electric factory, located on the west side of Vicuña Mackenna, just across from Horman's house. He said he arrived for work early that day. "We gave the workers a choice of going home or staying to resist," he said. "We were all at the factory, waiting for the weapons to arrive. There were about 20 of us who stayed to guard the factory. We had one revolver and one bullet. But the party told us [by phone], 'A green truck is coming, it will be carrying weapons.'"[97]

"Six young men arrived and said they wanted to fight," he said. "We told them about the weapons that were on the way." They stayed all night, making "Miguelitos," contraptions of bent nails to be strewn on highways to blow out tires. Nearby there was fierce fighting. The Sumar Textile factory was only a few blocks to the west, and they could hear explosions and automatic weapons fire. Orrego saw small military tanks heading in the direction of the factory. A military helicopter flew low overhead, receiving heavy fire from a water tower near the Sumar factory. Smoke poured out but the helicopter was able to fly away out of range. The fighting lasted all night. The next day, when the Army sent a larger attack force, the workers escaped into the La Legua neighborhood and held out for several days. The fighting at Sumar and La Legua was the heaviest show of resistance against the military. Many of the fighters had come to make a stand there after first gathering at the INDUMET factory a few blocks to the west on Santa Rosa Avenue.[98]

No weapons ever showed up at Standard Electric, and the workers planned to disperse when they could. Early the next morning, in a meeting of the MIR and Communist leaders who had taken charge of the factory, Orrego was instructed to check on the situation at another Cordón factory, Textil Progreso. The factory was one of the largest in the Cordón, employing about 1,000 workers, most of them women. On the morning of the coup Mireya Baltra, Allende's Labor Minister and a Communist, had come to the factory. "The workers begged me for weapons," she said in a later interview. Instead, she had to be smuggled out wearing a blond wig to avoid capture. About 80 workers agreed to stay to protect the factory.[99]

The streets were quiet as Orrego made his way north on Vicuña Mackenna toward Textile Progreso. No Army or police units were in sight to enforce the curfew. Orrego arrived about 7:00 a.m., after a quick half-mile walk. The situation was not encouraging. The remaining workers had food and an underground shelter, but no weapons.

In early afternoon, a large force of Army soldiers and Carabineros arrived in trucks, small tanks and buses lined with hay bales as makeshift armor. "They shouted, 'You're surrounded, surrender, turn over your weapons,'" Orrego recounted. "We all filed out into the street, hands behind our heads." There were hundreds of workers lined up in the street, many from the large IRT electronics factory on the other side of Vicuña Mackenna Avenue, which had also been raided.

They watched as Carabineros marched a man out into the street. He was black, so the soldiers thought he must be one of the Cuban "international combatants" the military had been denouncing. "Run, you Cuban son of a bitch," Orrego heard them shout. Terrified, the man stumbled forward, and the soldiers raked him with automatic weapons fire. The man was Enrique Meza Carvajal, a Venezuelan who worked at a small factory nearby. He was among the first of the 50-some foreigners killed after the coup.

The soldiers ordered the prisoners to lie face down on the sidewalk. Several hours later Orrego and the other workers were herded into green Carabinero buses and taken to the Estadio Chile, a small stadium that was already packed with detainees. Workers and their leaders made up the largest number of prisoners in the early part of the repression. Orrego was one of tens of thousands of workers and activists held for more than a year in various makeshift prisons, including the National Stadium and Chacabuco, a desert town in the north.

All of these events occurred within a mile and a half of Horman's Vicuña Mackenna home. During our tour, I went with Orrego to the address where Horman had lived. The two houses were gone, replaced by a row of small but sturdy homes now common for working-class families in Chile. Orrego recognized the side street, Pasaje Eduardo de Calixto. He had attended political meetings in a small house a block from Horman's that functioned as a kind of local headquarters for workers affiliated with MIR. Orrego and I talked to an elderly man who had lived on the street since

1973. He vividly remembered when, two days before the coup, Army units drove by on their way to raid the nearby Sumar factory looking for weapons. Shots were fired, and the workers came out of the MIR house and lined the street to watch the action.

In the weeks and months prior to the coup there had been much rhetoric about weapons and armed resistance. Allende's vague pledge in June that "the people will have weapons" was never acted on. Caches of military weapons, however, indeed existed, according to later reports. The Socialist Party military arm had received three deliveries from Cuba prior to September, including 200 AK-47 assault rifles, six Soviet anti-tank rocket-propelled grenade launchers and a variety of pistols. Half of the weapons went to Allende's personal guard, called the GAP. Cuban sources also said Cuba delivered 3,000 weapons to units of MIR, the Communist Party and MAPU. In addition, hundreds of Chileans had traveled to Cuba for military training. More RPGs and automatic rifles were stockpiled inside the Cuban Embassy for the Communist Party's use, but the Cuban sources said the party never retrieved them, nor was there a plan or strategy for their use. Despite the word in the factories that green trucks were on the way, in the end no distribution occurred, probably on Allende's order. There were enough weapons for a bloodbath, but never remotely enough to successfully turn back the united Chilean Army.[100]

· · · · ·

All armed resistance in the Vicuña Mackenna Cordón had ceased by the time Horman arrived home at midday on September 16. It is unclear how much he was able to learn about the violent events that had transpired in the nearby factories. Terry Simon provides an anecdote from the taxi ride from the center up Vicuña Mackenna Avenue. As the taxi neared the Horman address, the driver pointed out the window to the right and said, "That's the Sumar Nylon factory over there. My brother worked there and he died in it when the military bombed it."[101] The streets were quiet, but the Army was conducting daily military operations.

Reunited with Joyce, Horman recounted the events in Valparaiso and his disgust at the U.S. military officers' enthusiasm for the coup. He talked separately with housemate Lluis "Lucho" Mestres, who recalled him saying he thought the U.S. officers he met were "advising on the coup."[102]

Notes attributed to Simon described the afternoon and evening:

> Joyce, Lucho and Bob High were there. CH (Charles) is high strung and nervous. Calls Joyce first and then Lucho into bedroom and describes trip.
> Shortly thereafter Joyce and Lucho leave to go to (a friend's house) to bathe and get the story boards for their cartoons. Charlie goes into a small "bodega" next to the house to burn some books and papers....
> Joyce and Lucho return approx. 6:10 pm.[103]

That evening Joyce and Charlie went through their books and papers to decide what to get rid of. Charles decided to keep his notes on the Viaux plot and the Schneider murder, since it was from library research and not compromising. He also didn't want to part with his freshly acquired copies of books by Marx and Engels.[104]

· · · · ·

Horman had returned from the States determined to push for the completion of the film project with Walter Locke and Jorge Reyes. At some point Horman contacted Reyes, the director, and they arranged a meeting. Reyes said the meeting occurred just after Horman had returned from Valparaiso, placing the meeting on either Sunday, September 16, or Monday the 17th. He said shooting for the film, eventually released with the title *Avenue of the Americas*,* was 80 percent finished, and much of the footage was safely out of the country thanks to Walter Locke. Reyes said he and others had continued filming, but after the coup the mounting repression had made their situation unsustainable and the new material was in danger of being lost. He described the meeting with Horman:

---

* Locke and Reyes finished work on the film in 1974, with additional camera work in the United States by Don Lenzer and research by David Hathaway and Judith Brister, among others. Released in June 1975 and distributed by New Line Cinema, it was shown in local theaters in Cambridge, Massachusetts, and on German television. Some of the footage was also used in another production by the California-based Lucha Films collective, called *Chile with Poems and Guns*. The title was taken from a Pablo Neruda poem.

Logically, the sole subjects of conversation were how we could save the material which had been filmed and the possibilities which the Chilean resistance had of consolidating itself, in forming an international fighting front, or, if nothing else could be done, what were [the] chances of abandoning the country. Quite logically, we all thought that those who had the greatest chance of leaving the country alive were Charlie and Joyce, as they were both North American citizens. This was to be the last time we ever saw each other.[105]

Reyes, who would seek asylum in the Argentine Embassy a few days later, was able to bring Horman up to date. Persecution of Chile's leftist filmmakers had begun early, centered on the vast studios of Chile Films. Horman had never worked directly at Chile Films, but he had deep connections to those who did—including Jorge Reyes and their mutual friend Pablo de la Barra. Reyes was able to report on recent violent events affecting the close-knit community of leftist filmmakers. Army units had raided the Chile Films campus on the morning of September 11, probably because it was known to be a center of leftist militancy whose director, Eduardo "Coco" Paredes, had been Allende's trusted ally as former head of the investigative police. The military was convinced there was a cache of weapons on the premises, said staff filmmaker Douglas Hubner. The soldiers tore apart sets and ripped open the flooring in the 100-yard-long sound studio—where Hubner knew military exercises had been conducted only days before with real weapons. They found nothing. Instead they began to burn film stock—as many as 400 canisters of recent work and historic footage of news reels from the 1960s.

Other Chile Films workers had arrived earlier and managed to save some of the most important filming projects, however, notably the many hours documenting the Chilean experiment by Patricio Guzmán. They carried the priceless footage to the Swedish Embassy, which got it out of the country to be made into Guzmán's masterpiece *The Battle of Chile*. The military searchers found boxes of special effects, such as realistic-looking blood, guns and bullets, which Hubner assured them were fake. To his great relief, someone had removed the dozen or so real weapons hidden in the studio.

Paredes, meanwhile, had gone to La Moneda the morning of September 11 and was detained with a large group of Allende's close advisers and members of GAP, the personal guard. The group was taken to Tacna Army base, whose troops had attacked the presidential headquarters. On September 13, Paredes and 23 others were shot in groups of four made to stand at the edge of a pit, in what is considered the largest mass execution of the early days. The next day *El Mercurio* falsely reported that Paredes and a colleague had attacked a Carabinero patrol car and were killed "while fleeing."[106]

There was also disturbing news about Pablo de la Barra. His production studio, a small house on Constitución Street, not far from Chile Films in the Bella Vista neighborhood, had been raided and ransacked. De la Barra was not at the studio, but he may have been a target for two reasons, the filmmaker said. Two days before the coup he had shot a dramatic final scene for his film *Queridos Compañeros* (Dear Comrades), which involved a police raid on a poor people's squatters encampment. One hundred extras playing the Carabineros wore authentic green uniforms and carried realistic-looking automatic rifles made out of wood. A second factor may have been that Alejandro de la Barra, Pablo's brother, was a prominent member of MIR's inner circle and had gone underground at the time of the coup.[107] The film was set in the late 1960s when MIR's revolutionary tactics, including bank robberies and land occupations, were at their height. According to de la Barra, "It was a film that portrays the nature of the political militant and specifically the militants of the MIR, the Movement of the Revolutionary Left of that time. It told the story of them robbing a bank."

Horman may have visited the production house a few times, de la Barra said, but did not work on the film. Still, there were several indirect connections stemming from their close friendship. Horman's housemate Janet Duecy was a major financial backer of de la Barra's project. In earlier filming, de la Barra shot a scene at the Horman-Duecy residence, portrayed as a MIR safe house, in the posh neighborhood of Las Condes. In the sequence, police raid the house, and a Mirista tries to escape by jumping over the back garden wall but is captured. In the real-life raid on de la Barra's production studio, the soldiers confiscated some fake guns and uniforms that were stored there and destroyed the audio tapes for the film. The footage for the almost-complete project was elsewhere and was saved, however, and smuggled into the Venezuelan embassy.[108]

PART II   The Search

The Embassy of the United States of America . . . has the honor to inform the Ministry . . . that no persons have been granted asylum in the American Embassy at Santiago.

DIPLOMATIC NOTE TO THE FOREIGN MINISTRY, September 28, 1973

The lists of patrols and detentions were right there. It was easy to know who arrested him [Horman].

RAÚL MENESES, the Chilean sergeant who identified the body

We were told, fairly early on in the Horman part of it all, that we were not to ask personal questions or look behind the letter of what was told us.

U.S. CONSUL FRED PURDY, unpublished memoir

8 Missing

Monday, September 17, was to be the first back-to-work day following the coup the previous Tuesday. The new Interior Minister, General Oscar Bonilla, called on all Chileans to return to their normal activities and said Santiago could resume its daily rhythms. He said that he understood that there might be fear in the minds of some people, "although very few."

"We understand your distress and we reach out our hand to you," he said in a lengthy statement in the right-wing newspaper *El Mercurio*. He mentioned government workers, poor people, the mothers of prisoners. He assured them that the new government would not persecute ideas, or political affiliation, but only actions. *El Mercurio* chose to put the next sentence in a large three-column headline:

**THEY HAVE NOTHING TO FEAR
WHO HAVE DONE NOTHING**

Four thousand people already had been imprisoned in the Santiago area, the general said, claiming improbably that the majority had been captured in connection with sniper activity in the city. He urged the citizenry to have patience. "Interrogation teams" had been organized to question the thousands of prisoners. Many would be released, he said, "as soon as they have been sufficiently interrogated."

If this message was intended to be reassuring, it came across instead as profoundly ominous and threatening. "Who should fear us?," he said, then answered his own question. "Very few: the extremist, who insists on violence . . . ; the foreigner, who has abused our hospitality, to whom we will show no mercy. We will pursue them to the end."[1]

The key word in the general's statement was "interrogation." The mass arrests of the first week now gave way to targeted military operations based on real-time actionable intelligence. Teams of officers from SIM, the Army's intelligence service,* were conducting interrogations of the thousands of prisoners crammed into the National Stadium. Major Pedro Espinóza was one of the lead officers in charge of this grim work.[2] Torture was applied systematically although not universally. Interrogators gleaned information about leftists still at large, working from lists of those associated with the former government or thought likely to form part of the resistance. SIM also compiled the thousands of tips from informers—neighbors and coworkers—that poured in from all over the city. The lists of targets grew longer as new information was accumulated. SIM officers translated the intelligence into orders to send heavily armed squads of soldiers and Carabineros to detain specific people at specific addresses.

A system was set up to determine which military commands had jurisdiction in each section of the country. It was called the Commandos of Area Jurisdiction of Interior Security (CAJSI, for its Spanish initials). The CAJSI for the Santiago metropolitan area—by far the area of the most intense ongoing military activity—was divided into sectors and subsectors, each under the control and responsibility of military garrisons set up

---

* The Army's intelligence service was known by two acronyms. The most common was SIM, Servicio de Inteligencia Militar (Military Intelligence Service), which is the designation found most often in U.S. and Chilean documents and in interview references. Its less common official name was DINE, Dirección de Inteligencia del Ejército (Directorate of Army Intelligence). Both names refer to the same entity, which was by far Chile's largest intelligence service at the time of the coup. In this text, to avoid confusion with DINA, Pinochet's notorious security and intelligence service officially created in 1974, I use SIM, "military intelligence" or "Army intelligence" to refer to the service acting at the time of the coup. See Pascale Bonnefoy, *Terrorismo de Estado: Prisioneros de Guerra en un Campos de Deportes*, 2nd expanded ed. (Editorial Latinoamericana, 2016), 20.

around the city, often in existing military facilities used for training and technical activities.[3] The police force, the Carabineros, were integrated into this overall command structure. Although some of the commands overlapped, it was a relatively straightforward process for those with access to the operational structure to identify which military unit had carried out a raid at a particular address in the city. Horman's address was in the sector assigned to the Eastern Group, headquartered on Antonio Varas Street in Ñuñoa.

Far from a restoration of calm, the repression that was to ensue in the days ahead would be as intense as and much more systematic than that of the first few days. Three thousand more prisoners would be taken to the Santiago National Stadium for a total of 7,000 by September 22, according to the Red Cross. Deaths by execution would reach 859 victims by the end of the month.[4] An unknown number of suspects remained missing—*desaparecidos* (disappeared), in the new lingo of repression. With resistance all but stamped out, many of the new killings were of prisoners, held and tortured at the National Stadium before being raked with automatic weapons. Their bodies were then dumped in the streets or rivers.

On Monday morning, workers in the militant factories that had been part of the Cordones had no choice but to show up for work and hope for the best. All of the formerly government- or worker-controlled factories had been quickly restored to their previous owners, who were provided with Carabineros or soldiers to stand guard over the returning workers.

Such a scenario played out at Elecmetal, the metallurgical factory on Vicuña Mackenna Avenue about two miles north of Horman's house. Owned by Ricardo Claro, one of the richest men in Chile, the factory was among the first to be taken over by the Allende government. It had a workforce of 500 to 1,000 and was one of the most important steel foundries in Latin America, manufacturing specialty equipment for Chile's copper mines. More apropos to the military, Elecmetal had functioned as the command center for the 12 Cordones Industriales around the city. In the wake of the Tancazo, Carlos Altamirano, the firebrand head of the Socialist Party, had chosen the factory to deliver a major speech to hundreds of workers from surrounding factories about the importance of the Cordones organizations as a "impregnable barricade against any insurrectionist attempt by the bourgeoisie." Armando Cruces, the Elecmetal union chief, had been the elected president of all the allied factories in the Vicuña Mackenna Cordón.

On the morning of September 17, as the workers arrived, the targeted union leaders were separated from the rest. In the presence of the owner's representative, Carabineros detained the union leaders and took them away in two vehicles, one of which was an Elecmetal company truck. Cruces had been among the group but somehow managed to escape and go into hiding. The next morning, the bodies of six men, riddled with bullets, were found on Avenida Macul and transported to the Santiago morgue. They were later identified as the Elecmetal leaders. *El Mercurio* reported that a similar process took place in all the Vicuña Mackenna factories, with large contingents of soldiers standing guard over the returning workers.[5]

Charles Horman rose early that Monday. He and Joyce had much to do in preparation to leave Chile. The reports of book burnings, the violence in the neighborhood, the killings and roundups of workers had converted their beloved Chile into a landscape of fear. He and Terry headed into central Santiago to check on possible flights. Joyce also left the house to do errands and visit a friend near Plaza Egaña, in the eastern part of the city.[6]

At the Braniff Airways office they learned the airport was still closed. There were rumors that a special flight was being organized for foreigners, and the U.S. Embassy might know about it. At the Embassy they were told—rudely, Terry recounted—that only the Consulate, located almost a mile away, could provide any information on travel options. In the lobby, they encountered Frank Manitzas, a veteran U.S. journalist on assignment for CBS. "We want to go home, we are afraid," Manitzas quoted Horman as saying. He gave them his card.[7]

Simon and Horman had lunch, then separated. Simon went to the Consulate, on Estados Unidos Street, to talk to one of the vice consuls. She had booked a room in the Hotel Riviera, near Santa Lucia Hill, and they agreed to meet there the next day or later in the week. Horman said he wanted to return home to talk over the next moves with Joyce.[8] Little is known of Horman's movements after saying goodbye to Terry. He may have had time for the meeting with his filmmaking comrades at a nearby café before catching a bus or taxi at the nearby Plaza Italia to return home.

Charles Horman arrived at his house at 4126 Vicuña Mackenna Avenue in mid- or late afternoon, and settled in to do some writing.

According to Lluis Mestres, he had said he intended to record the events in Valparaiso and the suspicious activities of the Americans he had met there for *FIN*. He wrote a five-paragraph "Dear Joyce" letter telling her he had put them on a waiting list for a flight with Braniff. He wrote that the Chileans were requiring a lot of "rigamarole" to leave the country, including tax papers, a *salvoconducto* (exit permit) and an interview at the police station. There might be a simpler way. He added, "Mrs Tipton at the consulate is compiling a list of U.S. citizens who want to get out and they would clear the whole list through the Chilean bureaucracy at the same time. Seems like less fuss and bother to me." He mentions what appear to be possible office times—2:30 and 4:30—when they can talk to her at the Consulate and sign up.

In a reference to Terry that Joyce would understand, he said "sweet pea" was at the Hotel Riviera near Santa Lucia Hill. A final paragraph was pensive, with a kind of sign-off. "I went through some of the books on Chile while I was here. Some really fascinating shit. Wish I had time to just sit and read for a few days. See you soon. Love." There was no signature.[9]

Sometime shortly after Horman finished the note, a squad of soldiers, led by an officer, arrived and banged on the gate. The soldiers went into the house and returned a few minutes later with Horman in custody. At least five neighbors who lived in apartment houses across the road from Horman's house saw the arrest from their windows and balconies, which looked down into the property. They pegged the time at around 5:00 p.m. All coincided in describing what happened as an Army operation. The soldiers wore Army uniforms, carried rifles and were transported in vehicles typical of military operations. The neighbors did not have to imagine what military activity looked like. Since the military coup dozens of such operations had been carried out in the Vicuña Mackenna industrial neighborhood. Witness Victoria Osorio said there was frequent military activity near her apartment, located less than a block from the ITT Standard Electric factory and about 70 meters (230 feet) from the Horman house. Traffic of military vehicles had been "constant" on Vicuña Mackenna Avenue in front of her building.

One of the witnesses said she saw Horman, the "norteamericano," arrive at the house, and that soon thereafter a military truck and a jeep with as many as a dozen soldiers pulled up in front. The neighbors knew

Horman as the young man renting the house from Dr. Núñez, who was well known as a provider of medical care to low-income residents in the area. The soldiers put Horman in the truck and drove off to the north in the direction of Central Santiago. Two soldiers remained posted at the iron gate. One witness happened to be in a taxi traveling behind the truck and testified the truck turned off to the east on a street leading to the National Stadium. Several witnesses said a similar truck returned later, and soldiers spent a good amount of time carrying things—books, household effects and personal items—out of the house and loading them on the truck.

Horman was alone when he was detained. Ariela Vecchi, the wife of their landlord Dr. Núñez, testified she and her husband had left the house that morning after receiving a warning that a military raid was about to happen. She said the warning came in a telephone call from a Carabinero as a favor to Dr. Núñez. Joyce Horman wasn't able to make it home that night because of the curfew. She said later that she and Lluis were running errands and visiting friends in the Ñuñoa neighborhood.[10]

The eyewitness accounts indicated Horman seemed to be the target of a planned military operation, not the victim of a random patrol. The size of the military unit and soldiers' actions, even the reported warning by a policeman, all indicated the military unit was executing a detention order specifically aimed at Horman. Later accounts from military sources confirmed that the order to detain Horman was the result of intelligence information.[11] The Vicuña Mackenna factory district was one of the most dangerous areas in Santiago after the coup, and the military was encouraging sympathizers to inform them about neighbors they suspected of being leftists, especially foreigners. Everything that happened was consistent with the many other military operations in the area, including raids on dozens of Cordón factories, at the same time when several thousand prisoners were being rounded up and packed into the improvised cells at the National Stadium.

The location and timing of Horman's arrest, at the same time as the worker roundups at the nearby Cordón factories, was one of several clues pointing to possible reasons to target the North American. Another clue, emerging from events the next day, pointed to Horman's film work and his perceived connections with Chile Films.

The next day was September 18, Chile's national independence day. Early that morning, at approximately 8:00 a.m., a good friend of the Hormans received an ominous call. Isabella Rastello and her husband Mario Carvajal lived near the Hormans' old residence on Paul Harris Street, and Joyce and Charles had visited them often to use the telephone since they did not have a phone in their own house. Rastello said the man on the phone spoke to her in an "angry and arrogant" voice: "You are speaking with the Military Intelligence Service. We have detained an extremist North American with a beard. What is your relationship with him?"

The man demanded to know why her name was in his address book, and asked if she knew that he was a leftist extremist who worked in films. She was shaken. She responded that no doubt the man was referring to her friend Charles Horman, and she explained he and his wife were friends and used their telephone. She said Horman's film work was in documentaries, but she didn't know anything about his politics.

Around the same time another friend, Warwick Armstrong, a New Zealander who worked at the UN economics office CEPAL, also received a call. It was from the Frenchman who was renting a house that Armstrong had previously occupied and still owned. Armstrong's number at that house also would have been in Horman's address book. The Frenchman said the caller, who refused to identify himself, said, "You should go to the nearest police station (Ñuñoa). Here they have a friend of yours who makes films." Armstrong was afraid going to the police station might result in his own arrest, so he did not go. Instead, around noon, he called the U.S. Consulate to report Horman missing and possibly detained.[12]

Joyce Horman had been unable to get transportation home the night before and was in danger of missing curfew. She had met up with Lluis Mestres at a friend's house. Heading home, they made it only as far as the Plaza Italia area. They tried another friend's apartment there, but no one was at home. They knocked on another door. People in that apartment were unwilling to let strangers stay the night but gave them a blanket. They ended up trying to sleep in the stairwell on the fourth floor.

Finally arriving at the Vicuña Mackenna house at about 8:30 a.m., they discovered that Charles was missing and their rooms had been ransacked. Unnerved, Joyce talked to neighbors but was not sure what had happened to her husband. In one statement she said no one told her that the soldiers had taken Charles prisoner. She thought that, like she and Lluis, he might have been unable to return home the night before because of curfew. The squad had conducted a thorough search of the house, and many things were missing. "There were broken dishes, books and papers were scattered all around, the sheets had been torn off the beds, and, as I recall, even the mattresses had been pulled off the beds. It was a total mess," she later testified. She listed the stolen items: a Pentax camera, a tape recorder, a record player, a number of books about socialism, including books by Karl Marx in English, a clock radio, a wristwatch, an electric heater, and three portable radios, among other things. Curiously, perhaps, a box with two bottles of Scotch and a few dollars in cash was left untouched.[13]

Mestres, a native Spanish speaker, understood clearly that Charles had been taken prisoner and that the neighbors were warning them to get out of the house because the soldiers already had come several times and might be returning. Mestres and Joyce took a bus back to Santiago and went to the house of a friend, Heliette Saint Jean, in the affluent Vitacura neighborhood—a haven of relative safety given the circumstances. There she called her former neighbors Mario Carvajal and Isabella Rastello, to see if they knew anything about Charles's whereabouts. Carvajal said he had important information but didn't dare give it to her over the phone. Joyce wanted to go to meet him immediately, but her friend Heliette, a psychologist, said she was too tired and upset. She sent her son, who later returned with the frightening news about the call from military intelligence. It was only then that Joyce became convinced the military had abducted her husband. Heliette urged her distraught friend to rest and gave her a sedative. She then called the U.S. Consulate to report the missing U.S. citizen—the second such call to U.S. authorities that day.[14]

. . . . .

Far away across Santiago, in the western, once elegant part of the city, only a few hundred yards from the massive General Cemetery, the Santiago morgue was overwhelmed with the arrival of hundreds of bullet-riddled bodies. The modest facility had a small public entrance and a larger driveway providing access for ambulances and large vehicles leading to a basement area with a few refrigerated units. Before the coup, it customarily handled seven to ten bodies a day. All bodies were given an autopsy and if necessary their fingerprints were checked against the national identification database generated by identity cards, a universal requirement for all Chileans and residents.

In the weeks after the coup, thirty to forty bodies were brought to the morgue each day, often in groups of five to ten transported by police or military trucks. The medical examiners could no longer keep up. Mutilated bodies were lined up on the floors in corridors and any available space.[†]

By 11:00 a.m. on Tuesday, September 18, the festive national independence day in normal times, fifteen new bodies had arrived, all recorded as being found in *la vía publíca* (the public street) and most unidentified. The legal authority in charge of the bodies was listed as the military court or a local police station. The Macul Carabinero station delivered six of the bodies at 10:50 a.m. Logged in with registry numbers 2653–2658, the six men were soon identified as the union activists detained the previous morning at the Elecmetal factory in the Vicuña Mackenna Cordón.

At 1:35 p.m. three more unidentified bodies arrived. Again, the log book listed them as found in a public street and brought in by *militares* (military personnel). Body number 2663 was listed as NN—unidentified—and would remain so for a month. It was Charles Horman. An autopsy performed a week later determined he had died of multiple gunshot wounds to the head.

. . . . .

David Hathaway had obeyed the general order to the populace to return to work. He was nervous at first but knew if he didn't show up it would raise suspicions. All seemed relatively normal at the MADEMSA factory,

---

[†] The blog *Archivos Chile* documented the scene: "The entrance was frightful. The oval corridor running through the building was lined with corpses along both walls, from the door entrance to the back. The room where the refrigeration chambers are, which numbered about 90, was also full, and not all of them were working. In each unit one, two, three, four bodies were placed. In that room there were also bodies on the floor," said Dr. José Luis Vásquez, a staff coroner (https://archivoschile.com/dentro-del-instituto-medico-legal-primera-parte). The author is the director and founder of ArchivosChile, a Santiago investigative center in conjunction with the University of Chile journalism faculty.

and for a few days he was contemplating that it might be possible to stay in Chile. His partner Olga Muñoz was five months pregnant, and he began to envision getting married and raising their child in Chile. He liked his job as a skilled machinist, for which he had taken a training course. He also had been doing translations, paid in dollars, at the Ford Foundation. The combination of intellectual and working-class jobs fit his self-image as a committed revolutionary.

"We were nervous for sure, but we had not decided to leave the country," Hathaway said. "We figured let's see what's gonna happen.... I actually—it must have been the 17th or 18th—I went back to work at MADEMSA. I was taking the bus to be there by 8 in the morning, and I worked my shift. The situation at work was eerily normal. I was careful not to be in touch with anybody I was politicly related to there. I was just kind of laying low."[15]

Teruggi had spent the week checking on friends. Several of his *FIN* colleagues lived in an apartment in the high-rise Torres de San Borja, just across from the UNCTAD building on Alameda Avenue. The apartments had been a haven for foreigners and were therefore extremely vulnerable. Frank helped one of his colleagues transport "huge bags" of books on Chile, and anything that appeared to be Marxist, for safekeeping in the nearby *FIN* office. When the building had been raided on September 13, soldiers broke down doors and set an enormous bonfire of books they had thrown down from the apartment balconies.

The colleague, who did not want to be identified, was one of the last to see Teruggi alive. "Frank was always helping people," she said. "He would do anything to help a friend. He was dignified and sometimes seemed older than the rest of us because, though young, he was so quiet and serious. Frank was a true democrat. That is, he believed that the real power to bring about change belonged to the people and not the leaders of a country." But he could also be abrupt and argumentative, when he thought he was in the right. Though slight and not very tall, he was not afraid to "talk back" to authority figures. "He was the kind of guy who would have said 'Fuck you' to the military," the colleague said, adding that "a bunch of us thought that." And some of those friends feared something like that might have happened when he got arrested.[16]

On Thursday evening, September 20, Hathaway, Olga and Frank were sitting in the living room listening to shortwave broadcasts from Radio

Havana, which provided nightly updates on the Chilean situation. They heard a loud buzz indicating someone was at the front gate. Since it was after curfew, when only government authorities were on the streets, they quickly turned off the set. While Olga went to the gate, Frank and David pulled down the wires strung along the walls that served as an antenna. It was five Carabineros, who politely asked if they might search the house. Olga noticed there was a well-dressed woman with them who looked like she was from the *barrio alto*, the rich section of Santiago. Later Hathaway learned that a neighbor woman had told the police that suspicious foreigners lived in the house and they should check it out because they might be dangerous extremists. They were all frightened, but David was somewhat reassured that the police had rung the bell instead of breaking through the gate.

Inside, the policemen were especially deferential to Olga, who was visibly pregnant. They searched, but it didn't seem to Hathaway that they had any particular objective. Olga said they found her jewelry and some money, but returned them to her. "They always treated us very well." The only thing they found that seemed to attract their attention was in Teruggi's room. His packages of books wrapped to be sent to the United States were stacked on the desk and floor. He had sent a package that day from the post office.

"That's what they picked up on, were all these packages with books inside them in his bedroom, and on the bookshelves," Hathaway said. "A policeman said, 'Ah ha, he's got all this Marxist literature.'" The books included Teruggi's complete set of Lenin's writings, and a recently acquired biography of Leon Trotsky. They packed up the books and took them "as evidence." They also took Teruggi's camera and tape recorder. But a stack of leftist magazines in Hathaway's bedroom was untouched. One of the policemen said to Teruggi, "I have seen you before, I know you." They told Hathaway and Teruggi they had to come with them to the station. Olga could stay in the house. No one was mistreated or even put in handcuffs. Frank and David were loaded into a green bus typical of those used by Carabineros. The policemen rode at the back of the bus, where bales of hay had been placed against the windows for protection.‡ The only

---

‡ Around the same time, but in broad daylight, a dozen Carabineros in a similar green bus raided and searched my house on Julio Prado Street, in the same neighborhood. I noticed the bales of hay. The policemen were far from polite in our case. They charged into

prisoners, Teruggi and Hathaway were ordered to kneel facing the windows near the front, so that—they were told—in case of a terrorist attack they would be the first to be hit.

The bus took them to a police headquarters in the neighborhood, known as the Non-Commissioned Officers School, near the Plaza Zañartu. There the treatment changed. A uniformed Carabinero officer demanded to know what they were doing in Chile and if they were activists or extremists, and punched each of them in the chest, hard enough to leave Hathaway gasping for breath. None of the questions were specific. After a while they were put back on a bus and taken to the National Stadium, which was only a few blocks away. It was past midnight and they spent the night in the passageway outside the locker rooms that were being used as improvised prison cells for foreigners.

Their guards and interrogators were uniformed Army soldiers and officers. In the morning their questioning focused exclusively on Frank, who was asked about the calluses on his hands, which indicated he knew karate. They showed him photos from the house, and asked him to identify people appearing in them. Hathaway was taken aside and asked questions about Frank's political activities, but virtually nothing about himself. "They were preoccupied with the Marxist books in Frank's possession. I said that Frank didn't have any political activity in Chile, that he had never told me about any political activities," Hathaway said in early statements. The officer told Hathaway he believed Teruggi was a member of an unnamed leftist political party. When they were left alone, Frank and David talked about what they could safely say and how to avoid contradictions. "We talked about both of our stories, trying to make sure that things were coordinated so that we would not implicate any of our Chilean friends." Frank told him the officer didn't ask any questions about Hathaway, only about his own activities.

They spent the morning in the corridor, and then were placed in the cell for foreigners—one of the large dressing rooms under the bleachers intended for athletes using the stadium. They were not blindfolded, nor

---

the house demanding to know "¿Donde estan las armas?" (Where are the weapons?) They burned some of our books in the backyard; one book that attracted their attention was entitled *A Revolution in Psychology*. None of the Chileans who lived in the house were at home, and no one was detained.

were their hands tied. Hathaway estimated there were about 200 prisoners in the room, all foreigners. Sometime in the early evening an officer called Teruggi's name and took him away for further questions. Hathaway thought it was a prelude to their being released. He never saw Teruggi again.[17]

Frank Teruggi's lifeless body was logged into the morgue together with those of five other young men late the next evening. The log book noted the bodies had arrived at the same time—9:15 p.m., September 22—and they received consecutive registry numbers 2828–2833, indicating they were part of the same delivery of bodies, probably in a military truck. All were initially NN—unidentified—and listed as found in the street.[18] The military court was listed as the legal authority for the cases, as had become the rule for bodies brought in by police or military since September 11. The morgue workers noted that all had signs of beating or torture and had died from multiple gunshot wounds to the head and chest.

Teruggi was number 2832. Four of the men in the same delivery had been detained at a government-controlled factory, Aerolite, which manufactured car batteries. They included the government controller and two of his assistants, both lawyers. The sixth man was a 22-year-old Marine who had tried to resign before the coup and had turned himself in the previous day. The man's body showed signs of a ferocious beating with clubs, in addition to multiple bullet wounds.[19] The six bodies were the last of 38 delivered to the morgue that day, Saturday, September 22. At the time, half of them were unidentified.

· · · · ·

Testimony later surfaced that other prisoners had seen Teruggi in another part of the stadium during the 24 hours after he left Hathaway. The reports indicated that he had been taken to a circular building adjacent to the Velodrome, the track for bicycle racing. The military had converted the facility to a torture and interrogation center. The details, from two separate sources, were sparse but horrific. Several prisoners said they saw a North American named Frank, whom the interrogators referred to with curses as *gringo*. They were able to talk to him between interrogation sessions. He had been tortured with electroshock and so brutally beaten that he was semiconscious. The prisoners, many of them Communist Party activists, were also being questioned under torture. They were among the hundreds rounded up at the Technical University on September 11.

"He asked us, if anyone was released, to say that among the foreigners there were not only Latin Americans but also several North Americans, and that he was confident that the Embassy of the United States would do something for him," according to the account.[20] One of the witnesses was later identified as Victor Velastín, a Communist official from the city of Los Andes.[21] Another account came from Andre Van Lancker, a Belgian citizen who was imprisoned because of his job as a textile engineer in the Allende government. In an affidavit obtained in 1975, Van Lancker related what he heard from his fellow prisoners:

> The military took him for interrogation the same days as for me, i.e. about the 20th to the 23rd of September 1973, to the "caracol," a kind of corridor of the velodrome. . . . An officer whose identification was "Alfa-1" or "Sigma-1," I do not remember anymore, was in charge of the interrogation where Frank was heavily tortured by blows and electricity shocks. Finally Frank was in such a bad condition that the officer commented that he (the officer) had gone too far and he shot him with a burst of machine gun—as used in such cases. Afterwards, fellow prisoners told me the military commented among themselves, their fear of having troubles with the government of the U.S.A., that is why they did not want to recognize Frank's presence in the stadium.[22]

Two Americans had now died. The efforts to find their bodies and get an explanation for why they were killed naturally focused on the Embassy of the military government's principal ally, the United States.

9 The Embassy

Three years earlier the U.S. government had tried and failed to prevent Allende from taking office. The attempted coup resulted in the murder of General Schneider—the case Horman had been investigating for a possible article—which, if anything, helped rally support for Allende and democracy. After that debacle, U.S. officials concluded they had "virtually no capacity to engineer Allende's overthrow in the present situation." Instead Kissinger designed and Nixon approved a policy to show a public face of "cool but correct" diplomacy, while taking action behind the scenes to undermine and destabilize his government. The plans, as summarized by a top State Department official, "posit as their minimum goal the creation of pressures and circumstances which might cause or force Allende to fail or to modify his goals and as a maximum the creation of circumstances which might lead to his collapse or overthrow more easily later."[23]

The U.S. strategy as implemented was not sufficient by itself to bring Allende down, but was intended to provoke Chileans to act. Over three years, the tactics were varied and mostly covert, to avoid creating public sympathy for a besieged Popular Unity. The CIA funneled money to opposition parties, to newspapers for anti-Allende propaganda and to radical right-wing groups. The administration used its influence to cut off investment and veto international loans to Chile. The Pentagon groomed Chilean military leaders with offers of future military aid and clear signals that the U.S. would have their back should they decide to act against Allende. In September 1972, for example, General Pinochet, then the Army Chief of Staff, was invited on an official visit to the Panama Canal Zone. While there U.S. officers wined and dined him, and told him the "U.S. will support a coup against Allende 'with any means necessary' when the time comes."[24]

After September 11, Nixon and Kissinger exchanged the equivalent of high fives by telephone.

KISSINGER: Of course the newspapers are bleeding because a pro-Communist government has been overthrown. . . . I mean instead of celebrating—in the Eisenhower period we would be heroes.

NIXON: Well we didn't—as you know—our hand doesn't show on this one though.

KISSINGER: We didn't do it. I mean we helped them. [U.S initiatives] created the conditions as great as possible.

NIXON: That's right. And that is the way it is going to be played.[25]

Pinochet turned his mind quickly to his U.S. ally as well. The day after his successful coup, the general reached out to establish direct contact with the U.S. government, summoning an officer of the U.S. MilGroup, Colonel Carlos Urrutia, to his headquarters to ask him to transmit a personal message. He expressed the desire for strong and friendly ties with the United States, and his hope the U.S. would provide immediate help to relieve Chile's international debt. He seemed almost to apologize for keeping the U.S. in the dark about the coup: "Gen. Pinochet also referred to the fact that he and his colleagues had not even hinted to us beforehand of their developing resolve to act and said he thought it had been better that way."[26]*

---

* New U.S. declassified documents shed light on the still controversial question of a possible U.S. role in the coup. They show that as late as the day of the coup U.S. intelligence reports to President Nixon were uncertain if a united Army under Pinochet would join the Navy and Air Force in the move against Allende. President's Daily Brief, September 11, 1973: "Plans by navy officers to trigger military action against the Allende government [redacted] reportedly have the support of some key Army units." This long-withheld document presenting

Other generals came into the room to brief Urrutia on military progress. He said they were "pleased at the way things are going," and that they were facing only isolated pockets of resistance.

· · · · ·

The disappearances of Horman and Teruggi were reported as soon as possible to the U.S. Embassy. Embassy officials were well-positioned to get to the bottom of what had happened, especially considering the U.S. government's already close relations with the new military regime. Traditionally U.S. Embassies have taken very seriously their responsibility to protect U.S. citizens living in foreign countries. And Americans abroad almost instinctively expect that their U.S. passports provide them with a certain status and shield perhaps not available to citizens of other less powerful nations.

In this case, however, the reports of two missing Americans, together with the mounting evidence of massive human rights violations by the Pinochet regime, represented an awkward inconvenience, a snag in the U.S. determination to help the junta succeed. Teruggi's comment to his fellow prisoners indicated he had confidence the U.S. Embassy would come to the assistance of even those U.S. citizens, like him, who ardently disagreed with his government's policies. He was a committed leftist, but he had grown up in a family that believed in American values and opportunities and trusted the government.

The situation of the two Americans was not unique. The massive roundups of leftists and government sympathizers had quickly devolved into an international refugee and humanitarian crisis. At least 840 foreigners were swept into Chilean prisons and 49 were killed. Most were

---

intelligence conclusions to the president was released in September 2023 at the request of the Chilean government. On the question of the U.S. role, Kornbluh, in *The Pinochet File*, 111-116, concludes that the U.S. government was directly involved in creating a "coup climate" and destabilization. Not so in the coup itself: "By the most narrow definition of 'direct role'—providing planning, equipment, strategic support and guarantees—the CIA does not appear to have been involved." The authoritative study by Tanya Harmer, using Chilean as well as U.S. documents, reached similar conclusions. See Harmer, *Allende's Chile and the Inter-American Cold War* (UBC Press, 2011), 223-230. I concur with Kornbluh and Harmer in concluding that U.S. actions fell short of direct involvement in the coup.

Latin Americans from neighboring countries whose military governments would later form the transnational Condor alliance to continue the campaign against exiled leftists. Argentina, Brazil, Uruguay and Bolivia accounted for almost 500 of the total, and their governments dispatched military officers to Santiago to interrogate the prisoners from those countries.[27]

But citizens of prosperous democratic countries were also targeted by the repression. Twenty-five American citizens were detained, most in the National Stadium. In addition to Americans Horman and Teruggi, citizens of France, Great Britain, Spain and Italy were also killed. The foreign prisoners included 90 Europeans, 25 of them French. Drawing on a century of diplomatic precedent, the European countries and some Latin American countries reacted by quickly opening the doors of their embassies to people—not only their own citizens—who felt their lives were in danger. The embassies would eventually give asylum to more than 3,000 Chileans and 1,000 foreigners. The most crowded embassies were those of Argentina, Mexico, France, Sweden, West Germany and Italy. In addition, the UN High Commission for Refugees sent a representative to Santiago to organize a network of safe houses, in conjunction with the Catholic Church, which harbored 3,500 Latin Americans and their families who had been living in Chile as exiles with refugee status.[28]

The U.S. government, closely identified with the new regime, took a radically different approach. The United States wanted to convey to the world that the violence in Chile, while necessary to put down subversion, would soon be under control. Americans who showed up at the Embassy were assured that they would be safe in their homes and that they would be able to leave the country if they wished when things calmed down. Joyce Horman was an example. When she went to the Consulate to report her husband missing, she asked for protection and was refused.[29] Embassy officials were instructed that U.S. diplomatic facilities would not be used to harbor those seeking protection, even American citizens. In a diplomatic note to the new government, the Embassy wrote: "The Embassy of the United States of America presents its compliments to the Ministry of Foreign Affairs of the Republic of Chile and has the honor to inform the Ministry . . . that no persons have been granted asylum in the American Embassy at Santiago."[30]

The detentions of both Horman and Teruggi were duly reported to the U.S. Consulate, with the expectation that U.S. officials would contact the police and military to make inquiries. For most observers and journalists, it would seem naïve to expect that Chile's police or judicial system would honestly investigate killings most likely committed by the new military authorities, who were in firm control of every aspect of Chilean society. If anything was to be done, if any semblance of truth or justice was to be accomplished, the only realistic chance would be decisive action by U.S. Embassy officials, who had unique access and influence with the new authorities.

. . . . .

The U.S. press quickly learned, in the early days after the coup, that a number of American citizens were among the thousands of detainees, and pressed the State Department about what they were doing in Santiago to protect them. The issue came to a head at a contentious press briefing at the State Department on September 20. In previous days, the Embassy had transmitted to Washington lists of Americans reported detained. Horman's name was listed in a cable the day of the briefing. One list had 17 names. The one with Horman had nine.

The reporters wanted to know how many Americans were being held and whether the Embassy had "any contact" with them. (Diplomatic protocols require a country that detains a foreign citizen to allow consular officials from that person's country to visit the prisoner to ensure their welfare.) In answer, the State Department official minimized the number of reported detainees, saying "perhaps as many as six have been detained by the Junta." He couldn't say whether there had been any consular contact. A reporter said he was surprised the official had "no answer" to the question and insisted on knowing if the junta had blocked consular access to any of the prisoners. The State Department official waffled: "That's hard to say. It's a pretty confused situation. You know how you can run into anomalous situations. When I tell you that, I don't want you to think that we're having trouble."[31]

In fact, the cables from Santiago made clear that access to prisoners had been denied. U.S. officials, like Consul Fred Purdy, went repeatedly to the Stadium, but saw no prisoners, only lists that had been carefully scrubbed to exclude prisoners who had been killed.[32] Of Horman and other prisoners who were unaccounted for, the Embassy reported, "Chilean military authorities deny they are held in national Stadium and have no further info."[33]

In a subsequent cable, the State Department informed the Embassy its spokesman was "having a difficult time with questions" about the status of detained Americans and said the junta's "continued refusal to allow access" was hurting the new government's efforts to improve their image in the press.[34] More questions about the missing Americans were to be expected in coming days, the cable said, adding that it is "imperative that consular officers gain access to detainees so spokesman can say so."

There was a much more important reason to gain access. Had Embassy officials demanded access to the prisoners in the Stadium, they might have been able to save Frank Teruggi's life. The testy exchange about visits to American prisoners came on the same day, September 20, that Teruggi was detained and imprisoned in the Stadium. He was held there and tortured for the greater part of three days, until his execution late on September 22. It is not known what, if any, efforts were made by the Embassy during that time to overcome the junta's ban on visiting the imprisoned Americans.

· · · ·

The decisions about what to do and how to react to the new junta were in the hands of Embassy officials cast in new roles. Having been sent to Chile to support opposition to Allende, they now were tasked with defending the military government. Unavoidably, however, they also would have leading roles in the diplomatic and investigative drama of the Horman and Teruggi disappearances. For these officials, the saga would unfold in the first weeks and months after the coup and continue amid unresolved controversy for decades. We have already met one of the players, MilGroup commander Captain Ray Davis, who drove Horman and Simon from Valparaiso to Santiago in his car three days before Horman's detention. Primary responsibility for assisting U.S. citizens in trouble fell to Frederick Purdy, by virtue of his position as General Consul. Purdy was an experienced foreign service officer who had recently married a Chilean woman. He counted among his circle of contacts Michael Townley, an American expatriate and right-wing activist.[35] (In 1976 Townley, as an agent of Pinochet's security service DINA, would plant the car bomb that killed former foreign minister Orlando Letelier and Ronni Moffitt in Washington, DC.)

Purdy's deputy consul was James Anderson, who carried out work as an undercover CIA officer in addition to his consular duties.[36] During Allende's tenure, his circle of Chilean contacts included those working to "cause the economic collapse of Chile."[37] In the case of the missing Americans, Anderson's dual role was perhaps an asset, allowing him to work with Chilean intelligence operatives and to carry out key investigative tasks. He was credited with working hard on the case. Captain Ray Davis, his deputy Colonel Carlos Urrutia of the MilGroup and Military Attaché Colonel William M. Hon were well-connected with officers in the top echelons of the Chilean military.† Their liaison role, routine under civilian governments, was elevated to many times its normal importance in the wake of the military takeover. Nor did the U.S. officers hide their sympathy for their Chilean counterparts and enthusiasm for the demise of the Allende government. Captain Davis was by all accounts a competent career officer who sometimes exhibited conservative political views.

At the pinnacle of the Embassy was Ambassador Nathaniel Davis, a career diplomat who in his private life was considered somewhat liberal. He was not related to Captain Davis. Early in his career he helped the Kennedy administration organize the Peace Corps, and was sent to Chile to run the Peace Corps office there. Returning as ambassador, he presided over a diplomatic team deeply embedded with the opposition to Allende, including far-right groups, working to foment unrest and undermine the economy. With the coup, Chile went from adversary to cherished ally of the United States, deserving of enormous gratitude for having delivered a Cold War victory and deadly blow—in the perception of U.S. policymakers— against international communism. Davis treated the murders of two Americans as an obstacle to accomplishing U.S. policy, which was to

---

† Colonel Hon and Captain Davis were same rank in their respective services. A captain in the Navy is the equivalent of a colonel in the Army. Thus Captain Davis was the superior of Lieutenant Colonel Ryan, a Marine, who served in the U.S. MilGroup.

shepherd the new military government into international respectability.[38] More than murders to be investigated, the deaths of Horman and Teruggi were a problem to be finessed and an obstacle to be removed. Following his lead, the U.S. government persistently refused to acknowledge—for almost 20 years—that Chile's military had killed them.

Davis's second-in-command was Herb Thompson, the Deputy Chief of Mission. A World War II veteran who had spent time at the National War College, his cables displayed sympathy for the military and aversion to the families of the victims and to leftist Americans in general. He would take charge of the Embassy in November for several key months after Davis returned to the United States to take up a new post.

In general, Embassy personnel lined up easily behind U.S. policy. The middle and lower levels of political and economic officers, as well as the younger CIA officers, tended to side with the new military rulers for social and cultural reasons. Defending the junta, said Jeffrey Davidow, the lowest-ranking political officer in 1973,

> quite frankly fit in with the mentality in the Embassy. Most of the people in the Embassy, you know, as good middle-class Americans, looked on Allende with horror. And all of our Chilean friends were anti-Allende because of what we saw that Allende had done to Chilean society, which was really tragic. So there was a predilection to not come down hard on the military, or at least in the very beginning as the outrages grew.

Davidow was assigned the portfolio of human rights officer—a new position. Looking back, he came to feel guilty about not taking the job as seriously as he should have under the circumstances.

> We would go talk to Chilean officials. Not so much me, but the ambassador. I think we played a role in getting some people out [of prison], but we never, I think, went to the Chileans and said, look, we're your friends, yeah, but if you want a decent relationship with the U.S., clean up your act. I don't think we said it. . . . To which the Chilean government, I'm sure, would say, the hell with you. We've got Kissinger, we've got Nixon.

Davidow, who rose to ambassador rank and became the State Department's Assistant Secretary for Interamerican Affairs, later became a behind-the-scenes critic, especially of the Embassy's lackluster approach to the Horman-Teruggi cases. "So, you know, people's opinions change. And then I think it really took a couple of years for it to sink in just how beastly they were."[39]

Finally there were a few officials, both in the Santiago Embassy and in Washington, who even at the time were increasingly uncomfortable with U.S. failure to publicly confront the Chilean military about Horman and Teruggi and human right violations. Their dissenting reports were drafted in the heat of events but would be kept secret for decades, until their release in 1999 among thousands of declassified documents on Chile.

One of the dissenters, Robert S. Steven, spoke on the record to give an inside view of Embassy actions in those tumultuous days. Chile was Steven's second posting in Latin America. Son of a Massachusetts Unitarian minister, he sought the Chile assignment because of interest in the Allende experiment and its fraught relationship with the United States. He became one of the few human rights idealists in an Embassy full of Kissingerian pragmatists.

On the morning of September 11 he made it to the Embassy early and posted himself at a window in the upper floors overlooking Constitution Plaza. He saw troops and tanks converge in front of La Moneda and begin firing. The Hawker Hunter fighter bombers roared almost directly overhead as they launched the missiles that ended the battle. He also witnessed firsthand the callous treatment of American citizens who contacted the Embassy seeking protection. On this issue, he said:

> Our record is not a good one, it's not a handsome one.... One of the very best examples, being the day of the coup, when Americans came—I know this is a very controversial question, but I was there, I saw it—some Americans came to the embassy and asked to be allowed to come in for refuge because there was shooting in the streets, and [they] were refused entry. They were told, "No, just go home. They're not going to bother any Americans. As soon as things quiet down, you'll be all right. It's not necessary for you to come in here," and they left. In some cases they went to other embassies. We had Americans taking refuge in other embassies, and we had cases of Americans who had friends on the embassy staff, going to their houses.[40]

Steven said Ambassador Davis gave the instructions to refuse asylum by phone from his home on the day of the coup because he was not able to make it downtown to the Embassy. Even though neither Horman nor Teruggi had asked for such protection, the policy was frequently cited as an example of the Embassy's callousness and indifference to the plight of leftist Americans in Chile, two of whom were murdered. And in fact, Steven said, with Bostonian understatement: "I don't believe you will find much evidence that we put pressure on them to do things. . . . The result, I believe, for several years was that the Chilean military went happily on their way abusing and planning what amounts to a fascist political system, thinking that the United States would support them or at least didn't care."

. . . . .

In mid-September 1973 these Embassy officers faced their ineluctable duty to help the Americans known to be detained by the military and to investigate what had happened to the two—Horman and Teruggi—who were still missing. At the same time Washington was unequivocal in its instructions to the Santiago Embassy to deal lightly with the new military leaders. Ambassador Davis was immediately ordered to tell the new authorities, "The USG [U.S. government] wishes make clear its desire to cooperate with the military junta and to assist in any appropriate way." Henry Kissinger, in the first full policy meeting on Chile on September 14, stressed support and avoidance of criticism: "The first thing for us not to do is to give the appearance that we are putting pressure on them."[41]

The Embassy's duty to help its citizens was on a collision course with its orders to cooperate with the government that was detaining and—in Horman's and Teruggi's cases killing—U.S. citizens. By the time a consular official was able to enter the Stadium to look for the two Americans, they were already dead.

10 Investigations

What is most surprising about the Horman-Teruggi case is that there was any official investigation at all. Chile had a system of civilian investigators and forensic institutions that, under judicial supervision, was designed to go into action to investigate any unexplained death, such as a body with bullet wounds found in the river or on a street. That system continued to function after the coup, although it was under tight military control and was overwhelmed in the face of hundreds of violent deaths during the aggressive military repression. Yet it is now known that Chile's Investigative Police (PICH)[42] conducted several investigations of the Horman murder, on orders from the interior minister, General Oscar Bonilla. Moreover, General Lutz, the chief of military intelligence (SIM), acting on orders from General Pinochet following his meeting with the U.S. ambassador, also assigned officers to track down what happened to Horman and find his body. That those Chilean investigations took place is at least partially to the credit of the U.S. Embassy; that the Embassy made no attempt to follow up on any of the numerous substantive leads generated by those investigations is to the Embassy's shame. The Embassy even ignored and withheld from the families information gathered by its own personnel.

On receiving notice of detained Americans, including Horman, Consul Fred Purdy had his staff call police stations and the PICH. The top U.S. military officers, Defense Attaché Hon and MilGroup commander Davis, made inquiries as well among their military contacts. Hon contacted his counterpart in Army intelligence and sent him a photo of Horman. Captain Davis, whom Simon knew from the ride from Valparaiso, had several meetings with Joyce Horman and Terry Simon and helped them. Davis drove Horman to her house with an escort of Chilean soldiers to retrieve belongings. And he hosted the two women for dinner at his home and invited them to stay overnight because of the early evening curfew.[43]

Consul Purdy and Vice-Consul James Anderson made several trips to the National Stadium on Grecia Avenue. Purdy said the first visit was September 16, to check on the American couple Adam Schesch and Patricia Garrett, University of Wisconsin graduate students who had been reported detained the day before. Purdy entered the Stadium with an escort and saw some prisoners at a distance, but was blocked from talking to them. Likewise on September 19, when he was looking for Horman. He was shown informal handwritten lists of detainees, none of which had Horman's name.[44] Hon's contact, Colonel Juan Henríquez of Army intelligence, reported on September 20 that he had been told Horman was not in custody at the Stadium or in "any other detention centers."

Purdy's calls to PICH produced similar denials, but unbeknownst to Purdy the agency had begun an investigation. On September 20 two detectives showed up at the scene of the detention at the Vicuña Mackenna house, according to one of the owners, Ariela Vecchi.[45] She said the men interrogated her about the events at the house and took her husband Dr. Núñez away for several hours for further questioning. It was the first indication that Chilean authorities were treating the case with special concern.

Horman's name was included in a September 20 cable to Washington reporting nine Americans missing or detained. In New York City, Horman's father Edmund Horman was informed his son was missing and from September 21 on was in daily contact by phone with the State Department. Horman also called Jacob Javits, the Republican Senator from New York. Horman's congressman, Edward Koch, wrote a letter to Secretary of State Henry Kissinger, and gave a speech on the floor of the House calling attention to Horman's disappearance.[46]

The detention of Frank Teruggi and David Hathaway on Thursday, September 20, was reported to the Consulate the following Monday, September 24, by their friend Steve Volk of *FIN*. The same day, a Foreign Ministry official informed Purdy that Teruggi was being held in the Stadium. When Purdy visited the Stadium the next morning, a social worker there he called the "gray lady" told him "interrogations have been completed" for both Hathaway and Teruggi. The Chilean Embassy in Washington had also informed the State Department that Teruggi was being detained in the Stadium. The reports were false. In fact, Teruggi had been executed on Saturday, September 22, and his body dumped in the street. Teruggi's name never appeared on any Stadium list, but there was apparently no attempt to hide his body, as was the case with Horman.

The Consulate received a call on Tuesday, September 25, from the Santiago morgue to inform them that Body 2832, which had arrived the previous Saturday, had been positively identified as American citizen Frank Randall Teruggi. Fingerprints from the body had been matched to fingerprints Teruggi had provided to the Civil Registry office to obtain his resident identity card.[47] The morgue also reported the identification of Teruggi to International Police, and Purdy viewed the matching fingerprint card at that office.

Out of deference to the (false) Foreign Ministry reports that Teruggi was still at the Stadium, however, Purdy reported to Washington that "Teruggi's death should be regarded as unconfirmed." Other Chilean officials contacted on September 26 and 27 continued to give the Embassy reasons not to believe the fingerprint information showing he was already dead. "Embassy informed by Chilean authorities that there [are] no non Chilean dead officially reported," said one telegram to Washington. "Military authorities at National Stadium (now) say he was released the evening of September 21."[48] The information from the Foreign Ministry was false—the first of a series of contradictory and willfully deceptive communications about Horman and Teruggi. In contrast, information provided by the Civil Registry, the morgue, and the Identifications Bureau, all bureaucratic offices under the aegis of the Ministry of Justice, would turned out to be accurate in all cases related to the Americans' murders.

Meanwhile David Hathaway was still imprisoned in the Stadium locker room with the other foreigners. He had not been questioned again and thought that Teruggi had already been released. On Wednesday, September 26, the military released Hathaway and several other Americans into Purdy's custody. According to Hathaway, Purdy said he believed his friend Frank had been released and had traveled to the south of Chile. Somewhat later, at the Consulate, Purdy told Hathaway there was a body in the morgue whose fingerprints had been identified as Teruggi's.

The next day Purdy took Hathaway to the morgue to look at the body purported to be that of his friend. But he couldn't be sure:

> He took me to go see the body. I took a pill, one of those things to calm you down, like a Valium. I wasn't out of it, but when we got there I was more and more out of it because we walked all around the morgue. There were hundreds and hundreds of bodies just stretched out. Many of them torn to pieces. We came to the body they said was Frank. I wasn't sure. He had shaved his beard off. I said let's check his ankle [for signs of the wound he had received at the time of the Tancazo]. I checked his left side, and [a morgue worker] was there on the other side. He said there's no scar.[49]

Purdy wanted him to look for Horman's body, too, but after walking through the corridors lined with bodies he saw no one he could recognize. Hathaway returned to Volk's apartment in the Torres de San Borja and expressed his consternation about not being able to identify Frank. He asked Volk if he would go and make another attempt.

Volk agreed. He went to the Consulate to ask Vice-Consul Anderson to accompany him to the morgue. Anderson went into an inner office to confer with Purdy, who refused permission. Volk was able to overhear the conversation: "He shouted I don't care what [he] wants to do, and Mr. Volk can go to hell." Anderson later confirmed Volk's account, but said he got around Purdy's refusal. In a memo to his CIA superiors about his actions, Anderson said he was able to convince Purdy that Volk should be allowed to view the body. The next day, October 2, Anderson took Volk to the morgue. Without difficulty Volk identified Body 2853, the same one Hathaway had viewed, as that of Frank Teruggi.[50]

Teruggi's relatively quick identification was an example of how Chile's bureaucracy was designed to work. Grinding out routine procedures, the morgue and Civil Registry were identifying hundreds of bodies even under the most stressful conditions. The morgue's fingerprint unit had more than doubled in size and was staffed by technicians sent by the Civil Registry's Identifications Bureau. It was attempting to catch up on the long backlog of cases since September 11. Most "NN" bodies arriving at the morgue were fingerprinted within 24 or 48 hours, and *fichas* (cards) were sent to be matched against central files at the main Civil Registry office. In almost all cases, the *ficha* was returned to the morgue's director within two or three days, containing the person's identity and data from their identity card, including number, date of birth and latest address.

In Horman's case, however, the bureaucracy was short-circuited. Morgue records show that his body may still have been in the morgue— but out of sight—at the time Hathaway visited there on September 27. Technicians had duly inked his fingerprints following standard procedure, and the fingerprint card for Body 2663 had been sent to the Civil Registry office and received there on September 25. Horman's Chilean identity card record was also at the Registry, with the corresponding fingerprint card. Yet the routine process of comparing the two documents was not completed. This was not an accident. Police investigative reports from 1973 show that a Foreign Ministry official instructed morgue and Registry officials to keep the results secret even from police investigators.[51]

Charles Horman was not missing; his body was being hidden.

11 Distract and Deceive

The discovery of Teruggi's body filled Joyce Horman with dread. She had been ricocheting between meetings in the Embassy, the Consulate and with Captain Davis, at first trusting, then pleading with them to help. Fifteen days after his disappearance it was increasingly difficult to cling to the hope that Charles would be found alive. And she became convinced that U.S. officials were deceiving her. In one hurtful conversation, a Consulate official suggested that her husband might have gone into hiding to get away from her. When Terry Simon, a source of emotional support, left to return to New York, Joyce moved to the house of her friends Warwick and Rosalie Armstrong, where she relentlessly worked the phones and continued the search on her own. She returned several times to the Vicuña Mackenna house to interview neighbors; she tried to enter the National Stadium, but guards turned her away. She pressed her Embassy contacts for details about what they were doing. As September turned into October, nothing seemed to be happening.

Behind the scenes Embassy officials had been making polite inquiries. Ambassador Nathaniel Davis convened the "country team"—the chief Embassy officers—and ordered them to check with their regular Chilean contacts about the Horman and Teruggi detentions. The ambassador's directive almost immediately produced a solid lead. Economics officer Judd Kessler had dinner with a friend, Enrique Sandoval, who had worked in the Education Ministry in the Allende government, and asked him to try to find out what he could. Sandoval wanted to help—he already had heard about Horman's disappearance from Horman's friend Warwick Armstrong. A few days later Sandoval discreetly contacted his brother, who was an officer in the Carabinero police force.

He called Kessler to tell him what his brother had told him, without identifying the source. He said "a highly placed source in the Chilean military had told him Horman had been executed in the National Stadium on or about September 20, 1973." Nelson Sandoval, working as an interrogator at the Stadium, was well placed to make inquiries.* Kessler immediately conveyed the information to U.S. Consul Purdy when they crossed paths at the Embassy. Purdy had the most up-to-date information on the cases, and the information placing Horman at the Stadium contradicted Chilean government denials. Kessler recalled that Purdy commented, "I'll bet that's right." But that was the end of it. By all accounts, Purdy did nothing with the information. He didn't inform the ambassador or even write a memo recording the conversation, which occurred around September 30. He told Joyce nothing about it, and in their next conversation he continued to stoke the possibility that Horman could have gone into hiding.[52]

Sandoval, intent on protecting his brother but skeptical that the U.S. Embassy would act on the information, also conveyed the report without specifying the source to Mark Dolgin of the Canadian Embassy. It would be weeks before the Horman family learned of this early report.

Meanwhile, Defense Attaché Hon and Captain Davis of MilGroup were moving up the chain of command in the Chilean military. After his initial conversations with Colonel Henríquez of Army intelligence, Hon was

---

* Nelson Sandoval, in his testimony to the Chilean court (3384), said another interrogator, a Marine, told him something like, "Captain, don't stick your nose in that. They shot that North American—he committed suicide, but with help" ("Mi capitán, no se meta en cosas, pues a ese norteamericano lo fusilaron . . . se suicidó, pero con ayuda"). He elaborated in an interview with Pascale Bonnefoy: "Stop looking for him. He was executed. He was one of those idealistic gringos. There was a file with very negative information about his activities in the movement against the Vietnam War. He had links to MIR and was sending information outside the country" (*Terrorismo de Estadio*, 194–195).

summoned to a meeting in the Armed Forces General Staff headquarters, where he met with General Nicanor Díaz Estrada of the Army and General Francisco Herrera of the Air Force. He pursued a logical line of questioning based on his knowledge of military operations. He asked the two generals to check which military command had jurisdiction in the area of Horman's house in Vicuña Mackenna, and which units carried out raids there. The Chileans were unhelpful, repeating only that Horman was not in the Stadium and had not appeared on any lists of detainees.

Joyce Horman had come up with a lead on her own. Retired General Camilo Valenzuela visited her, telling her a friend in Minnesota (Joyce's home state) had requested his help in locating Horman. It was a bizarre and disingenuous offer. Unbeknownst to her, Valenzuela had worked with the CIA in the 1970 plot to kidnap General Schneider and had been forced to retire because of his involvement.[53] He proceeded to unspool a series of falsehoods about the case. He claimed a Red Cross official had informed him that Charles Horman was alive and well in the Stadium as of the previous Saturday (September 29), and that he had been "checked out" of the Stadium and gone to Curicó, a city about 80 miles south of Santiago. (In fact, the Red Cross had no information on Horman.)

Valenzuela also talked to Colonel Hon and spun a similar tale with other details, one of which was at least partly true. He told Hon that Horman had been released and that he thought it was "very strange Mr. Horman would not contact his wife when he left the stadium." Hon said Valenzuela offered another detail: "Mr. Horman was working for and receiving pay from Pablo de la Barra, who is a known Communist." This detail about Horman's filmmaker friend, reflecting intelligence Valenzuela most likely received from the military, was wrong about the alleged pay to Horman and about de la Barra's political party (he was a Socialist, not a Communist).[54] Valenzuela's comment was also intriguing in light of an order about Chile Films only a few days earlier from General Díaz Estrada, chief of the Armed Forces General Staff and one of the highest-ranking officers in the new regime. Díaz Estrada's order directed the various intelligence and police agencies "to undertake the necessary measure to detain the foreign personnel working in Chile Films." It added that Chile Films personnel were transporting suspicious packages to and from the coast and it was of special interest "to determine whatever support or connection existed with other undesirable foreigners and/or movements in opposition to the current Junta."[55]

Colonel Hon was in a position to know General Valenzuela's notorious history, but conveyed no hint of what he knew to Joyce Horman. Hon also met with the head of Army intelligence, General Lutz. The general was clearly a well-informed source, if he would cooperate. Hon told Lutz that Embassy personnel had interviewed witnesses who had seen "Army personnel" carry away Horman from his house in Vicuña Mackenna Street on the late afternoon of September 17. General Lutz "promised to conduct an investigation and inform of the details," Hon wrote in a memo.[56]

Captain Davis was pursuing the same line of questions about operations in the vicinity of Horman's home, noting that witnesses had seen Army personnel detain Horman. MilGroup officer Colonel Carlos Urrutia channeled the questions through General Pinochet's top military aide, Colonel Enrique Morel, to ensure they would reach the appropriate Chilean commanders for the Santiago military area. Colonel Urrutia had a direct line to General Pinochet's office, having been the first U.S. government official to meet with Pinochet the day after the coup. Davis and Urrutia were posing the right questions to the right Chilean officers. They knew that the command structure and rigid procedures for operational after-action reports would provide the correct answers if the officers chose to reveal them.[57]

Instead, the military commanders, via Colonel Morel, transmitted outright falsehoods to deceive their U.S. military counterparts. They stated that no military or police operations were conducted at 4126 Vicuña Mackenna, despite the multiple eyewitness accounts. And they embellished the denials with the beginnings of a phony cover story designed to blame the left:

> Colonel Morel indicated that it is possible that the personnel involved in the search at Mr. Horman's quarters and removal of Mr. Horman from the scene are impersonators and not members of the Armed Forces and Carabineros. *There is a record of this tactic being used by sympathizers of the former regime.* Mr. Horman, being a U.S. citizen, was a good target for the impersonators, under present circumstances.[58] (Emphasis added)

In fact, there had been no such incidents of leftists attacking with military uniforms, and the U.S. officials were well-positioned to know that.

The top commanders also repeated the government's consistent theme that Horman did not appear on any lists of detained persons. For anyone paying attention, it was obvious that the military itself created and controlled those lists, and it could be expected that the names of executed prisoners had been removed. Hathaway's release, for example, had exposed the speciousness of such official assurances based on the lists. His name, too, had been missing from the lists Purdy and other officials inspected at the Stadium, but at the time he was released, his name began to appear and stayed on official lists thereafter. Similar discrepancies were pointed out by Vice-Consul Anderson. In a chronology note for September 21, Anderson says he was able to arrange for the release of four Americans: two of them—John Cerrutti and Henry Warlow—did not appear on any list, but the American couple Adam Schesch and Patricia Garrett were listed. The Stadium officials clearly were maintaining two sets of records, an accurate set for the interrogators and the military, and another, sanitized list to be shown to the Red Cross and diplomatic officials making inquiries.[59] Later investigations in Horman's case would also show such a double listing.

Anderson, whose CIA intelligence training perhaps equipped him to have a more critical approach toward the Chilean military, documented another discrepancy in tracking prisoners. He and another consular officer spent Monday, October 1, investigating various sites associated with the cases. In Teruggi's neighborhood, he went to the Carabinero Non-Commissioned Officers School, where Hathaway had said he and Teruggi were taken. Officers there were forthcoming and did not hesitate to show their arrest records to the U.S. Embassy official, according to Anderson: "They had kept track of the Americans held at the school. These records were checked and showed that the Garrett-Schesches had been detained there and then taken to the National Stadium. Records also showed that David Hathaway and Frank Teruggi had also been detained there and then sent to the National Stadium on September 20."[60] Anderson's findings contradicted the official claim from the government that there was no record of Teruggi. Anderson did not, however, ask further about the reason for Teruggi's detention or track the information to the next step, the Stadium.

Joyce Horman was doing her best to conduct her own investigation. Using a driver provided by the Embassy, she tracked down witnesses to her husband's arrest and located a woman who had seen the Army vehicle carrying Horman in the direction of the Stadium. She contacted military officers at their offices and tried to confront them, but her pleas were ignored. Sometimes she ended the day in tears. Her frustration deepened when Captain Davis, in a meeting on October 1, just after Terry Simon's departure, began to question her about her relationship with her husband, according to her written statement:

> He said he was asking this because he wanted to know if I was aware that Charles and Terry Simon had stayed in the same room in Vina del Mar. I said of course I knew that they had stayed in the same room, that we three had been friends for years and that it in no way reflected on my relationship with Charles. Davis commented that he would nonetheless have to include this in the report on the investigation and suggested it would look very bad to other people.[61]

Davis did indeed make the point about the hotel room in reports to other U.S. officials, who more than once suggested that Horman had left to get away from his wife. Davis hinted it could cause Embassy investigators to take the case less seriously and give credence to Chilean claims he was in hiding.[62] The focus of the investigation seemed to shift away from the Chilean military to the couple's personal life. Davis pressed her to give him a list of the couple's friends in Chile, a predictable request but one that put Joyce Horman even more on edge. She thought it could put her friends in danger and refused.

· · · · ·

The U.S. inquiries failed to produce any useful information but clearly the numerous and repeated inquiries by the U.S. Embassy had gotten the attention of the new military authorities. On October 3, the Foreign Ministry issued what amounted to the first of several official—mostly false and often contradictory—cover stories. In two official communiqués to the Embassy, the Ministry acknowledged that both Horman and Teruggi had been held in the National Stadium, but then claimed against all evidence that they had been released unharmed.

The two notes—numbered 15125 and 15126—used the exact same words for both cases. Horman (likewise Teruggi) "was detained, in the

National Stadium, on the 20th of September for violation of the curfew. The next day he was released because there was nothing to hold against him." The statement about Teruggi added it was "possible" he had been shot by curfew patrols and taken to the morgue. In the case of Horman, who was still missing, the Ministry assured the Embassy that the Investigations Service—the PICH—was undertaking "relevant procedures" to locate him. This was true and the first official indication PICH, under the aegis of the Ministry of Interior, had been brought into the case.[63]

As a coverup, the statements were awkwardly framed. Teruggi indeed had been picked up on September 20, but Horman was known to have been arrested three days before, on September 17. At the time the statements were issued, Teruggi's body had already been identified in the Santiago Morgue. The Embassy was negotiating the expatriation of his body to his family in the United States. The Foreign Ministry was asking the Americans to believe that both men had been in custody at some point (contradicting their own previous denials) but somehow had failed to contact any of their friends after their release and before being killed.

Publicly the Embassy avoided saying anything to cast doubt on the Chilean denials of responsibility. Embassy documents reflected the Chilean cover story and began to refer to "unidentified persons wearing Army uniforms" and "uniformed persons." A clear pattern was emerging by which the Embassy looked for answers to the mystery in every scenario except the most obvious, namely that the best evidence pointed to the Chilean military having killed Horman and Teruggi in much the same way they had killed hundreds of other pro-Allende foreigners and Chileans.

12 Mr. Horman Goes to Chile

Edmund Horman decided it was time to go to Chile.

His conversations with Terry Simon when she arrived in New York were disturbing, especially her report about contacts with U.S. officials. His daily calls to the State Department only increased his frustration that the U.S. government was making a show of activity but was not really pushing the Chilean military for answers. U.S. officials in Washington told him there was a "growing sense Charles Horman is in hiding," echoing what his daughter-in-law was hearing in Santiago.[64]

His son was still missing, and the discovery and identification of Teruggi's body only increased his foreboding that something similar had happened to Charlie. There is no worse nightmare for a father than the loss of a son in the prime of life. And while father and son had been close, there had been differences—both political and cultural—that weighed on him. Horman was a prosperous businessman whose life was well-ordered. His son was a writer and observer with a taste for adventure. Despite his Harvard education Charles had shown no interest in a lucrative career in business and finance. A job in his father's successful industrial design business in New Jersey was far from his mind. Both were strong personalities and their political arguments had sometimes been bitter, not unlike those of establishment fathers and counterculture sons and daughters all over America at the time. Ed Horman had made sure the gulf did not get too wide. When Charles had announced he was giving up his job at King TV in 1967, his father flew to Portland, Oregon, so they could drive across country together, a seven-day journey of continuous conversation. When Charles and Joyce quit their New York jobs and set out for South America he thought it was an ill-conceived plan, but one he could accept from his adult son. Charlie's recent visit to New York had been a joyous reunion, but the elder Horman was unable to dissuade his son from returning to Chile.

Author Thomas Hauser spent many hours with Ed Horman, whose odyssey in search of his son in Chile inspired the movie *Missing*. Their interviews for Hauser's 1978 book portray him as a thoughtful, determined man on the eve of his departure:

> I tried very hard not to indulge in sorrow. Certainly my hopes had dwindled, but I was committed to pursuing every last chance that Charles might still be alive.... Maybe I fantasized a little about where our relationship would go if Charles were rescued and brought home alive. Fortunately, I had the satisfaction of knowing that, while we suffered the wear and tear that was normal between members of our respective generations, the bonds between us were strong.[65]

The elder Horman was a doer, an entrepreneur, a well-spoken and respected person who was comfortable dealing with power and men of influence. He had been calling everyone he knew in that category, including New York Senator Jacob Javits, Congressman Edward Koch and eventually Massachusetts Senator Ted Kennedy. Charles's television colleagues were also generating expressions of support. The State Department received telegrams of concern signed by almost 100 people.[66] Ed Horman had the force of that solidarity campaign at his back when he touched down in Santiago on October 5. Consul Fred Purdy met him at the airport. He was 67 years old and had just gotten off a 12-hour overnight flight, but he immediately launched into a tireless round of meetings with Embassy officials, reporters and Chilean contacts. U.S. ambassador Nathaniel Davis received him and his daughter-in-law Joyce in his office within hours of his arrival.

Ambassador Davis reviewed the multiple contacts by Embassy personnel with Chilean officials. To Horman, it seemed like the ambassador was accepting the Chilean story that the military was not involved at face value. He asked the ambassador how he could square the denials with the phone calls to people in Charles's address book, purportedly from Chilean intelligence, the morning after his son was detained. The ambassador said he didn't know anything about those calls, and asked Purdy to check on them. The meeting was cordial, but Horman was put on notice that the Embassy actions were more pro forma than aggressive.[67]

What he was told was far from the whole story. Ambassador Davis did not mention that the Chileans, only three days before, had sent the Embassy an official note on the case, admitting Horman's detention, but misstating the date and claiming implausibly it had been for a curfew violation and that Horman had been released the next day. Purdy neglected to mention Judd Kessler's report from the previous week that a military officer said Horman had been executed in the Stadium. Purdy later testified that he didn't take the report seriously because it was second-hand.[68]

Horman spent a week touring hospitals and talking to U.S. and Chilean military officers. He appeared at the National Stadium to call out Charles's name over a loudspeaker. There was no answer.

Purdy drove Horman to several of the meetings in his car. He set up a meeting with a British journalist, Tim Ross, who purportedly had contacts with the clandestine "pipeline" hiding fugitive leftists and helping them escape the country. In the meeting, Ross claimed that his contact had talked to Charles Horman, who was awaiting secret transfer out of the country, but that Horman, according to the contact, had refused to send back a message to the Embassy. The origin and motivation of that story is not known, but it was completely bogus and the elder Horman saw it as another distraction.

With inquiries leading to dead ends, the focus of the search would shift to the morgue, autopsy and fingerprints. Two of Horman's friends, David Hathaway and Steve Volk, had gone to the morgue to look for him. But neither saw him among the approximately 150 bodies they inspected. Ed Horman said he wanted to go to the morgue himself to look, but Consul Purdy said he would have to go alone. Horman declined.

In the first week of October, the FBI sent a copy of Horman's fingerprints from his service in the Air National Guard by diplomatic pouch. The Embassy asked twice more that Chilean authorities check Horman's prints from his Chilean identification card and from the new FBI set against unidentified bodies at the morgue. Without confirming that such a check had actually been done, Chilean authorities said the result was negative.[69]

The real movement in the case was behind the scenes. It began when Ambassador Davis finally raised the issue of the disappeared Americans directly with General Augusto Pinochet, the head of the military junta. Pinochet, not Davis, had requested the meeting, asking Davis for "a quiet moment to talk," when they met on October 12th at a Columbus Day holiday reception. The junta leader was the supplicant. He said Chile greatly needed economic and military aid from the United States, and Davis described the usually brusque dictator as "gracious." Davis said the United States wanted to be helpful, but there were "political problems." He brought up the Horman and Teruggi cases, pointing out that Horman was still missing and Teruggi's killing was unresolved. Concerns about human rights were increasing in intensity in the United States, and the Embassy was feeling the pressure. Senator Ted Kennedy was gathering support for a complete ban on military aid, citing human rights abuses. Pinochet responded with irritation. He railed that a heavy hand was needed because weapons caches were still in the hands of leftist extremists. The military intervention had prevented "a million deaths" that would have occurred if the left's "self coup" had succeeded. (Such a leftist plot did not exist; it was invented as a disinformation tactic by the military.)

But Pinochet had gotten the ambassador's message that the still missing American was an obstacle, urgently to be removed.[70] Pinochet appears to have turned the matter over to his head of Army intelligence, General Augusto Lutz, to be resolved. The day before he met with Davis, Pinochet had called Lutz out of a meeting in which Colonel Hon was briefing him about the Horman and Teruggi cases. Hon said the meeting resumed a few days later. Lutz said he was aware of all the details the U.S. officer was providing him and the government was "following up on this information." According to Hon, Lutz said, "Everyone in Chile is looking for Horman, to include the Embassy, Horman's father, *Investigaciones*

[Investigative Police], the military, Carabineros and friends. . . . Some of these groups will find the useful lead."[71] That General Lutz was annoyed and impatient at all the fuss about the two Americans comes through in Hon's rendition of his words. As events unfolded, the "useful lead" was not hard to find, and it was Lutz's own men who would produce it. The civilian detective bureau, the PICH, was also assuming a more important role.

It might seem surprising that in the most brutal days of the new military government a civilian detective and two military investigators would embark on an honest investigation. But that is what they did, not in overt defiance of orders, but—in their minds—in compliance with what they were instructed to do and in service to the judicial system they had served long before the military takeover.

On or about October 15, the day he met Hon, Lutz issued orders that led within a few days to the discovery of Horman's body. We know about these orders and their results because of the statements of two of those men, both lower-ranking officers in Army intelligence. Their key role has been almost entirely unknown and ignored until now. The two men would eventually provide us with the most credible inside view of what happened to Charles Horman.

The officers were Jaime Ortiz and Raúl Meneses Pachet, both master sergeants with Department IV of the Military Intelligence Service (SIM). Meneses and Ortiz were assigned to find out what happened to Horman and locate his body. They succeeded and personally told Edmund Horman they had confirmed that his son had been executed in the Stadium.

Officers Meneses and Ortiz assumed a unique role in this story and are among the few military witnesses who are still alive and have been willing to share what they know. Their accounts are well-documented. The two met several times in 1973 with Joyce and Ed Horman, using their real names and identifying themselves accurately as investigators from Army intelligence. Ed Horman describes those meetings in his "diary" relating the events in Chile. Then, 14 years later, in 1987, Meneses, by then retired, approached a U.S. Embassy political officer to offer what was described as exclusive information about the Horman case. The officer, David Dreher, described the meetings with Meneses in a series of memos and cables. The memos, once declassified, allowed the author and a colleague to identify and locate both Meneses and Ortiz. Both men talked openly in interviews with reporter Pascale Bonnefoy in 2016, and Meneses gave an additional interview in 2024. Documentation about all of these encounters—the diary of Ed Horman, Embassy memos and cables, and the interviews—are now available and are the basis for the account that follows.[72]

· · · · ·

Edmund Horman was the epicenter around which the events revolved. His arrival and the pressure building in the United States had moved important Chilean protagonists into action. October 15 was the day things started to happen. In the morning, Horman met again with Ambassador Davis. It was a tense encounter. "I told him that I had no doubt that the Chileans know exactly where Charles is, that the American government should be able to force an answer from them. No meaningful reply," he wrote in his diary.

In the early afternoon he and Joyce visited Chilean Army Major Luis Contreras Prieto. Joyce had already met Major Contreras because his brother worked in a bank in New York and friends of Ed Horman had put them in touch. Contreras had been active in the coup operations and was at home recuperating from an injury. He had given Joyce incorrect information earlier that Charles was safe and would be released, a "misidentification" for which he now apologized. Ed Horman appealed to him "on the grounds of plain humanity" to help the Hormans get a straight story from SIM. Contreras picked up the phone immediately and called a contact. After a short conversation he turned to Ed and said someone from Army intelligence would contact him "very soon."

The SIM contact, whose name Horman records in his diary, was Captain Hugo Salas Wenzel, a veteran intelligence officer who years later became director of CNI, the main intelligence security force and successor to the notorious DINA. He was then the direct superior of Meneses and Ortiz. On or about October 16, Captain Salas gave the two men the assignment to find the missing American citizen Charles Horman. The order had come from the top, from General Pinochet to General Lutz to Captain Salas. Ortiz said he was shown a Foreign Ministry cable to Pinochet describing U.S. pressure on the Horman case, with the junta leader's annotation "DINE [Army Intelligence]: Investigate."[73] The assignment was to "find the whereabouts" of Charles Horman. They did not expect it to be difficult. Meneses and Ortiz had already worked on "antisubversive" assignments before the coup. They were part of Department IV, an Army Intelligence unit that was searching for and confiscating weapons thought to be stockpiled in the Cordones Industriales.

"We began at the beginning, with the detention," Meneses said. Meneses and Ortiz drove to Horman's ransacked home in Vicuña Mackenna 4126, and interviewed neighbors, who described the military patrol that detained Horman.

Captain Salas had given them information indicating which Army units were operating in the Vicuña Mackenna area. It was the Eastern Grouping under the command of General Benavides. General headquarters for the grouping was in CIM, the Command of Military Institutes, which included the Military Academy. They were directed to the School of Telecommunications located on Antonio Varas Street.[74] There they talked to the commander of Department II, Intelligence, Colonel Fernando Grant Pimentel, who checked the operational logs. Grant told Meneses and Ortiz there had been an order specifically for Horman's arrest. It had arrived from the command center for the metropolitan Santiago region, known as CAJSI. Grant had assigned the raid to Lieutenant Enzo Cadenasso, of Department III, Operations.[75] Cadenasso happened to be there in the office and also spoke to Meneses and Ortiz. He remembered the detention. He said he had mustered a patrol of himself, a sergeant and several enlisted soldiers and drove to the Vicuña Mackenna address in a truck to pick up Horman and take him to the National Stadium.

"They beat him up hard because he resisted," Cadenasso told them. Ortiz said Horman was detained as an "extremist," but he didn't know the specifics. He said SIM must have had a file on him. In a matter of a few hours the two investigators had identified the military unit and the names of soldiers responsible for Horman's arrest. "The lists of patrols and detentions were right there. It was easy to know who arrested him," Meneses commented.

The next stop was the National Stadium, still crammed with thousands of prisoners. The officer in charge of the register of prisoners found Horman's name in his records. He said Horman had been "checked in and checked out." There was no doubt, Ortiz said. "I saw Horman's name in a notebook at the National Stadium." Meneses and Ortiz knew what it meant that Horman had been transferred out—it meant they would probably find Horman in the Santiago morgue.

When Meneses spoke to Embassy officer Dreher in 1987, he added other details implicating his chief, Captain Salas Wenzel, in Horman's detention. He said Salas Wenzel was in charge of an intelligence unit conducting weapons investigations in the Cordones, and he provided the information leading to the order for Horman's arrest. Meneses also said the decision to execute Horman was made by Captain Pedro Espinóza, a ranking intelligence officer assigned to the Stadium. He said Espinóza was "the person at the Stadium who made the decision on who was to die."

Before going to the morgue, they needed to talk with Horman's wife and father, who were expecting them because of Major Contreras's call to Captain Salas the day before. Meneses and Ortiz visited Ed Horman in his room at the Crillon Hotel on October 16, according to Horman's contemporaneous diary:

> At 10:30 am two men from Military Intelligence, Manesas [*sic*] and Ortiz by name, arrived. They spent 1½ hours asking detailed questions of Joyce. As they were leaving, Ortiz asked Joyce what she knew about FIN. This was the name of the small news clipping service with which Charles had worked at times. The question confirmed our feeling that the Chileans were entirely familiar with whatever happened to Charles.[76]

Meneses and Ortiz went from the hotel to the morgue. They were zeroing in on records of bodies arriving around the time of Horman's detention that had not yet been identified. While there they recognized a detective from PICH. His name was Mario Rojas and he seemed to be keeping track of what they were doing. They narrowed their search to one body that seemed a possible match. Meneses and Ortiz returned to the Crillon for a second conversation with Joyce and Ed Horman. At their request, Joyce gave them a description of the clothes Horman was wearing. They asked Ed Horman if he could obtain Charles's fingerprint record. While they waited Horman called Fred Purdy at the Consulate—not far from the hotel—and the fingerprint record based on Horman's Air National Guard file was quickly messengered to the Crillon and given to the two officers.

Ed Horman had been searching in Santiago for almost two weeks to no avail. Now the increased activity involving the morgue was an ominous sign his search was nearing the end that he most feared. Earlier the same day, visiting the offices of the Ford Foundation in Santiago, he had gotten another signal of what was to come. One of the Ford program officers, economist Lovell Jarvis, took Horman aside. He said a friend who worked for an "English speaking Embassy, not the American Embassy" had some information. Jarvis said the friend had a friend with contacts in the Chilean military, who had told him that "Charles had been shot in the Estadio Nacional on September 20th." It was a third-hand report, but taken together with the visit from the two military investigators, Ed began to prepare himself for the worst.[77]

Meneses and Ortiz, during several visits to the morgue, noticed resistance from employees to showing them records for unidentified bodies. Captain Salas went with them in their final visit to use his military rank to persuade the civilian employees to cooperate. The obstacle removed, Meneses and Ortiz obtained autopsy records, fingerprint cards and a description of clothing. They were finally able to match the copy of Horman's prints provided by the Consulate to the morgue's records for Body 2663. The records showed that the body had been found in the street and delivered by military vehicle to the morgue at 1:35 p.m. on September 18, the day after Horman was detained. Time of death was listed as 9:40 a.m. In an interview Ortiz stated: "We skimmed through the records rapidly and *a la mala* (under the table)—because we weren't supposed to have access to them—looking for those that corresponded to the unidentified bodies, until we came across an autopsy record of an N.N. with clothes similar to what his wife had described to us."[78]

A final step remained. They took the Horman fingerprint record to the Identifications Bureau of the Civil Registry office, where they made a definitive match. The prints provided by the FBI not only matched those of Body 2663, but they matched Horman's fingerprint record in his Chilean identity card file in the central Civil Registry.

The SIM investigators returned to the morgue to inform the director of the match. Despite the chaos of the time, the morgue kept relatively complete records, which showed that Body 2663 had already been transferred to the nearby General Cemetery on October 3 at 11:00 a.m. Meneses and

Ortiz determined from the records that Horman had been buried in a wall niche identified as Patio 23, but they did not attempt to view the body.

Charles Horman's body finally had been found and identified. The director of the morgue immediately informed the Consulate of the now official determination, based on Meneses and Ortiz's findings. Fred Purdy went to Horman's hotel to inform him of the confirmation of his son's death. It was the afternoon of October 18, a month and a day after Charles had gone missing. Purdy informed him, according to Horman's diary, that a positive identification from fingerprints had been made of a body "almost certainly that of Charles; that he had been shot in the Estadio Nacional on 9/18; that he had been interred in the wall of the Santiago cemetery on 10/3."

The next day, Meneses and Ortiz visited Horman a final time at the Crillon, to tell him personally what they had found and convey their condolences. They told him, in answer to his questions, that his son "had been shot in the Estadio Nacional on September 18 and . . . his body interred in the wall of the Santiago Cemetery on October 3."

While they were still there, Purdy called to say he had gone to the fingerprint division of the Identifications Bureau that morning. He was allowed to inspect the fingerprint card and autopsy on Body 2663. He also saw the card with prints from Charles Horman's Chilean identity card. And he brought with him the photo reproduction of Horman's fingerprints provided by the FBI. The three sets were identical.[79] With this final check, there was no room for doubt.

In his later written reports, Purdy omitted any mention of Horman having been shot in the Stadium, and would deny he had said that in his conversation with Ed Horman. In fact, the Embassy would refuse for years to say anything directly challenging the Chilean military's official denials, despite compelling evidence from multiple sources pointing to military responsibility.

The two soldiers expressed their sympathy to the grieving father, and offered an apology. "I'm sorry, things like this shouldn't happen," Horman remembered Ortiz saying. He wrote in his diary, "when Ortiz and Manesas said goodbye to me, Ortiz was so affected that there were tears on his cheeks."

Horman called family members in New York to tell them the search was over. He said he and Joyce would be flying home as soon as they could get a flight.

PHOTO 1. Charles Horman grew up in New York City. He graduated Phi Beta Kappa from Harvard in 1964. After a stint in the Air National Guard, he embarked on a career in journalism and filmmaking, getting his start as a writer for King Broadcasting in Portland, Oregon. There, he worked on prize-winning political documentaries with a group of talented colleagues, who remained his close friends.

PHOTO 2. Frank Teruggi was younger than Horman and more political but equally brainy. He entered college in 1967 and combined honors-level grades with heavy involvement in the antiwar movement and radical politics.

PHOTO 3. Frank was a ham radio enthusiast, and set up a shortwave receiver when he went to Chile. Notre Dame High School for Boys, near Chicago, exposed him to a liberal strain of Catholicism known as liberation theology. His teachers were from the Holy Cross Order, whose priests ran an elite but progressive high school in Santiago, Chile.

PHOTO 4. Teruggi's father, a typesetter and fervent union activist, was also Frank, so young Teruggi was called Randy, his middle name, at home.

PHOTO 5. Teruggi protested at the Democratic National Convention and joined a Chicago group supporting social justice in Latin America. Soon he was learning Spanish, saving money and planning a trip to Chile, where a "real" revolution was happening.

PHOTO 6. Horman had a more gradual but steady evolution toward the left than Teruggi. He attended the Chicago protests and wrote about them. Back in New York he got a job at a business magazine, where he tried unsuccessfully to move its coverage in a more progressive direction.

PHOTO 7. Horman's father, Edmund, was a successful businessman who probably would have been comfortable with the label of liberal Republican. He and Charles were close, but discussion about politics, in the cauldron of late 1960s activism and polarization, was often contentious.

PHOTO 8. Joyce Hamren, from Minnesota, and Charles Horman were married, with good jobs, but settling down was not in their plans. They outfitted a Chevy truck as a camper and headed to South America. They met more and more people who talked about the wonderful, peaceful and democratic revolution going on in Chile.

PHOTO 9. Among those enthusiastic about Chile's democratic revolution was Richard Pearce (*second from left*), Horman's colleague from King TV, who had filmed two documentaries in Chile. He posed with members of the crew after filming at the recently expropriated American Screw Factory in Santiago. Horman, on his arrival, did volunteer work at the factory.

PHOTO 10. Teruggi registered for economics classes, hoping to finish his degree, and joined a militant student organization affiliated with MIR. There was also time to hike in the high Andes near Santiago.

PHOTO 11. Salvador Allende was elected president of democratic Chile in September 1970, survived a clandestine effort by the CIA to keep him from taking office and began his presidency with a year of economic expansion and growing popularity.

PHOTO 12. Allende's revolution seemed possible. Thousands of young foreigners were flocking to Chile, many of them political exiles. They wanted to contribute to the revolution. Teruggi (*far left*) teamed up with Brazilians Carlos Beust and Jorge Alberto Basso and Paulina Vidal, a Chilean, for volunteer work and political organizing among farm workers.

Fernando Alarcón

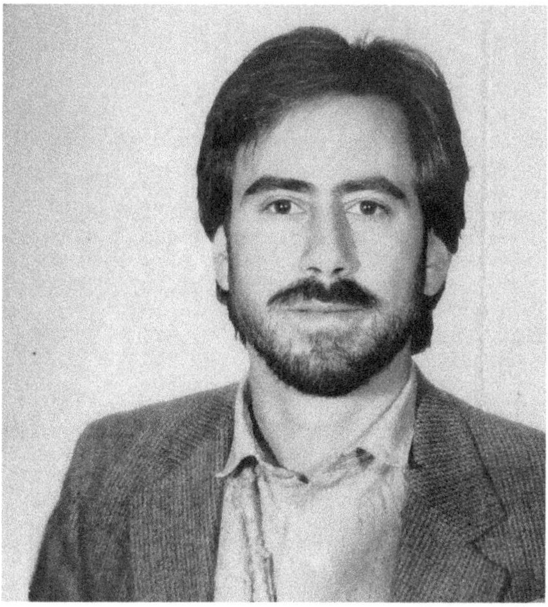

PHOTO 13. Fernando Alarcón, one of Teruggi's housemates, described himself as a "professional revolutionary." One of several MIR militants who shared a house with Teruggi, he was a member of MIR's "Central Force," which attempted resistance after the coup.

John Dinges

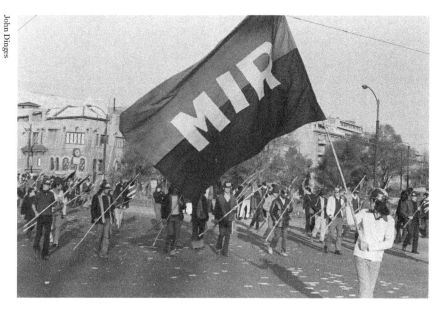

PHOTO 14. The Marxist party MIR, the Movement of the Revolutionary Left, was supportive but skeptical about Allende's democratic road to socialism. Hedging their bets, they prepared for armed struggle, creating a clandestine "Central Force," some of whose members received military training in Cuba. MIR-affiliated groups organized farm workers and worked in the poorest neighborhoods. They welcomed many foreigners. In frequent marches, their chants proclaimed the need for weapons. But MIR members paraded with poles instead of rifles.

Nov 6

Dear Don,

Well, this week is sure a bummer. You have Nixon and we have three generals. No telling what any of them will do.

Inspite of all the comments and dissections which have floated down here, I guess I don't quite understand Nixon-by-a-landslide. I guess McGovern made some mistakes; and I guess Nixon scored some points with his trips and being able to come up with something vaguely like a peace treaty a few days Before the election, but still that doesn't really explain it to me. There's something working underneath for Nixon to have had that kind of victory — a prodigious weariness, a pervasive cynicism.

I've been doing voluntary work during the big crisis here the past few weeks. This past weekend, I found myself assigned doing factory work at — of all places — the American-Screw Company, now estadicized and producing screws for Chile. It's the first time I've ever done anything like factory work and let me tell you I'm glad I was doing it for some greater goal, like keeping Chile going, rather than for just good old money, because everything they tell you about it is true. It's a drag. Very noisy, very dull. American Screw had been pretty stingy about capital investment, so the machines there are very old. I worked on a machine which can make 15,000 little screws a day. It's almost automatic, but it fucks up so you have to have some one to watch it and make sure the little blanks which are milled into screws feed in properly and stop the machine if they don't.

Everyone working with me was enormously friendly. Some were volunteers, some regular factory workers. I've never been called comrade so much in my life. They have gorgeous lunches there — not just on voluntary work days. Rice and fish in a tomato sauce with a fried egg slung on top and some salad. Up to then I'd been working doing loading and unloading, mainly sugar, maggi bullion cube cartons, nestles, and powdered milk. A few times, to my deep regret, 250 gallon drums of oil. I got a lot of sun, though.

I've been totally unable so far to find some one to write for from down here; but I've gotten fascinated in a line of research. I've been reading the trial transcripts and talking to people about the Viaux case — an attempted coup against Allende when he was first elected before he took office, in which the head of the army was murdered. The details of the case are incredible. Very much like Z in the kinds of people involved. Small fascist groups, the sons of the rich, the generals, even Christian Democrats. For now I'm happy reading about it, but later, if I keep finding out interesting stuff, I may do a long, long piece on it almost novelistically getting into the details of their meetings and network.

Whew, fraid that election has me on a bummer. Four more years indeed. Oh well. Fuck!

Charlie

PHOTO 15. Horman's many letters to Don Lenzer, another King TV colleague, often veered into sardonic humor, as he vividly described the political scene in Chile. He was doing research, but frustrated he couldn't find an outlet in the United States for his writing.

PHOTO 16. The workers' movement was the heart of the Allende revolution; this large march took place in the weeks before the coup. Union leaders and government managers controlled hundreds of factories, which were in turn organized in a dozen industrial belts, or *Cordones Industriales*, around the periphery of Santiago. The goal was a mixed economy of socialist and private enterprise.

PHOTO 17. Allende's experiment stalled in the face of unrelenting U.S.-sponsored destabilization and growing opposition. The *Cordones*—San Joaquin and Vicuña Mackenna among the largest—were cast as the bulwarks where the workers' movement would resist a military coup. Horman was asked to raise money in the U.S. to arm the workers, and he agreed.

PHOTO 18. In September 1973, the economy was in decline as inflation soared. People took to the streets to defend or oppose the government in rallies that sometimes clashed violently. Allende's coalition was split. One faction, opposed by Allende, advocated arming the workers. The other warned of civil war. The situation was grim as hundreds of thousands marched to salute their embattled president on his third anniversary in office.

Cristián Montecino

PHOTO 19. On September 11, 1973, a united Chilean military, led by General Augusto Pinochet Ugarte, struck down the Allende revolution in a paroxysm of killing and mass arrest. Neighbors denounced neighbors, targeting especially the many foreigners and exiles who sympathized with the workers movement. The fiercest onslaught was launched against the *Cordones* factories and their shantytown neighborhoods. Pockets of resistance were quickly overcome.

Marcelo Montecino

PHOTO 20. At least 7,000 prisoners were packed into the National Soccer Stadium in the first two weeks. Hundreds of riddled bodies were taken to the Santiago morgue. The bodies of Charles Horman and Frank Teruggi arrived a few days apart, on September 18 and 22. Horman, detained in the Vicuña Mackenna workers neighborhood where he had recently moved, went missing for a month as the military covered the tracks of their murder of two Americans.

PHOTO 21. Henry Kissinger (*right*) oversaw first a violent but unsuccessful CIA effort to prevent Allende from taking power in 1970, then three years of well-funded covert activities to destabilize Allende and prevent the success of his socialism-cum-democracy model. In line with Kissinger's policy of defending the new dictatorship, U.S. embassy officials feigned ignorance of what happened to Horman and Teruggi and deceived the families. Kissinger displayed his embrace of dictator Augusto Pinochet at a meeting in Santiago in June 1976.

PHOTO 22. U.S. consul Fred Purdy, shown with his Chilean wife, Gigi Mohn Purdy, had the responsibility of helping American citizens in trouble. But Ambassador Nathaniel Davis ordered Embassy officers to deny protection to any Americans seeking it. The ambassador did not challenge the implausible Chilean story that leftists disguised as soldiers killed Horman and Teruggi. Purdy later wrote that he had instructions not to question the Chilean version too closely.

PHOTO 23. Intelligence officer Pedro Espinóza (*right*) was one of the officers who determined who survived and who was executed at the Stadium. Among the most notorious of Pinochet's security officers, he was later convicted in dozens of killings, including those of Horman and Teruggi.

PHOTO 24. General Augusto Lutz, who died under mysterious circumstances in 1974, was head of Army intelligence at the time of the coup. A civilian intelligence agent, Rafael González, claimed he saw Horman in Lutz's office. He also said, then later retracted, that a CIA agent was there and that Horman was killed because "he knew too much."

PHOTO 25. Joyce Horman (*center*) with Ed and Elizabeth Horman in 1986. The Horman and Teruggi families never stopped looking for the truth. Ed and Joyce Horman searched for Charles in Chile and came away with the theory that U.S. officials may have fingered him for execution—a plausible scenario at the time that was strongly asserted in a 1978 book and the Hollywood movie *Missing*. This book reinvestigates—and refutes—that widely accepted theory, with newly available evidence. It is able to tell, finally, the untold story of how it all happened.

13 Disappeared in Plain Sight

Why had it taken a month to find Charles Horman, while Frank Teruggi had been so quickly identified? Questions about the fingerprint delay were posed by some Embassy officials and also by civilian detectives brought into the case. The delay was not simply because of the unavoidable chaos of the early days after the coup, as the Embassy led Horman's family and the press to believe.

Both Charles Horman and Frank Teruggi had been executed while in the custody of the Chilean military. That was the clearest interpretation of the available evidence. Though equally tragic, there was also a difference between the two cases. Teruggi was tortured and killed in circumstances that are known in part. Witnesses saw him in the Stadium and talked to him. He expressed the hope that the power of the U.S. Embassy would be brought to bear to save his life. In fact, as Teruggi was being held, more than a week after the coup, embassy officials were still being barred from talking to Americans in custody. Had they insisted, at least Teruggi's life might have been saved. Instead, he was executed and his body taken to the morgue on September 22. Once there the morgue's bureaucracy followed procedures established by existing—pre-coup—laws. Officials identified his body in less than two days and notified the U.S. Consulate. That was the way the system was designed to work. Nevertheless, because the Chilean government was telling the Embassy a different story, U.S. Consul Purdy delayed confirming Teruggi's identity and did not inform his family for a week after his identification.

Morgue and Civil Registry officials also fulfilled at least part of their legal obligations. The Teruggi autopsy specified the cause of death as "numerous bullet wounds in thorax and abdomen, with complications." Fragments of bullets were found in the body. In such cases of evident homicide, the designated legal authority, usually a court, normally would begin a criminal investigation to determine who fired the bullets and their motives. The legal authority in both Horman's and Teruggi's cases was the Military Court, but that court conducted no investigations.[80] Nevertheless, the morgue quickly identified the body and at the request of the Teruggi family shipped his body to the United States. Teruggi was buried in his hometown of Des Plaines, Illinois.

In contrast, Horman was "disappeared" after his execution. In the early 1970s, human rights advocates had not yet developed the legal vocabulary to describe such situations. In English, the word used for a person who could not be found was "missing." But Horman did not go missing as if he had been lost in a battle or after an earthquake. The evidence shows that those who killed him *caused* his body not to be found for a month. The military government intentionally "disappeared" Charles Horman. It was one of the early cases that exhibited this new tactic that would soon become systematic among the dictatorships of the Southern Cone, a tactic that eventually was labeled "enforced disappearance."

Disappearance entails the deliberate hiding or disposing of bodies of victims after they have been executed. The Pinochet government did so on a massive scale in subsequent years, eventually "disappearing" more than 1,400 victims, of whom only 307 have been found even after 50 years.[81] In the weeks after the coup, this began in a relatively primitive form. The military executed hundreds of persons after detention and dumped their bodies on public streets, in irrigation canals and in the Mopocho River. Police or military details that had not participated in the executions would recover the bodies hours later and deliver them in trucks to the morgue, thus breaking the chain of custody between the executioners and the bodies. The executioners also seemed to take care to strip from the bodies anything that could identify them—such as ID cards, jewelry, and sometimes even their clothes. Arriving at the morgue, such bodies were logged in as NN—unidentified.

This procedure was carried out so frequently that it can be fairly assumed it was the result of a general order from the highest level. Its purpose was to allow the military to deny responsibility for the mass killing—for example to claim that Horman and Teruggi had been released from military custody before they died. Delivering unidentified bodies to the morgue delayed but did not usually prevent their identification. Routine fingerprint checks led to the identification of the immense majority of NN bodies within a few days of their arrival. That is what happened in Teruggi's case.[82]

In Horman's case the military government took additional action to prevent his body from being located. Those blocking actions eventually were circumvented by Meneses and Ortiz, allowing them to identify Horman's body on October 18. It might seem strange that one layer of the government took investigative action that potentially embarrassed another layer, but the facts are unmistakable, and perhaps point to a bureaucracy still operating under old procedures. After Horman's body was located, Chilean military officials at the highest level switched from concealment to misinformation. They took great pains to provide U.S. officials with a plausible cover story to explain the deaths as the action of malevolent leftist forces, and in the process to paint Horman and Teruggi as anti-American extremists.

First, the story of the misplaced fingerprints.

A civilian detective, Inspector Mario Rojas, played a key role in discovering what happened. He worked for PICH, the civilian detective bureau that historically had been independent of the military security services. The junta considered it to have been an instrument of the Allende government and accused of functioning as a "political police." Its former chief, Eduardo "Coco" Paredes, was one of the first officials to be executed following the coup. The junta put an Army general, Ernesto Baeza, in charge of PICH and quickly fired two dozen detectives on suspicion of lingering loyalties to the former government. PICH was the Chilean counterpart to the FBI and served as liaison to U.S. law enforcement on international criminal matters. Despite the upheaval after the coup, it retained its civilian status as an agency under the supervision of the Interior Ministry.

Its role in the Horman-Teruggi investigation has been little known. Ed Horman says he and Joyce Horman met with Inspector Rojas around the time Horman's identity was finally established. Rojas questioned Joyce Horman and wrote a report,[83] but neither Horman knew anything about his more substantive role in the investigation.

Rojas's contemporaneous reports establish that PICH was running a parallel but less successful investigation at the morgue at the time that Meneses and Ortiz were trying to locate Horman. Rojas and PICH were assigned to the case by Minister of the Interior General Oscar Bonilla, who was the one general in the top ranks of the coup known to be uncomfortable with the extent of the killing. Bonilla ordered PICH to work on the case when the FBI sent copies of Horman's fingerprints via diplomatic pouch in the first days of October. Rojas was instructed to conduct inquiries to find the current whereabouts of Charles Horman, "who has disappeared"—virtually the same instructions received by Meneses and Ortiz of SIM.[84] In repeated inquiries Rojas submitted the set of FBI fingerprints to be checked by the morgue and Civil Registry. As late as October 16, he was told the results were negative—no matches. But subsequent events cast doubt on whether those agencies actually checked the FBI prints against unidentified bodies.

On October 18 and 19, Rojas and the two SIM officials were at the morgue and the Civil Registry offices at the same time. They noticed each other, although they do not say they exchanged words. Likewise, employees at those agencies were aware of the heightened interest in the Horman case and that two teams of investigators were asking about him. The SIM officers were first to have success. But Rojas followed their tracks and noticed that something was amiss about the way Horman's fingerprints had been handled.

At the Civil Registry office he looked up Horman's identity card file. He found that the morgue's *protocolo* (record) for Body 2663 had been received by the fingerprint department on September 25, but the *ficha* showing the official identification of the body as Horman was dated October 19, the same day he was there and 23 days after the request for fingerprint identification had arrived—an extraordinary delay. In fact, Meneses and Ortiz already had evaded roadblocks in order to match the fingerprints, finally doing so "under the table." The official *ficha* certifying identification appears to have been drafted as a result of their action. To investigate further, Rojas reported, he went to the morgue to find out more details about "circumstances, place, date and cause of death," but there the morgue secretary presented him with another roadblock, saying she had been told not to provide information: "[My] inquiries . . . failed to deliver any positive result because the secretary of said establishment, Miss Eliana Housset Mera, abstained from revealing [the information] *in accordance with instructions received directly from a Mr. Goycolea of the Ministry of Foreign Relations*" (emphasis added).[85]

Rojas wondered why the Foreign Ministry was intervening in the case, and why a morgue official was refusing to give information to a police detective. A few days later Rojas interviewed the Foreign Ministry official, whose full name was Luis Goycolea Grez, chief of the Americas Department, the entity responsible for diplomatic interchanges with the U.S. Embassy. Goycolea admitted telling Housset not to give out any information about "the Horman case," saying the information had to be withheld until the government was informed: "The reason . . . was solely and exclusively for the purpose of *preventing the information from being revealed to officials of the U.S. consulate or embassy* before government authorities themselves had a correct appreciation of the facts" (emphasis added).[86] Goycolea added that such a revelation would be "highly inconvenient."

Housset's job as morgue secretary was to update the log book and oversee paperwork traffic among the various agencies involved in identification procedures. From her and other morgue officials, Rojas learned that she had blocked the identification of Body 2663 in another instance. Around the same time, one of the coroners had instructed an employee to write in Horman's name in the autopsy record, but she instructed the employee not to enter the annotation, saying it would be a violation of procedures.

In the interview with Rojas, Housset pointed to a lack of trust among the various officials dealing with the matter. She confirmed that the SIM officials had returned to the morgue with a copy of the *ficha*—the Civil Registry certification of Horman's identification—but they refused to give it to her. They appear to have given the document directly to her boss, the director of the morgue, because he quickly called Purdy at the Consulate to inform him Horman had been identified.

In his long final report to his PDI superior, dated November 29, Rojas summarized the results of his "expanded" investigation to find Horman's body. He says he found out at the Ministry of Defense that the Eastern Grouping of CAJSI had jurisdiction for operations in the area of Horman's Vicuña Mackenna address. Records there did not have Horman's name as a detainee, but Rojas found a report signed by Lieutenant Colonel Roberto Soto Mackenney, chief of Department III Operations, saying that on September 17—the day of Horman's arrest—ten raids were conducted in the area and that among the persons "captured" was an unnamed "foreign extremist." Inspector Rojas was retracing the steps previously investigated by Meneses and Ortiz, but unlike the SIM officers he was unable to locate the actual patrol that made the raids on Horman's house, nor find any mention of Horman's name.

Among other details Rojas gleaned from official documents: military personnel had delivered Horman's body to the morgue; his body was among a large group of unidentified bodies arriving September 18, all of whose fingerprints were taken the same day they arrived; an autopsy was conducted on September 25, establishing that Horman died of multiple bullet wounds, including massive wounds to the head. The autopsy states that the time of death was 9:45 a.m., September 18.

Purdy and other Embassy officials did not know about these background details, nor did they make any effort to question any of the Chilean officials who could have informed them about the actions that delayed the identification. Embassy officials had the names of Meneses, Ortiz, Rojas, Housset, and the morgue's director, Dr. Oscar Novoa, but never asked them to explain what had transpired and why the Horman identification had been delayed for so long.

Purdy said that was in accordance with instructions from the ambassador: "We were told, fairly early on in the Horman part of it all, that we were not to ask personal questions or look behind the letter of what was told us. As a result we were severely limited in being able to check out the veracity of what was told us and thus to be able to check sources and details."[87]

The account presented above raises further questions about the handling of Horman's body, for example whether other junta officials intervened at earlier dates to sidetrack the identification by moving Horman's remains.[88] The bottom line is that at least two named officials, Goycolea and Housset, took actions to prevent or delay Horman from being identified until the two SIM sergeants were able to circumvent those efforts, with the help of fingerprints provided by the FBI. U.S. Embassy officials made no attempt to look into any of the anomalies.

· · · · ·

The second element of the Chilean approach was to throw mud on the victims. Even as lower-ranking officials had been enlisted in the effort to find the missing body of Horman, top-ranking officers were honing the details of an elaborate, but somewhat implausible cover story to present to their U.S. counterparts. General Lutz, chief of SIM, had met with the U.S. Military Attaché, Colonel William Hon, several times in October and had promised to deliver a formal written report on Horman and Teruggi.[89] Once Horman's body was identified, Colonel Hon pressed Lutz for the promised memorandum. He said Ambassador Davis's last day as ambassador was November 1, and suggested the document "should be in our hands prior to the Ambassador's departure." Cutting the informal deadline short, a Lutz deputy, Commander Sergio Herrera, delivered the two-page memo to Hon at 10:00 a.m. on October 31. In the style of intelligence organizations, the memo lacked any identifying markings; it was unsigned, undated and without addressee.

The memo, "Information on the deaths of two North American citizens,"[90] was a combination of denials, obfuscation, outright falsehoods and derogatory information portraying Horman and Teruggi as dangerous leftists, while absolving the military government of any involvement in their deaths. It appeared to be designed to give Embassy officers something on which to hang their defense of Chile's junta.

It was a difficult task. The report had to account for the known facts that witnesses had seen uniformed soldiers detain Horman at his home, and that Carabineros had detained Teruggi with his friend David Hathaway and taken them to the Stadium. Moreover, General Lutz's own agents, Sergeants Meneses and Ortiz, had tracked down Horman's body, seen his name in military documents, and interviewed the officers and soldiers who detained him. The officers said they had filed a full report to their SIM superiors.

On Teruggi, Lutz's report claimed he was indeed detained at the Stadium, "but subsequently he was set free and his death occurred while he was out of military or police control." In Horman's case, "evidence exists that Mr. Horman may have been detained by military personnel at his home located in the so-called 'Cordón Vicuña Mackenna,'" but this was an "abnormal . . . situation" since these uniformed persons supposedly arrived in a civilian truck, without identifying themselves and without leaving any documentation of the search. These actions violated military regulations, the report said, drawing the dubious conclusion that therefore "both American citizens died while out of military control."

Moreover, it said, a possible cause of their deaths could have been the rampant sniper and guerrilla activity in the period of September 11–20 and extremists "fighting against civilians" with weapons similar to those used by the military. These explanations were elaborations on earlier unofficial statements that the men who detained Horman were leftist extremists using stolen Army uniforms.

In apparent reference to the mission of Meneses and Ortiz, the Lutz report said the military intelligence service was in constant contact with Horman's parents and wife and had succeeded in locating Horman's body and identifying him through "meticulous analysis using fingerprint evidence." That part was true.

The coherence of Lutz's narrative was certainly questionable, but the Embassy's cable to Washington reported Lutz's explanations at face value without comment: "Memo notes that Teruggi had been detained and taken to National Stadium but then released. No indication that Horman was arrested was found. Memo suggests possibility that [the] two [were] killed by extremist snipers active during time period."[91]

This was a cover story that Chilean authorities would stick to with little variation for the duration of the military government. Moreover, U.S. officials in Santiago and Washington repeated the story in public comments in support of the idea that nobody could know how or why Horman and Teruggi were killed.

Perhaps the most intriguing part of the memo, however, was the part that suggested that the Chilean intelligence service had files on Horman and Teruggi, and had information about their political activities both in Chile and the United States:

Available records on both persons lead to the conclusions that they were involved in extreme leftist movements in our country, which they supported both materially and ideologically.

It is necessary, furthermore, to indicate that available and well supported records exist of an organization linked to North American residents in our country, with connections in the rest of the countries in the continent and led from the U.S., which has launched an offensive campaign tending to obtain the following objectives:

a. Help extremists and political leaders of the former government leave the country.

b. Carry out a campaign to discredit the Governing Junta, intending through those actions, to impede economic or other assistance from the U.S. to our country.

c. Discredit diplomatic procedures of the American Embassy in Chile, alleging that these have been weak and have permitted military action against North American citizens residing in Chile.

The memo said there were "concrete reasons" to assess that Teruggi belonged to the organization, and that the information was relevant to both men. The description of the "U.S. based organization" could plausibly fit CAGLA, the Chicago organization in which Teruggi was active before traveling to Chile. CAGLA and other leftist organizations were indeed involved in solidarity activities such as those described in the Lutz report and were critical of the role of the United States in Chile and elsewhere. It was later learned that the FBI was investigating Teruggi's activities in Chicago, including his connection to CAGLA and an umbrella group, the North American Anti-Imperialist Coalition (NAAIC). NAAIC members worked in the "international struggle against imperialism, which we view as class struggle," according to materials quoted in the FBI reports. Among NAAIC's goals was "material and propaganda support for liberation movements among oppressed peoples in the imperialist system."[92]

Lutz's memo claimed the information was based on unspecified intelligence files, although some of the information was implausible on its face. Horman and Teruggi were accused of activities that could only have happened in the few days between the coup and their deaths. Points (a) and (b) allege "discredit[ing]" the military junta and helping people flee the country. Frank Teruggi and other Americans indeed were engaged in helping people, including Latin American militants, get asylum in embassies after the coup, but there is no basis for the idea they were helping "leaders of the former government." Point (c) is somewhat bizarre, and perhaps a warning to the U.S. officials. It charges that Horman and Teruggi were engaged in a campaign to bring discredit on the American Embassy for failing to protect North Americans against the military. In fact, it was their deaths that had focused such criticism on the Embassy.

The Embassy kept Lutz's intelligence report about Horman and Teruggi secret, releasing it to the Horman family only in 1976. But it caused a stir among several officials in Washington and in the Embassy. Political officer Robert Steven examined the Lutz report in light of the FBI reports about Teruggi, which were disclosed to the State Department in 1976. He said he detected possible echoes of the FBI reports in Lutz's memorandum. He and Chile desk officer Rudy Fimbres would become dissenting voices pushing back against the Embassy's too-easy acceptance of the Chilean military's cover stories. In closely held, detailed memoranda on the case circulated only inside the State Department, Fimbres raised the sensitive question that perhaps a U.S. government agency might have provided intelligence information to Chile about leftist Americans.[93]

In 1973 Steven was on the receiving end of Chilean efforts to paint Horman and Teruggi as dangerous leftists. He reported on a conversation with a Foreign Ministry official, Enrique Guzmán, who said he was working hard on the Horman-Teruggi issue. Guzmán had spoken previously about the case, but in December 1973 he was "pushing" the idea that their links to the Cordones had gotten them into trouble with the left, Steven said.

> Both Horman and Teruggi had not only been deeply involved in leftist activities in the "Communist industrial areas" but perhaps had been shot by their own comrades of the left for some unexplained reason. For example, they may have known too much about leftist activities, or have "betrayed the cause" by failing to join in the fighting against the military. Guzmán had in the past hinted at their involvement with the left, but never before had suggested that they were killed by the leftist extremists.[94]

Again, in this behind-the-scenes exchange, the Chilean official is conveying a variation of the junta cover story—the falsehood that they had been shot by leftists. But he also was pointing the U.S. official to information that was at least partly true—both were interested in the Cordones, although it might be an overstatement to say either was "deeply involved." Steven understood the Guzmán comments as part of a larger effort by Chilean authorities to push derogatory information on the two Americans purportedly gleaned from Chilean intelligence files.[95]

There are other examples of Chilean officials giving U.S. diplomats information that appeared to come from intelligence files.[96] In Teruggi's case, information was conveyed that could have come from knowledge of Teruggi's interrogation during his detention. A government spokesman who had never met Teruggi described him as "a rebel, of quick temper, easily disturbed." And Interior Minister Bonilla, in a statement to the new U.S. ambassador, David Popper, said, "Teruggi's release had been delayed somewhat by the impression he conveyed that he was a Chilean of Italian extraction."[97]

These confidential exchanges left a plethora of unanswered questions and pointed to unpursued leads about the murders. Few of the actions by the Chilean government were consistent with an innocent explanation of their involvement in the deaths. Why had the fingerprint check on Horman been delayed? Two military intelligence investigators had finally accomplished the identification, and they had stated that Horman was held and executed by the military. Chilean officials were conveying a changing litany of cover stories that on the one hand betrayed they possessed inside information about Horman and Teruggi's political activities, but on the other hand claimed implausibly that the military had nothing to do with their deaths even though both had been, or "may have" been, in military custody at one point. A recurring element of the Chilean statements was the unsupported assertion that leftists had killed Horman and Teruggi, either while masquerading in stolen military uniforms or shooting people with military-style weapons.

• • • • •

The U.S. press began to play an increasing role, especially after Ed Horman's return from Chile.

U.S. officials filtered information about the case into the public realm in ways that preserved the Chilean cover story. Leaks to the press and official statements excluded the evidence pointing to military responsibility for the deaths (for example, the statements to Ed Horman from SIM officers Meneses and Ortiz). What they conveyed for public consumption uniformly defended and embellished the Chilean denials of involvement and cast doubt on the statements of Ed Horman, statements which were indeed supported by facts.

Horman had been initially wary of the two intelligence officers who visited him in mid-October in his hotel. He said they appeared to want to help, but he suspected they might be "making a smokescreen" for the military. So when Raúl Meneses and Jaime Ortiz did what no one else had been able to achieve—locate his son's body and establish a positive identification—Horman's suspicion turned to gratitude. When he arrived in New York on October 21, he gave credit to the two officers for telling him the truth. He said the two intelligence officers not only identified his son with "positive proof," but they informed him and Embassy personnel "with witnesses present . . . that Charles was executed in the Stadium." To a State Department officer coordinating press inquiries, he described the emotion one of the officers had exhibited, saying he "was in tears as he realized the enormity of what had transpired." Horman was keeping careful notes of what he learned: "Purdy, Ortiz and Manesas [*sic*] of SIM, Col. [*sic*] Mario Rojas of *Investigaciones* all told E. C. Horman that CEH (Charles) had been shot in the National Stadium on 9/18/73."[98]

Horman, therefore, was furious when the same State Department officer in whom he had confided contradicted him publicly in conversations with journalists. Press officer Katherine Marshall was quoted in the *New York Post* speculating that Charles had been killed not by the military but by leftists, thus repeating the line being pushed by Chilean officials.[99] Marshall also drafted press guidance—talking points to answer reporters' questions—saying the State Department "has no way of knowing at this time exactly what happened or the sequence of events which led to Charles Horman's death."

Using convoluted language, the statement of guidance continued: "We can say categorically that at no time *did anyone say that we had been informed* or that we had some *definitive* information as to the circumstances in which Charles Horman died" (emphasis added). Any "meaningful conclusions" would have to wait for the Chilean government's report, "which we sincerely hope will shed real light on this tragic event."[100] The wording was a dodge and pitted the word of the aggrieved father against that of the State Department. In fact, as we have seen, Embassy officer Judd Kessler had received information that Horman had been killed in the Stadium and passed this on to Purdy. Likewise, multiple witnesses saw both Horman and Teruggi in military custody just prior to their deaths.

Horman expressed his controlled frustration about State Department actions in a letter to Senator William Fulbright of the Foreign Relations Committee. He said Embassy officials had given inordinate weight to the credibility of the Chilean military and failed to press the government, even while withholding information from Horman. His indictment was eloquent and severe:

> It seems apparent that it is Department policy to clear the Chilean government of responsibility and, at the same time, clear themselves of their obligation to hold a foreign government to account for killing an American Citizen....
>
> So—from September 18 to October 5, the day of my arrival in Santiago, the American Embassy did *nothing* to verify the evidence which had been placed in their hands ... and which proved to be the key to the truth. From October 5 to the very end, their "efforts" produced no results beyond the repeated statements that they had contacted the Chilean government right up to General Pinochet, and had been told that the Chileans knew nothing about Charles or his whereabouts....
>
> I do not know the reason underlying the negligence, inaction and failure of the American Embassy. Whether it was incompetence, indifference or something worse, I find it shocking, outrageous and, perhaps, obscene.[101]

Ed Horman's accusations of Chilean responsibility and his indictment of his own government's inaction have been confirmed and reconfirmed over the years as additional evidence has emerged. He had traveled to Chile trusting the U.S. government; he came away suspecting the worst— that U.S. officials had not only covered up for the new Chilean junta but might have been involved somehow in the killing itself. Based on his interactions with Ambassador Davis and others, he gradually became convinced that the Chilean military would not have killed an American citizen without first checking with its strategic ally, the U.S. government.

PART III Unraveling the Truth

In my opinion, in the particular case of Horman, neither the State Department, nor the U.S. Embassy in Santiago, nor Mr. Kissinger had any participation whatsoever.

RAFAEL GONZÁLEZ, 2001, recanting his 1976 statements

The evidence presented here has established, to a high degree of certainty, that Horman and Teruggi were executed, without U.S. involvement, as part of the massive repression against leftists, foreigners and Allende government sympathizers in the days following September 11.

AUTHOR'S CONCLUSION based on his investigation

[The case against Captain Davis] is so weak that he could not be convicted. It would have been easier to convict Henry Kissinger.

JUDGE MARIO CARROZA, interview

14 The Making of "The Man Who Knew Too Much"

Horman's family first expressed their new theory in the *New York Times*. This was the idea that Charles Horman had learned something in Valparaiso about U.S. participation in the military coup against Allende's government, and that this knowledge may have led to his death a few days later. It later was expanded into the charge that Captain Ray Davis or other U.S. officials may have ordered him killed him to silence him, or approved such an order by the Chileans.

On November 19, about a month after Joyce and Ed Horman arrived back in Manhattan, the *Times* published two long analytical stories on the case. The first described Ed Horman's odyssey in Chile looking for his son and his respectful complaints about "lack of initiative on the part of the Embassy."[1] The second, headlined "2 Americans Slain in Chile: Unanswered Questions," described Horman and Teruggi as "deeply committed to the Allende cause, pacifists and gentle intellectuals not involved in Chilean politics."[2] This understated portrayal, based on interviews with friends, was not exactly accurate, but unsurprising at the time considering the fear, violence and chaos the friends had survived. The article then recounted Horman and Terry Simon's trip to Valparaiso and Viña del Mar and being trapped there by the coup. Joyce Horman told the reporter "her

143

husband brought with him information on American activities at Valparaiso on the eve of and during the coup." They had met Captain Ray Davis and the retired Naval engineer, Arthur Creter, who was quoted as saying, "We came down to do a job and it's done." Joyce Horman said the engineer's statement was "a reference to the coup."

The newspaper took pains to point out that it was not known if Horman "had obtained proof that the engineer was speaking of the military takeover." And an unnamed friend who had access to Horman's information from Viña (and who later identified himself to me as Steven Volk) was quoted as saying "Charlie's information is interesting as part of the general picture of United States intervention in the Chile crisis, but it did not warrant killing him off." Volk said in an interview that Horman's "information" consisted of the detailed notes by Terry Simon that he had transcribed on his typewriter and smuggled out of Chile in an empty Chapstick tube.[3]

The idea would not resurface for almost a year as coverage of the stories of Horman and Teruggi faded from the news. Then, in October 1974, marking the one-year anniversary of the events in Chile, the London *Sunday Times* revisited the issue in a long investigative piece about alleged U.S. intervention in Chile. Reporters Godfrey Hodgson and William Shawcross marshaled their considerable reporting power to argue that the United States, on Henry Kissinger's orders, had "sought to destroy the Allende government by all means short of a massive invasion." The U.S. tactics, culminating in the successful military coup, were summed up in the word "destabilisation," which was the headline of the 8,000 word article.[4]

Charles Horman, his family and Terry Simon figure prominently toward the end of the piece. The authors state the generally known fact that the coup was launched in Valparaiso by the Chilean Navy. They state further, however, that the Navy planned and executed the coup in coordination with the United States and in liaison with U.S. officers there. Horman and Simon's encounters with Captain Ray Davis and Marine Lieutenant Colonel Pat Ryan, the authors write, offer "a tantalizing glimpse of the dashing Colonel Ryan and his helpers at work." The article then reprises the main elements of Horman's Valparaiso experience: that Horman and Simon met a man who came to Chile "to do a job for the Navy"; that they spent time with Colonel Ryan and his colleagues, who boasted about their inside knowledge of the coup; and that Captain Davis brandished a Chilean Navy identification card at a roadblock when he gave them a ride back to Santiago. The information obtained by Horman was portrayed as potentially lethal: "Horman was later picked up by the Chilean military police and disappeared. His wife, parents and Terry Simon believe they may have killed him because he knew too much about American liaison activities."[5]

The sentence in the London *Sunday Times* may have been the first time the phrase, made famous by the 1922 story "The Man Who Knew Too Much" by G. K. Chesterton, was applied to Charles Horman. To be sure, it was couched as the family's belief, not as established fact. But it caught on, as a powerful idea that seemed to embody the family's suspicion of what might have happened.

Then, almost two years later, in June 1976, the idea received apparently strong confirmation from a source claiming to have inside intelligence information. The source was Rafael González, a 20-year veteran as a civilian intelligence agent for the Estado Mayor de la Defensa Nacional (EMDN, Armed Forces General Staff) and other intelligence agencies. As scores of reporters were gathering in Chile for an international meeting featuring Henry Kissinger, González gave interviews to three American reporters over the course of several days. Asked about the two murdered Americans, González volunteered an explosive charge: "I knew that Charles Horman was killed because he knew too much. And this was done between the CIA and local authorities."[6]

He said he knew that Horman was brought from Valparaiso to Santiago. "I saw the guys that brought them here to Santiago, and he disappear." He said he saw Horman in the office of General Lutz, SIM's top officer, and was present for a conversation in which Lutz ordered Horman to be executed. He recounted Lutz saying: "That this guy knew too much, and we have another kind of information, so this guy has to disappear."

In that and subsequent interviews, each time González referred to Horman's killing he repeated the phrase he "knew too much." The interviews were conducted in English, which González spoke fluently, if not always grammatically, because he had been stationed in the United States. The interviewers were Latin American correspondents for three major news organizations: Joanne Omang of the *Washington Post*, Frank

Manitzas of CBS News and Rudolph "Ru" Rauch of *Time* magazine. Manitzas knew the case well, having done extensive reporting on it in 1973. He pressed González to repeat what happened:

GONZÁLEZ: I just told you what happened.
MANITZAS: Well, please tell me again.
GONZÁLEZ: That they said this guy knew too much. So he has to disappear.

González said the meeting where he saw Horman took place "just a couple of days after the coup d'etat" in the Ministry of Defense, and that Lutz was in conversation with his deputy, Colonel Victor Barria, and an unidentified man who said nothing. The man dressed like an American, González said, and "I suppose it could be a CIA agent."

Manitzas broadcast several radio dispatches on CBS. Omang's story in the *Washington Post* would have the most impact. Omang's article bore the headline:

CHILEAN CHARGES GENERAL ORDERED AMERICAN'S DEATH

The story described González's statement as providing "the first real clue in the death of Horman."[7]

González's charges had enormous impact. They created a narrative that would dominate the story of Charles Horman and would be reiterated in elaborate detail in Thomas Hauser's 1978 book *The Execution of Charles Horman: An American Sacrifice* and in the 1982 film *Missing*. They led the State Department to open an internal investigation to determine whether U.S. intelligence officials may have played a part in Horman's death. The statements would form the core of two lawsuits, one accusing Henry Kissinger and other U.S. officials of collaborating in Horman's murder, the other a libel suit by Ambassador Davis, Captain Davis, Patrick Ryan and Fred Purdy charging they had been defamed by the movie.*

---

* In the libel suit *Davis v. Costa-Gavras*, 654 F. Supp. 653 (SDNY 1987), the court ruled the film did not defame the plaintiffs because it was a "docudrama," rather than a documentary, and thus could not be held to "strict fidelity to fact." Thus, the court decided the case without resolving any of the factual questions, such as the U.S. role in the coup or

With González's statements, the idea that Horman and Simon had witnessed something in Valparaiso about U.S. involvement in the coup and that Charles Horman was killed because "he knew too much" was repeated as fact and placed in the mouth of the head of intelligence of the Chilean Army. And González expanded the narrative to paint a picture of a U.S. official who was present for Horman's interrogation and who gave tacit approval to the proceedings. The family's speculation and suspicion now appeared to be confirmed by an authoritative source inside the Chilean military. The film *Missing*, the accompanying book and statements of the family thereafter strongly suggested that the American in Lutz's office was Captain Ray Davis.

· · · · ·

What the family and U.S. officials did not know was that González, by his own later admission, had fabricated the narrative about the man who knew too much, and would later retract his entire story about U.S. involvement in Horman's death. Moreover, in his five-page retraction written in 2001, González identified the source of his information about Horman's supposed knowledge about the coup: he said it came from an article by the prominent British journalist William Shawcross in the newspaper the *Sunday Times*.[8]

The October 1974 article provided González with details he inserted into his 1976 interview. Notably, it quoted family members about Horman and Simon's stay in Valparaiso and the fact that they had been brought back to Santiago by an American military officer. Most tellingly, the article gave González the powerful key phrase, that Horman "knew too much"—which the article attributed to the Horman family.

In June 1976 González was in a dire situation. He and his wife and their eight-year-old child had been given asylum in the Italian Embassy and had been languishing there since the previous September. The Chilean government considered him a defecting intelligence agent with damaging information and refused to give him the safe conduct pass he needed to

---

responsibility for Horman's death. See Professor Thomas Leicht, "What's Missing in *Missing*," in *The Films of Costa-Gavras: New Perspectives*, ed. Homer B. Pettey (Manchester University Press, 2020). The judge removed the Hauser book from the suit early in the case.

leave the country. His desperation at the time is palpable in his 2001 written statement and his subsequent testimony to the court in 2003, in which he says he was under pressure by Italian diplomats to tell a story that would get him out of Chile:

> Just then [during the OAS meeting] Mrs. [Livia] Meloni and a high official of the [Italian] Foreign Ministry called me and passed me an old *Sunday Times* article written by the journalist William Shawcross, where the death of the American citizen Charles Horman was reported. . . .
>
> When Mr. Kissinger was about to arrive at the OAS meeting in Santiago de Chile . . . the Italian high diplomat . . . forced me to receive journalists from the *Washington Post*, to whom I was supposed to speak about the Horman case and say that I had seen a CIA agent in Gen. Lutz's office when Horman was ordered executed—a fact of absolute falsehood. I never saw any American. What they wanted was to compromise the CIA.[9]

He said he wanted to be specific that nothing he had previously said should be used to prove the U.S. government had a role in killing Horman.

> In my opinion, in the particular case of Horman, neither the State Department, nor the U.S. Embassy in Santiago, nor Mr. Kissinger had any participation whatsoever.

About the accusations against Captain Ray Davis, he said:

> Let me make it clear that neither Cmdr. Ray Davis nor any other U.S. citizen was in that office. Cmdr. Davis was not the mastermind of Horman's death and had nothing to do with it.
>
> His death was not due to information coming from the CIA, the U.S. Embassy or Cmdr Davis. The information about Horman was local, and had nothing to do with how his wife and the movie *"Missing"* have portrayed him, namely that he spent his time writing poetry and drawing ducklings.

González repeated the retraction in his testimony before Judge Zepeda:

> The two officials . . . forced me to make declarations in accordance with an article by the journalist W. Showcross [*sic*] from the English newspaper *The Sunday Times*. . . . When said officials of the Italian Embassy brought the American journalists to me I had to give that version, which was false, and when the officials from the North American embassy came [to interview me] I had to repeat the same things for obvious reasons.

González said he had run afoul of DINA, the powerful security police, in the course of his intelligence work for other agencies, and sought asylum in the embassy out of fear he would be killed. These fears were not groundless: in 1974, a DINA informant who gave a confession to a human rights organization was murdered.[10] He said the Italian diplomats were pressuring him to do the interview and even threatened to throw him out in the street if he did not cooperate.

The recantation was categorical in regard to the accusations of a U.S. role—and it came from the person who had given those charges credibility and worldwide dissemination starting in 1976. Given such a complete turnaround, we must face the question of when González was lying and when was he telling the truth. The idea that he was pressured or even forced to give the interview and implicate the CIA was raised for the first time in his retraction affidavit. By the time the retraction came to light the Italian diplomats had died. It seems implausible, however, that Italian diplomats would threaten someone to whom they had given refuge. The Italian Embassy had given asylum to 250 people after the coup and the ambassador, Tomaso De Vergottini, was well known as a critic of the dictatorship.[11]

The core fact of González's retraction is his identification of the *London Times* article, which indisputably contains the key details and wording González used in his 1976 interview. That fact is strong evidence that González indeed was lying when he claimed that those details and the wording "knew too much" came from the head of Chilean intelligence, General Lutz. At the very least, in light of González's retraction, his statements could no longer be reasonably relied upon as evidence to implicate U.S. officials in Horman's death.

González says he was acting out of fear. He says he invented the story to bring international attention to his own situation as an embassy asylee unable to leave Chile safely. As his son Sergio said, speaking for his father in 2004: "He had to say that or they would have killed him."[12]

González has stuck to one part of his story: that he saw Horman in custody and that he was being held as a "subversive" based on "local" intelligence about him. That part of his testimony tied him to Horman's detention and caused Judge Zepeda to bring a criminal charge of complicity against him. In other words, the only part of his testimony he did not retract was the part that was most damaging to himself. And indeed it resulted in his conviction.

As a trained undercover agent González would have been familiar with techniques of mixing elements of truth and invention to give the story plausibility and to enhance its credibility. Whether or not that was his intention in this case, he was successful in creating a kind of circular confirmation. By taking something the family believed to be true and placing it in the mouth of a high-ranking source inside the Chilean military, González seemed to confirm for the family that Horman was killed because he knew too much.

Similarly, the reporter William Shawcross, without knowing that González had relied on his story, closed another circle on the narrative by writing a story about González's 1976 interview. Its headline:

MYSTERY DEEPENS OVER THE MAN "WHO KNEW TOO MUCH"

Shawcross quoted González quoting Lutz using the phrase, and called the statement "sensational . . . evidence that Chilean military officers intended the murder of a U.S. citizen."[13] Then he continued, echoing allegations of his own 1974 story, but this time attributing them to González as confirmation: "Even more explosive is the rationale now being suggested for Horman's murder: that he may have blundered upon evidence that American Naval intelligence officers had foreknowledge of the Anti-Allende coup."

To put it in the simplest terms, González was able to fool not only the family but journalists, diplomats and U.S. congressional actors with his initial accusations about Horman's detention and execution. His story of the man who knew too much and a possible U.S. role drove the Horman case into the highest tiers of public awareness, especially with the success of the Costa-Gavras film *Missing*. In turn, the film, which portrayed González's appearance as a dramatic turning point, was the framework for a judicial investigation by Chilean Judge Zepeda, whose final verdict in 2016 appeared to endorse the most explosive charges of U.S. responsibility in the death of the "man who knew too much."

González's retraction in his 2003 court testimony was made public at the time but received little press coverage.[14] Moreover, his detailed 2001 affidavit explaining how and why he invented much of his story has not been published until now.

. . . . .

Because the retraction radically changes our understanding of the case, we should examine how Rafael González came to form such an important part of the story of Charles Horman.

At the time of the coup González was working as a civilian agent for the Intelligence Department of the General Staff of National Defense (EMDN, in the Chilean acronym). He had been employed by the General Staff and other agencies, including SIM, for almost 20 years. On assignment for SIM he worked as a covert agent in New York from 1969 to 1972, presumably in a security role on behalf of the Allende government.[15] His son Sergio Daniel was born there, and thus qualified for American citizenship. At the time of the coup, he was given the task of collecting papers from Allende's office and says he saw the president's shattered body on a sofa.

"A couple of days" after the coup, according to his 1976 interview, he was called into the SIM director's office in case he was needed as an interpreter with a North American prisoner. At that time he was working again for EMDN, in counterintelligence. While González's credentials in EMDN have been verified, González is the lone source for the alleged September 1973 meeting with Horman in General Lutz's office, and there has never been any independent corroboration of it.

In contrast, González appears in a March 1974 incident involving Horman that is amply verified. After Horman's identification in October, the Chilean government had refused to give permission to ship the body to the United States. Interior Minister Bonilla met with the new U.S. ambassador, David Popper, in early March and admitted he had delayed the release for fear that the return of the murdered American's body to the family in the United States would be used "to the detriment of Chile abroad." He agreed to authorize the shipment on the ambassador's assurances it would be done "quietly and privately."[16] Rafael González was given the task of accompanying Consular officer James Anderson to clear the paperwork at the morgue and find the burial spot to retrieve the body. Anderson has verified this. He wrote that González appeared at the

Consulate on March 21, identifying himself as a Lieutenant Colonel in the Air Force. Anderson said González was forceful and professional in overcoming bureaucratic hurdles and was able to obtain written permission for the exhumation of the body.[17]

In September 1975, González resigned from his intelligence job (he had moved from EMDN to SIFA, Air Force Intelligence) and the next day entered the Italian Embassy asking for asylum for himself and his family. He explained in his interviews with Manitzas that he opposed the new intelligence service, DINA, which had been imposing a Gestapo-like reign of terror in Chile. He also aired complaints about homosexuals and Jews and claimed that the CIA had once "hypnotized" his former wife. Manitzas concluded that González was a defector, not a refugee, because as a veteran intelligence agent he had had access to many secrets about the workings of the military. González wanted to leave Chile, preferably to the United States, but said he feared he would be detained and killed if he tried to leave through normal routes.

Nine months passed and González and his family were still in the Italian Embassy, as the military junta refused to issue the safe conduct pass that would allow him to leave the country. He had various meetings with U.S. consular officials about the status of his young son, and was told the family would be able to enter the United States once they got out of Chile. In those meetings he repeated his claim about the CIA hypnotizing his former wife, which he said occurred during his assignment in New York and was an attempt to force him to give information about his work.

In June 1976, Italian officials gave permission for him to do interviews with the U.S. journalists Manitzas and Omang. The third journalist, *Time* correspondent Rudolph Rauch, interviewed him several days later, but his story was not published. The purpose was to call attention to the humanitarian plight of the González family and put pressure on the junta to allow him to safely exit the country. It was an optimum moment. Dozens, perhaps hundreds, of international correspondents were in Santiago to cover the OAS meeting and Kissinger's visit.

In the unpublished interview with Rauch, González gave the most detailed statement about his motivations: "I was retired from the Air Force on 2 September [1975], supposedly for disciplinary reasons. The real reason for my retirement was that I complained about immoralities at the highest level in the service in which I used to work."[18]

Despite the publicity generated by the interview about Horman, González remained in the Italian embassy an additional eleven months and was finally allowed to depart Chile for Spain in May 1978. He then agreed to submit evidence on behalf of the Horman family in the lawsuit *Horman v. Kissinger et al.*, and stayed as a guest with the Hormans in their New York City apartment. By that time he had been interviewed several times by U.S. officials and his story had started to wobble. According to declassified transcripts of four such interviews, he denied saying Horman's killing was coordinated with the CIA; he said he never mentioned Horman returning from Valparaiso. The statements to U.S. officials contradicted what he had clearly said in the recorded interviews with Omang and Manitzas. He also volunteered that he had never heard of Horman before seeing him in Lutz's office. But in a sworn affidavit in the Kissinger suit, he returned to his previous story about the CIA being involved and said all of the statements he made to Manitzas and Omang were true. His core story did not waver: in one short interview he repeated the phrase "he knew too much" five times as the explanation for how and why Horman was executed by the military.[19]

In 2003—24 years later—González appears again. He was living back in Chile. As the country transitioned back to democracy in the 1990s, Chilean courts had embarked on energetic prosecutions of emblematic human rights crimes, and case number 2182-1998 was opened about the Horman and Teruggi murders. In May 2003, Judge Jorge Zepeda ordered his arrest. Because González claimed he was present when Horman was in military custody in the Defense Ministry office, he was formally charged as an accessory to Horman's execution. González gave a long statement to police and handed over the affidavit containing his retraction, which he said he had written in November 2001. He was convicted in 2015 and sentenced to two years in prison, which was reduced to confinement in his home because of his age.[20] In summarizing the evidence against him, Judge Zepeda repeated the claim that a CIA officer was present in Lutz's office and other details that González had said were fabricated, but did not mention anything about González's retraction.

One finally has to ask, after all of González's twists and turns, did he ever see Horman at all? We cannot say based on confirmed facts, nor is credibility any guide. If González had been able to indicate he had told someone at the time—in 1973—about what he witnessed in Lutz's office, it might have enhanced his credibility, but he never pointed to anyone who could provide such corroboration. The evidence from Sergeants Meneses and Ortiz that Horman was taken directly to the National Stadium and was executed there is hard—but not impossible—to square with González's testimony about his supposed presence around the same time in the Defense Ministry, several miles away.

Sergeant Jaime Ortiz, who worked in SIM, and whose statements have been uniform and corroborated by contemporary witnesses, said he doubts that such a scene in Lutz's office ever took place, with Horman or with any other prisoners: "It is hardly feasible. Lutz did not even question members of the GAP [Allende's security guard] or Allende's ministers." Logistically the movements around different parts of the city with Horman in custody are hard to reconcile in González's and Ortiz's accounts.[21]

It is also strange that González—supposedly the go-to person on Horman—knew nothing about the inquiry by SIM agents Ortiz and Meneses to find and identify Horman's body. He first mentions them in a 2003 statement to police, saying he read about them in Hauser's book, and reproduces the misspelling of Meneses's name as "Manesas."[22]

In the Chilean court case, Judge Zepeda chose not to credit González's retraction and instead indicted him as an accessory to the crime based on his original statements in 1976. The judge viewed the retraction to be self-serving, since it came as González was arrested and charged. Yet the "self-serving" argument is undercut by the fact that almost the entirety of the evidence against González was his own voluntary testimony, and the most damaging part of that testimony—never retracted—was his unwavering claim to have been in the room with Horman shortly before he was executed.

15 How and Why

If Charles Horman and Frank Teruggi were not executed at the instigation or acquiescence of the U.S. government, why did the Chilean military actors detain the two U.S. citizens and decide they should be killed? And if the U.S. government actors were not covering up their own guilt in the murders, why did they embrace with such apparent enthusiasm the cover stories by the Chilean military denying all responsibility? Those are the most important questions that remain to be answered, to the extent it is possible with the available evidence.

The evidence presented here has established, to a high degree of certainty, that Horman and Teruggi were executed, without U.S. involvement, as part of the massive repression against leftists, foreigners and Allende government sympathizers in the days following September 11. Yet the U.S. Embassy, by any objective measure, failed to conduct an authentic investigation of what happened. Moreover, Embassy officials deceived the family on more than one occasion and acquiesced in Chile's cover-up of the crimes.

The actions of top Embassy officials, in particular Ambassador Davis, Consul Purdy and Colonel Hon, conformed to a policy dictated from Washington to protect the new military junta from criticism. As a consequence, they downplayed, concealed and in some cases misrepresented available facts to the extent those facts pointed to Chilean government responsibility. Over the ensuing years, U.S. authorities, irrespective of the party in power, failed to marshal U.S. resources, such as the FBI, to fully investigate the deaths of these two American citizens abroad. Instead, according to statements by insiders such as Consul Purdy and others, U.S. diplomats accepted the alibis of Chilean authorities at face value, declined to exert pressure on them to explain obvious contradictions and made little effort to check the veracity of what they were being told.

The U.S. inaction frustrated and enraged the families and stoked their suspicion that U.S. officials were directly involved not only in overthrowing Allende but in killing their loved ones. With the U.S. government intent on protecting the Chilean junta, and the Horman family and their advocates focused on proving U.S. involvement, little or no effort was devoted to investigating available leads and evidence, including from living witnesses, that could have brought those directly involved to justice and shed additional light on the circumstances of the killings. This diversion of energy is most evident in the court investigation by Judge Zepeda, which focused so heavily on proving the thesis of the man who knew too much that it missed the opportunity to locate and interview the two military officials—Ortiz and Meneses—who identified Horman and actually spoke to his captors, who were still alive.

There is a range of plausible motives, but no smoking gun, to explain the military's decision to detain and kill Horman and Teruggi. There is no first-hand account, much less a confession, by any of the military actors directly involved. For Horman, we can rely on the statements of Ortiz and Meneses, which provide the most credible but still incomplete factual account of what happened. Even those two officers were conveying what they were told by other Chilean military actors, who gave only vague explanations for why Horman was considered subversive. For Teruggi, we have the excruciating accounts of other prisoners who saw him near death.

With the relevant caveats, it is possible to outline the plausible motives, based on reporting already detailed in earlier chapters.

THE CORDONES CONNECTION

Horman and Teruggi, as well as many Chileans, viewed the workers' movement organized in the Cordones, the factory belts around Santiago, as the most likely centers of resistance to the coup. On the morning of the coup, Teruggi and some friends made the trek to factories in one of the Cordones, as did many Allende sympathizers (including myself), and were disappointed to find so few signs of resistance. In the early days, the most violent military raids were directed against the factories in the Cordones areas that were controlled by workers. Hundreds of workers were executed as a result of those raids, and literally thousands were rounded up and taken to the Stadium. This occurred around the same time that Horman and Teruggi were detained, and in both cases their bodies arrived at the morgue at the same time as the bodies of groups of workers killed at militant Cordones factories. Many other people were arrested in surrounding working-class housing areas, known as *poblaciónes*. Horman was arrested at his house, where he had lived for only a few days, in the midst of the Vicuña Mackenna Cordón. His presence as a gringo in a working-class area, near some of the most militant factories, was undoubtedly noticed and may have made him more vulnerable amid the intense military activity.

Moreover, the Chilean government raised the Cordones factor as part of its disinformation efforts following Horman's disappearance. A Chilean Foreign Ministry official tried to convince Embassy officer Robert Steven that Horman and Teruggi both were "deeply involved in leftist activities in the 'communist industrial areas'"—an unmistakable reference to the Cordones. The official then suggested falsely that it was their leftist comrades who killed them—the core premise of the junta cover story. The statement about leftists was incongruous. But it is notable that the Chilean official took pains to link both Horman and Teruggi to the Cordones movement, whose members accounted for so many of the victims in the early weeks. It is not known if the official's statement was based on Chilean intelligence files or was concocted to portray the two Americans in an unfavorable light.

In fact, Charles Horman had taken action to support the Cordones workers movement in a way that could have exposed him to danger if it had been known. He had raised funds in New York which he said were intended for political work and to buy weapons for the workers in the Cordones. We have no information about the identity of any worker contacts or intermediaries who asked him to raise the money. I tried to locate possible contacts by interviewing worker and political activists formerly connected to the Cordones movement. All were knowledgeable about resistance efforts in the Cordones, including efforts to procure weapons, but none of them knew anything about Horman or Teruggi.[23]

It is not known if Horman turned over the money he had raised to anyone in Chile. But we must consider the possibility that he delivered the money to the person associated with the Cordones who had asked him to raise the funds. If that person was later captured and revealed how he got the money, it would have been more than adequate reason to send a squad of soldiers to detain Horman. We do not know if that is what happened. But from Ortiz and Meneses we know the raid at the house was targeted at Horman by name and the arrest order was based on information from a SIM intelligence officer (Captain Hugo Salas Wenzel),[24] whose unit had carried out repressive operations before the coup to find weapons in the Cordones factories. The specific content of Salas's information is not known, including whether the reason for the arrest involved the Cordones.

The Cordones connection is not a certainty as a reason for the deaths of the two Americans, but it provides a plausible scenario for what might have happened, especially in Horman's case.

CONNECTION TO MIR

Teruggi had strong connections to the Movement of the Revolutionary Left (MIR), which was Chile's most radical political party. Horman did not, as far as is known. MIR advocated armed struggle and the Marxist strategy of dictatorship of the proletariat to achieve revolution. The movement was vocally critical of Allende's "reformist" adherence to the democratic process and was not part of Allende's coalition. Teruggi's links to MIR clearly were of a nature that could have put him in danger, although more by association than by his own activity. There was intense MIR activity in his house, and it had been noticed in the neighborhood. All of the housemates were related to MIR in some way, and Teruggi himself, while not an official member of the party, had participated as an activist in MIR's student organization FER since early in his sojourn in Chile. One of the housemates, Fernando Alarcón, was a cadre in the elite Central Force, which was MIR's military wing. Two women in the house, Olga and Maria Virginia, were engaged in sensitive tasks for the MIR Central Committee, including preparing false identity papers for use in underground activities. Blank forms for Chilean identity cards were found in the house after the raid, an indication that police may have found other such materials. Teruggi was arrested with his American roommate, David Hathaway, who was also associated with MIR but was mostly unharmed. Teruggi was singled out for special interrogation once he arrived at the National Stadium, and his death appears to be connected to something that happened during torture.

Horman's connections to MIR were tangential at best, but he could have been associated indirectly with the party through his filmmaker friends, including his colleague Pablo de la Barra. The military relentlessly targeted Miristas; hundreds were killed and thousands detained in the first year.

CHILE FILMS AND EDUARDO "COCO" PAREDES

Horman's film work and association with Chile Films and Pablo de la Barra was mentioned several times by people connected to the military. The director of the government-funded production company was Eduardo "Coco" Paredes, a figure hated by the right, and the film production company was considered a hotbed of leftist activity. In calls to friends the day after Horman's arrest, men identifying themselves as Army intelligence agents alluded to his work as a filmmaker. The calls were threatening and pointed accusingly to his film work while labeling him a foreign extremist. General Camilo Valenzuela, a sinister figure implicated in the 1970 plot to prevent Allende from being inaugurated, told U.S. officials Horman was receiving pay from de la Barra, "a known communist"—a doubtful assertion that is denied by de la Barra, who was not a member of the Communist Party. The repeated allusions are an indication that the military had a file on Horman that included details about his film work.

Defense Minister Patricio Carvajal issued an order to investigate foreigners employed or associated with Chile Films, a category that would have included Horman. Weapons training had taken place at Chile Films. Horman's close friend Pablo de la Barra, who had a strong but unofficial connection to Chile Films, was working on a film portraying armed revolutionaries, and his brother was a leader of MIR who was later disappeared. In a separate incident that probably occurred after Horman's disappearance, de la Barra hid several guns in a camper van that had been lent to him by Horman.[25] Police discovered the guns, and de la Barra turned himself in and eventually was expelled from Chile.

There is strong evidence, then, that the military knew of Horman's film work at the time of his detention, but it is harder to see how it could have been a reason to kill him.[26] No one was killed during the raid on Chile Films, even though weapons had been stored there. Nevertheless, Eduardo Paredes was executed shortly after the coup, and two other people connected to Chile Films were disappeared at a later time.[27] In those cases, political activities not related to Chile Films were thought to be the motive.

BEING A FOREIGNER, POSSESSING LEFTIST LITERATURE

There is no question that the military targeted foreigners aggressively in the early weeks. More than 800 were rounded up, dozens were killed and thousands sought refuge in embassies and UN safe houses. Americans did not necessarily feel as threatened by the junta's broadcast calls to turn in "foreign extremists," but at least 20 Americans were detained in the National Stadium. I know from personal experience and conversations that military squads raided the houses and apartments of many other Americans, often because of denunciations by neighbors. Meneses said "extremist materials" were found in Horman's house, and explained, "He was therefore considered a foreigner/extremist and the order was given to execute him." He also commented: "They only knew he was a foreigner and an extremist."[28] Both Horman and Teruggi were known to have a considerable library of Marxist literature. Neither considered their books dangerous enough to dispose of them in the days before their arrest. Teruggi was proud of his collection of the complete works of Lenin. In both raids, however, police and military confiscated large quantities of books.

As arbitrary as it may seem, the military's campaign against foreigners and the confiscation or burning of extremist literature were factors frequently mentioned in early repressive operations, resulting in many deaths, and in Horman's and Teruggi's cases both factors were present.

DOSSIERS ABOUT ACTIVISM

Junta officials claimed to know about both men's political activism in Chile and back in the United States. "The Junta clearly had or quickly acquired derogatory information on Horman and Teruggi, and frequently mentioned it to Embassy personnel," wrote Frederick Smith in his internal State Department report, kept secret until the year 2000. Besides calling them "extremists," which was a general label applied to almost anyone detained or killed, various military and government officials alluded to both men's activities on behalf of the Cordones, work in *FIN* (the newsletter translating U.S. leftist articles), and association with pro-Allende groups. Intelligence officer Ortiz asked Joyce Horman about her husband's association with *FIN*, indicating he already had some information about it from his files. The memorandum from Army intelligence chief General Lutz contained detailed allegations about Teruggi's work with a U.S.-based organization that was engaged in assistance to leftists in Latin America and campaigns to discredit the junta and the U.S. embassy. Other officials offered information about Teruggi's personality, calling him a "rebel" with a fiery temper.

Enrique Sandoval, whose brother had conveyed information about Horman from inside the Stadium, came to New York in 1976 and met with Ed Horman. According to Horman, Sandoval said there was a "dossier" on his son. "He said that Charles had been interrogated in the upper part of the Estadio [stadium] where Military Intelligence was stationed. He said that a dossier had been presented which spoke of Charles' participation in the March on Washington and his activity in civil rights and anti-Vietnam war movements. He said that it also referred to Charles as a member of MIR."[29]

All of this information about their activism, while hardly incriminating, seemed to confirm the existence of Chilean intelligence files on Horman and Teruggi, and perhaps other Americans. And it fed suspicion that some of the information about activities in the United States might have come from liaison with U.S. military intelligence or the CIA. Meneses said other intelligence officers told him there was a list of suspicious American leftists, which they said came from the Embassy.[30] The U.S. government has denied that any information on Americans was given to the Chilean government before or after the coup, but an extremely uncomfortable set of documents emerged in 2000 showing that the FBI had conducted an investigation on Teruggi and had obtained his address in Chile. The FBI documents described his connections to activists in Germany helping U.S. soldiers to desert. Desertion and troop disloyalty was a particularly sensitive issue for the Chilean military, since MIR was known to be organizing soldiers inside the barracks, and some of the soldiers collaborating with MIR were tortured and killed.

The CIA denied providing any information about Horman and Teruggi to Chile. But the CIA has a dubious record of telling the truth on such issues, so it must remain an open question whether and to what extent U.S. officials shared intelligence with their Chilean military counterparts about leftists that may have put them in danger. I will return to this issue in chapter 18.

ARBITRARY CRUELTY

There is credible testimony from other prisoners that Frank Teruggi was killed by a sadistic torturer who executed him because he was an American and the signs and effect of his torture could not be hidden. Such executions to hide the evidence of torture, or to dispose of a prisoner whose information was no longer useful, became extremely common in subsequent years, especially in Chile and Argentina. The tactic was often the prelude to disappearance—the intentional hiding of bodies after execution. I have been able to document many such cases in my other books. In Teruggi's case, while such action likely explains his death, it does not shed light on the motive for his detention and interrogation, particularly since his housemate David Hathaway did not receive similar treatment.

· · · · ·

The above theories are all supported, at least in part, in the available evidence. It is important to recall that the two Americans were killed in a specific time frame in which hundreds of Chileans and foreigners were executed and thousands were being rounded up and thrust into prisons. Many Chilean citizens were executed for reasons similar to those described here. Others were executed who had little or no political connections or activity. Still others survived capture and imprisonment after being found with far more incriminating evidence. It is known that Latin American military personnel, given license to torture and kill with impunity, often exercised their power with caprice and irrationality.[31]

There are other theories that should be considered far less probable. Mistaken identity, for example. Meneses was told by other military personnel that Horman's captors thought he was Brazilian and did not know he was an American citizen until after he was dead. Implicit in the story is the idea that they would not have killed him if they had known he was an American. Horman spoke fairly good Spanish with an American accent, and had light skin and fair hair. He was targeted for arrest with an order naming him, and soldiers confiscated large quantities of English-language books and other materials. So it is extremely unlikely that those who captured him did not know they were executing a *gringo*, a North American.

HOW MUCH DID HORMAN KNOW?

As demonstrated in previous chapters, the once widely accepted theory, based on the 1976 statements of Rafael González, was that a U.S. official approved Horman's execution because he knew too much about the U.S. role in the coup. González later retracted both elements of that theory, saying he used a 1974 press report to invent a false story about Horman's death.

The theory of U.S. approval, therefore, lacks a factual basis. But we should consider the issue independently of the false statements by González. Did Horman in fact know something that could have put him in danger, either from the Americans or the Chileans? The most obvious first thought on the issue is this: Terry Simon saw and heard the same things as Charles Horman during their stay in Viña and Valparaiso, but her notes and statements at the time and since do not point to any potentially dangerous knowledge. The military officers they met were joyful backers of the coup; one of the men (Creter) bragged he had information about how it unfolded, but his information was not particularly significant (the timing of the takeover of Valparaiso) and was factually inexact. According to the early accounts of those who talked to Horman just before his death, he expressed disgust—not fear—at the attitudes of the military personnel he and Simon met. Both Horman and Simon suspected that the U.S. military officials they met had advance knowledge of the coming coup, which was later confirmed by one of those officials, Colonel Ryan, who said he had been given six or seven hours' advance notice. None of that information was dangerous or exclusive. Nor did any of the information they heard in Valparaiso constitute evidence of the American officers' direct participation in the coup.

Nevertheless, Ed and Joyce Horman became deeply suspicious of the U.S. Embassy officials they dealt with in the long search for Charles's body. They became convinced that Charles's death may have been related to something that happened on the coast and expressed their suspicions in newspaper interviews. When Rafael González spoke out in 1976, the family believed him; they had no way of knowing that he was fabricating his story about the "man who knew too much" and that he had used a newspaper article quoting the family's own suspicions as the basis for his statements. González's statements at the time seemed plausible, even probable.

Now we know otherwise. Besides González's now retracted statements, there is no factual basis for the idea that Charles was killed because of his purported knowledge obtained in Valparaiso about the coup.

There is another element to the theory, however, which is the suspicion that Horman's research into the Schneider assassination and a possible CIA connection to the plot may have given the Chilean military and/or

U.S. officials a motive to kill him. This theory gained prominence in 1976, when the Church Committee report *Covert Action in Chile* revealed that the CIA had indeed been directly involved with those who carried out the kidnapping that resulted in Schneider's death.

Did his research in 1972 about Schneider provide a possible motive to kill him? Author Thomas Hauser, writing in 1978 after the publication of the Church Committee report, states that Horman, in his library research, "had come to believe that the United States had masterminded the 1970 assassination of General Rene Schneider." But as evidence Hauser quotes a letter from Horman to his parents saying, "An interesting thing is the enormous number of people who knew about it at the time, including [former president Eduardo] Frei, his Ministers, the CIA, the American Ambassador, and several Senators."[32] Indeed, suspicion and denunciation of possible CIA involvement in the events surrounding Schneider's death were widespread in Chile in 1972 and were included in a book on the case. The book, *El Caso Schneider*, was published in September 1972, around the time Horman began doing research on the case.[33] Secret documents about CIA intervention in Chile, known as the "ITT Papers," were published by the *New York Times* and *Washington Post* earlier in 1972 and were widely republished and discussed in Chile. The *Times* piece, headlined "Papers Show ITT Urged U.S. to Help Oust Allende,"[34] said, "The papers reveal that ITT dealt regularly with the Central Intelligence Agency and, at one point, considered triggering a military coup to head off Allende's election." In other words, the idea that the CIA was promoting subversion in Chile was more or less an open secret. Suspicions about the CIA were so widespread that they caused Chileans to speculate that any American working in Chile might be a covert agent; I was accused of being a "CIA agent" more than once.

Finally, the earliest accounts do not support the idea. Reporter Frank Manitzas interviewed Joyce Horman and Lluis Mestres in October 1973. He asked them what Horman had said on his return from Valparaiso. Manitzas writes: "In his talks with friends and his wife, Horman never said anything alarming about what had happened in the port, or what they might have seen in their two-and-a-half hour drive from Valparaiso to Santiago. What everyone seemed to remember was Horman and Simon talking about the 'attitude' of the American military personnel, especially their expressed 'pleasure' that Allende had been overthrown."[35] Mestres said Horman thought the American military men he met were "advising" on the coup.

On the Schneider research, Joyce Horman said she had been asked at the Consulate if there was "anything in the house that might have irritated the soldiers." "No, absolutely nothing," she said. But later, she changed her mind: "After thinking further, I mentioned that Charles had a short study on the Viaux/Schneider case. It came to mind because the previous Sunday [the day before Horman's detention], we had gone through the house looking for anything that might prove offensive in any way. Charles and I decided, after some discussion and after looking at the pages, that all the information included was public and common knowledge, so we had not destroyed it."[36]

In neither case is there any evidence that Horman possessed any specific information indicating U.S. involvement. None of what he knew could reasonably be seen to have put him in danger. That is the factual record.

16 Scenario for a Movie

Over the ensuing 40 years, the Horman case was memorialized in a book, a Hollywood movie and three trials, all having as their central focus Rafael González's accusation of U.S. involvement in the murder. All were built on an architecture of possible scenarios of what happened based on not unreasonable assumptions emerging from González's stunning, yet fabricated, declarations. The fundamental assumption, shared by many at the time, was that González was telling the truth.

First, a word about assumptions, which quickly began to displace factual investigation as the case gained public notoriety and justice tended to be defined as a matter of establishing that the United States government had killed two of its own citizens in Chile.

Assumptions are very strong mental instruments. They are formed from our experiences and preliminary understanding of a given situation and are useful in guiding the direction of our thinking and even our conclusions. They are also shaped by our passions.

Most of my investigative work, for example, has been directed at dictatorships and human rights crimes in Latin America and has been critical of U.S. government relations and sometimes complicity with the perpetrators of those crimes. One might presume that the investigation in this book would aim to confirm the worst-case scenarios about the U.S. role in the Horman and Teruggi tragedies. In fact, when I began this investigation in the early 2000s, I expected I would be able to find the proof of a guilty U.S. hand in the killing of two Americans. That was my assumption, but my assumption was proven wrong when confronted by the facts uncovered in my investigation.

Likewise, the assumptions surrounding the U.S. role in the collapse of Chile's democracy are reasonable and very powerful. The U.S. government, under the leadership of Richard Nixon and Henry Kissinger at the time, was deeply invested in the success of the Chilean military both in overthrowing Allende and in replacing his leftist model with a durable regime that would be dependably pro-American and anticommunist. That known fact led, not unreasonably, to the assumption that the Chilean junta would not kill two U.S. citizens without getting the go-ahead from their main ally and defender. It could also be presumed, as a hypothesis, that the intimate relationships between U.S. intelligence—the CIA, State Department and military agencies—and the Chilean military was such that information flowed freely back and forth. As a corollary, it could be further presumed that United States officials provided intelligence dossiers on leftist U.S. activists living in Chile to their Chilean counterparts, who in turn kept U.S. officials informed about major actions affecting U.S. interests, for example the execution of U.S. citizens.

Such assumptions should not be mistaken for fact, but they can be valuable as guides in the formulation of possible hypotheses about what happened. In the end, however, an investigator is obliged to build an architecture of solid facts to support such hypotheses. Or, in the absence of supporting facts, to look in another direction. And even when evidence is found, it must stand the test of potentially contradictory facts and scenarios, which also must be honestly pursued. In the end, the ultimate objective is the pursuit of truth, conclusions based on facts, not a "truth" of deeply held but subjective opinion. That is the purpose of the present inquiry.

Having assumptions and following their lead to construct possible scenarios and hypotheses is an honest process. It is what Edmund Horman did, painstakingly, in the weeks and months after he learned of Rafael González's statements putting a CIA agent in the room when his son's death sentence was pronounced. González is the key, he told author Thomas Hauser:

> Reread González's testimony. The answer to why Charles was murdered is there. González says that Charles was killed "because he knew too much." And that he was "brought from Valparaiso to Santiago." Clearly, someone thought that Charles's stay in Valparaiso and Vina del Mar was significant. Otherwise it would never have been mentioned in front of González. If you want to find out why Charles was killed, take a look at what he and Terry learned in Vina.[37]

The elder Horman was a meticulously organized man, and in December 1976 he compiled his thoughts and the known evidence in a 31-page typewritten report he entitled "The View after Three Years."[38] He listed and summarized all the declassified documents he had received, and he reprised what was said by Embassy officials, Rafael González, the two SIM officers Ortiz and Meneses, and others. He quotes a cable that seems to weigh against the case he was building: "González statement to Consul sounds plausible, but in view of his reputation we cannot assume it is accurate."[39]

From the information he formed a hypothesis, which he called a "scenario." Writing in December 1976, the elder Horman shows an impressive command of the known facts but drafts his scenario with unabashed forays into the realm of assumption and speculation. In the following text, I have italicized assertions not based on known facts but rather Horman's assumptions about what might have happened, including the statements, later retracted, of Rafael González.

> Charles Horman and Terry Simon were caught in Viña de Mar by the coup. At the Hotel they met Creter of the U.S. Navy who talked freely and indiscreetly *about participation of the U.S. government in the coup.* His remark, "we came to do a job and we did it," was later confirmed by Captain R. E. Davis, Commander of *Mlgrp Viña, and a member of Naval Intelligence.* . . .
> Creter's indiscretions were overheard by a woman who accompanied him and she interrupted the conversation. *Later she probably described the incident to Lt. Col. Patrick J. Ryan, USMC second in command of Mlgrp Viña. Col. Ryan reported the matter to Captain Davis, either by telephone to Santiago or personally when* Captain Davis came to Viña later in the week.

Captain Davis drove Charles Horman and Terry Simon to Santiago September 16. *Alerted by Col. Ryan's report on Charles Horman's talk with Creter, he checked with CIA and was given the information which later were presented as a dossier at Charles Horman's interrogation (see p. 11). Arrangements were made to have Charles Horman arrested and turned over to SIM.* . . .

They took him directly into the Estadio Nacional. . . . He was taken directly to the upper level and interrogated by S.I.M. The dossier mentioned above described his activities in the U.S. in the civil rights and anti-Vietnam war movements, his participation in FIN in Chile. He was condemned to be shot *but the interrogators were unwilling to carry this out on their own authority. They therefore sent him and their files to the office of General Lutz, Director of Army Intelligence, in the Ministry of Defense building. Recognition of the gravity of murdering an American citizen* who had been arrested under circumstances where there might have been witnesses (as there were) is evidenced *by the fact that Charles Horman's file was reviewed by General Lutz, by Col. Barria, his second in command, and by an American intelligence agent. They decided that Charles Horman "knew too much" and confirmed the sentence of shooting him.*[40]

The plausibility of the scenario was strengthened in Horman's mind when he met in New York with a key figure in the investigation, Enrique Sandoval, who had left Chile and had sought exile status in Canada. Sandoval's brother Nelson, a Carabinero officer stationed at the Stadium, had obtained information about Charles's execution. Enrique Sandoval had conveyed his brother's information to Embassy officer Judd Kessler in late September.[41] The fact that U.S. officials did not act on that information and withheld it from Ed Horman when he arrived in Chile greatly enhanced his suspicion that those officials were not forthright with him and were perhaps covering up other secrets about U.S. involvement. The information from Sandoval finally reached Horman more than two weeks later by another channel, on the same day Charles's death was confirmed by Sergeants Meneses and Ortiz. In their personal meeting Sandoval gave Horman further details about the "dossier" on his son, which accurately described Charles's antiwar activity.

Thus, when Horman read about Rafael González's explosive statements in June 1976, he placed the new development alleging U.S. involvement in a rich context he had already compiled. He was eager to share what he knew when *Washington Post* reporter Lewis Diuguid called him a few days after the news about González broke. Diuguid wrote the first truly investigative story about Horman's case, appearing in late June with the headline "The Man Who Knew Too Much." Quoted in the story, Horman for the first time directly pointed to U.S. involvement in Charles's death. "Considering the information I have gathered and what I have seen and heard," he said, "the only conclusion I can draw is that the United States fingered him."[42]

Diuguid was the first journalist to bring together the known facts, interview critical sources and reveal new documents that had been released to the Horman family. Horman showed Diuguid a copy of the "Lutz report"—the SIM-prepared document accusing Horman and Teruggi of supporting extremist activity in Chile. Diuguid interviewed a former embassy official who supported the idea that a dossier existed: "An official close to the case recently has acknowledged that the CIA had considerable information on him [Horman]."[43]

Ed Horman completed his "scenario" with a pointed indictment of Embassy officials. He said they made no real effort to follow up on leads, failed to "bring the Junta to book," cast doubt on accounts pointing to junta responsibility, and reinforced suggestions that Charles had been killed by leftists. The man who had begun his quest with full confidence in the U.S. Government came away believing its officials had killed his son and were engaged in a coverup.[44]

My purpose in this exegesis of Ed Horman's statements is not to cast doubt on his veracity, much less to question his sincerity. In every aspect in which his scenario touched on known fact, he represented those facts accurately and without shading. His foray into unsupported conjecture based on assumptions was a rational exercise by a man of conservative temperament.

Those assumptions turned out to be wrong. In subsequent years and in multiple declassifications and three judicial investigations no additional facts have ever been uncovered to prove any of Horman's speculative statements above. For example, nothing ever emerged to indicate Creter was referring to U.S. involvement in the coup in his much-repeated comment. Nothing showed that Davis and Ryan were concerned about what Horman knew and targeted him for detention and execution. Nothing backed up his speculation that Davis arranged for Horman's arrest. As shown already, the supposed presence of a CIA official and his approval of Horman's death sentence in Lutz's office has been categorically retracted years later by the lone source for that charge—González.

Nevertheless, Ed Horman had created an immensely compelling narrative, which would soon obtain a much larger audience in a successful book and a blockbuster Hollywood movie.

. . . . .

In late 1973, Thomas Hauser, a young lawyer soon to become a prolific author, called his friend Terry Simon after reading about the Horman case in the *New York Times*.[45] Born in New York City, Hauser graduated from Columbia University and Columbia University Law School and worked for several years in a law firm. With Simon's backing, Hauser met Ed Horman and got his cooperation. Hauser's book, *The Execution of Charles Horman: An American Sacrifice*, was published and widely reviewed in 1978. It was renamed *Missing* after being adapted for the film by Costa-Gavras in 1982.

The book was investigative in format, and the author made clear his theory of the case, writing on the first page:

> It has been alleged with increasing credibility that Charles Horman was executed with the foreknowledge of American Embassy officials because he stumbled upon evidence of the United States involvement in the Chilean coup.[46]

Ed Horman's scenario is presented at key junctures of the narrative and his verdict is quoted:

> I am now convinced that the United States government had foreknowledge of and possibly planned my son's execution.

And on the last page, Hauser acknowledges he framed the book to reflect the Hormans' views:

> If I appear to have emphasized the opinions of Ed and Elizabeth Horman, it is because they are people without a voice in high councils of power and are possessed of a view that I believe merits further investigation. I invite rebuttal by all interested parties.

In spite of such framing, Hauser's book is a critical investigative endeavor. The author gathers facts and acknowledges when the facts that do not fit his central hypothesis. He says he conducted 75 interviews, including key embassy and U.S. military officials. The list of relevant U.S. officials is impressive: Ambassador Davis, Captain Ray Davis, Patrick Ryan, Navy contractor Arthur Creter, Consul Fred Purdy, Judd Kessler, John Tipton, James Anderson, Herbert Thompson. All denied the thesis of U.S. involvement. Hauser does not cite any research or interviews conducted in Chile and seems to have relied on books and publications in English for background on Allende and the Popular Unity government. There are no footnotes, although sourcing is generally clear in the text.

Hauser lays out Ed Horman's theory, but does not claim his research was able to prove it. The stories about Creter, Davis and Ryan in Valparaiso are presented factually, as told both by Simon and the men themselves. He allows:

> Viewed in a vacuum, these facts hardly prove that United States military personnel were directly involved in the coup. Moreover, such participation, even if established, would not necessarily mean the American officials were responsible for the death of Charles Horman.

He repeats several times, moreover, that the circumstances require further investigation, and in interviews after publication he says he hoped and intended that his book would lead to thorough official inquiries inside the U.S. government.

The book was released around the time of the fifth anniversary of the 1973 September coup, and attracted a considerable amount of attention. In statements to the press, Hauser was less nuanced about his accusations. A UPI story reproduced in several newspapers put it this way:

> Hauser charges junta troops arrested and killed Horman—probably with the knowledge of U.S. officials and perhaps under their orders, because Horman had stumbled onto signs Washington was involved in the coup.[47]

If Hauser's book was objective for the most part, filmmaker Costa-Gavras produced a political thriller that delivered a powerful message with little ambiguity.[48] *Missing*, released in 1982, starred A-list actors

Jack Lemmon and Sissy Spacek, playing Ed and Joyce Horman, and was one of the most successful films of the year.

The film stated its claim to facticity in opening credits:

> This film is based on a true story. The incidents and facts are documented. Some of the names have been changed to protect the innocent and also to protect this film.

Over the two-hour film, there is no letup in the atmosphere of tension and terror—terror in the portrayal of military brutality in the days following the coup, and tension in Ed Horman's unfolding realization that U.S. officials, who he thinks at first are helping him find his son, are actually misleading him. Horman and his daughter-in-law, whose name was changed to Beth at Joyce Horman's request, are seen as hostile to one another—he, the conservative willing to trust the established U.S. authorities, and she, unremittingly suspicious of Ambassador Davis and "Captain Tower" (Ray Davis), who at one point seems to make sexual overtures to her and Terry Simon.

As the plot develops, it hews almost exactly to the real Ed Horman's hypothetical scenario. As Charles takes notes, the Arthur Creter character says a variation of his line, "The Navy sent us down here to do a job and . . . uh . . . she's done," delivered with sidelong glances and other clues that make it unmistakable he is referring to U.S. participation in the coup. "Beth" drives the point home by explaining to her bewildered father-in-law, "Ed, all those American officials were probably involved in the coup." Much of the focus is on the Captain Tower/Davis character, who appears in almost every scene involving U.S. diplomats and by the end is clearly the cinematic villain.

Rafael González appears as "Agent Perez," a "desperate man" who has received asylum in the Italian embassy already in October 1973. The scene in Lutz's office is presented in flashback. We see Horman tied up in an adjoining room while Perez, Lutz and the American officer discuss his fate. The officer could be Captain Tower, but his face is not clear. Lutz says Horman knows too much and must disappear. Switching back to the Italian Embassy, Perez/ González is asked if the Chileans would order an American disappeared without consulting U.S. officials first. "Oh, no, no, no, they wouldn't . . . they wouldn't dare," he says.

Beth and Ed Horman exchange bitter words. At one point he accuses her of "sloppy idealism" and thrusts at her a question about Charles's relationship with Terry. She responds, "Why did you come here. . . . Why don't you just go back to New York?" But they reconcile as the film moves to a denouement. There is a heartwrenching scene in which they are searching through hundreds of bodies at the morgue. Beth finds Frank Teruggi's body, but not Charles. "I sold you short," Horman tells her, as he begins to accept the inevitable. A man at the Ford Foundation is the first to tell him Charles was shot at the Stadium, but cannot reveal his source.

Meeting with the ambassador shortly after, Horman explodes in anger when introduced to a sketchy-looking journalist who says there is "good news" that his son is hiding in the north, waiting to be smuggled out of the country. Horman orders the journalist to get out, and confronts Ambassador Davis and Captain Tower/Davis in a controlled fury:

> I have reason to believe that my son was killed by the military . . . and I do not think that they would dare do a thing like that unless an American official co-signed a kill order. I think you knew he was dead from the start.

The charge is devastating in its weight, and made more compelling as it sums up the accumulating evidence of the movie so far. Horman's transformation is complete. The conservative who believed in the establishment now accuses the U.S. ambassador of murder.

The ambassador denies the charge, but lectures Horman on the realities of U.S. economic interests and the need to defend them. Tower/Davis, his face darkened, lashes out with a non-denial, sealing his character's sinister identity:

> Your son was a bit of a snoop. He poked his nose into a lot of places he didn't belong. If you keep on playing with fire, you get burned.

Meneses and Ortiz are not referenced in the movie, nor is their role in identifying Horman's body. "Consul Putnam" (Purdy) delivers the news by phone that Charles has been identified by a recheck of fingerprints. Ed and Beth Horman embrace in deep sadness and he announces they are going home. Horman refuses the condolences of Embassy officials and says he intends to sue them all. A narrator reads lines closing the film:

Ed Horman filed suit charging government officials, including Henry A. Kissinger, with complicity and negligence in the death of his son.... After years of litigation, the information necessary to prove or disprove complicity remains classified as secrets of State. The suit was dismissed.

Missing won an Academy Award for Best Screenplay Adaptation, and the prestigious Palme d'Or at the Cannes Film Festival. Because of the film the events surrounding the killing of Charles Horman and Frank Teruggi are known even today as the "*Missing* case," or "*Caso Missing*" in Chile. Indeed it is hard to imagine a grander public stage for the case than a Hollywood movie opening in more than 700 theaters and viewed by millions of people, first in the United States and subsequently in international distribution. In the United States it was the third-ranked movie in its opening week, and remained in theaters for almost a year.[49]

The film was banned in Chile. *Time* magazine, which was sold in Santiago kiosks, was confiscated the week it published a review of *Missing*.

· · · · ·

The lawsuit referred to at the end of the movie was *Joyce Horman et al., v. Henry Kissinger et al.*, civil case 77-1748, filed in Washington, DC, federal court on October 3, 1977.

The Horman family was represented by lawyers from the Center for Constitutional Rights, a highly respected progressive law firm based in New York.[50] The 35-page complaint alleged that U.S. officials, through actions and failure to act, were responsible for Charles Horman's death. Among the specific charges were that officials kept files and compiled a dossier on Horman's political activity in the United States and in Chile and made it available to the Chileans. On Henry Kissinger specifically, the complaint alleged "on information and belief," that defendant Kissinger had knowledge of the arrest, detention and execution of Charles Horman, and either instructed the defendants and other U.S. officials not to seek Horman's release and/or to adopt a passive attitude, which resulted in his death.

The events and scenarios involving Creter, Davis, General Lutz and the unknown CIA agent are described as leading to Horman's death because he "knew too much."

The complaint listed as defendants 11 U.S. officials and two still unidentified U.S. agents. In addition to Kissinger, the defendants were Ambassador Davis, Kessler, consular officers Purdy, Anderson, Shaffer and Marian Tipton, military officers Hon, Ryan and Ray Davis, and State Department official Jack B. Kubisch. (Creter was not named as a defendant.)

Because the suit was brought in civil court, the defendants were accused of criminal and noncriminal actions that had caused injury to the plaintiffs, who included Charles Horman (postmortem). The plaintiffs asked the court to award compensatory and punitive damages in the amount of $4,540,000.

The Horman family sought to prove their case by asking the court to force the U.S. government to reveal secret files about the events of September and October 1973, including participation in the military coup and intelligence contacts with the Chilean military before and after the coup. The strategy was stymied by the administration of President Jimmy Carter, which refused to release many of the most relevant documents. In July 1980, Secretary of State Edmund Muskie submitted an affidavit to the court, part of which was itself secret, asserting "a formal claim of privilege." In effect, the "privilege" was an assertion (finding) by the highest level of the U.S. government that the documents requested by the Hormans involved U.S. secrets whose disclosure would damage U.S. national security and foreign relations.

Secretary Muskie then assured the court that, in effect, there was nothing to see here. He stated:

> The responsible State department officials who investigated and considered this matter have found no evidence of involvement by any United States Government personnel in the disappearance and death of Charles Horman. Specifically, the State Department is not aware of any foreknowledge of or participation in Charles Horman's death by any United States Government personnel.[51]

Muskie's denial of documents covered all agencies, including the CIA. Earlier CIA director Stansfield Turner testified, issuing an even more general denial, saying that no evidence had been found to support the lawsuit's contention that CIA personnel had foreknowledge of Horman's abduction and death.[52]

The U.S. government decision precluded the full exploration of evidence of alleged crimes by officials of that same U.S. government. It thus presented an insurmountable obstacle to the Hormans' lawyers. They filed a motion admitting they faced an impossible task:

> Without full discovery plaintiffs are in a "Catch 22" situation.... From the beginning of this tragedy, a great deal of information has been and continues to be concealed from plaintiffs. They have been urged to believe as fact contentions which responsible members of the State Department who personally investigate this case have called virtually incredible.[53]

The Hormans' lawyers therefore asked the judge for a "voluntary dismissal without prejudice." The legal stratagem was hardly a normal way to end a civil suit, since it left open the possibility the suit could be resumed in the future. In the final decision three months later, U.S. district judge Thomas Flannery granted the motion and dismissed the case, declaring:

> Dismissal without prejudice has been allowed to give plaintiff an opportunity to secure new evidence after he has found, by discovery or otherwise, that he cannot prove his present claim.[54]

Having been unable to prove any of their charges, the Horman family embraced the possibility they could still prove their scenario of U.S. government responsibility in the future.

They would get another chance, but it would be in Chile.

17 A Trial in Chile

Years passed. Chile returned to elected government in 1990. Investigations of human rights crimes began in a halting way. The National Commission of Truth and Reconciliation compiled a report with careful documentation demonstrating that the civilian-military government was responsible for the deaths and disappearances of more than 3,000 persons, validating the claims of the families of the victims that had been ignored for so long. Charles Horman and Frank Teruggi were included in the first lists made public in 1991. The commission found they had been executed by agents of the military government.

The law creating the commission prevented it from naming or accusing the individual perpetrators, even when eyewitnesses and other evidence were available. That was to be the task of the Chilean court system, which was constrained by the presence of many holdover judges who had collaborated with the dictatorship. General Pinochet retained considerable power as Commander in Chief of the Army until resigning in 1998, and was not shy about letting civilian authorities know he would not tolerate trials of those who had carried out his orders.

That same year, however, Pinochet was arrested during a trip to London. Having finally stepped down as military commander he was a private citizen, albeit with the self-conferred title of "senator for life." A Spanish court pursuing violations of international human rights laws asked for his extradition for crimes associated with Operation Condor, the alliance of Southern Cone dictatorships founded in Chile. The arrest deflated the dictator's façade of power and impunity. Returned to Chile after more than a year of house arrest, he faced a newly empowered and vigorous court system. Pinochet and his top officers suddenly were vulnerable to multiple judicial investigations and charges.

In December 2000, the Horman family filed charges of murder and kidnapping in a Chilean court. The case was accepted by Judge Juan Guzmán, of the Court of Appeals, who was handling the most important human rights cases against Pinochet. Frank Teruggi's case was added later. The original defendants included General Pinochet; General Herman Brady, the ranking officer overseeing CAJSI operations of mass repression; and Major Pedro Espinóza, the SIM officer in charge of interrogations at the Stadium.[55]

Judge Guzmán launched the investigation by compiling newly released U.S. declassified documents. He showed particular interest in the film *Missing*, and arranged a viewing in the presence of Joyce Horman so she could answer his questions about what was factual, according to her experience and Hauser's book. Guzmán summoned filmmaker Costa-Gavras to testify in person and asked similar questions. The director freely acknowledged he had taken artistic license in some scenes. He couldn't indicate a source for Captain Davis's statement that Charles Horman may have staged his own disappearance to embarrass the junta, and he said Davis's inflammatory line in which he called Horman a "snoop" was "my invention." But he firmly defended the factual basis of the story, saying it was true to Hauser's book and his interviews with the Horman family.[56]

Guzmán investigated the case for almost two years, but was increasingly occupied with other major cases against Pinochet, including the sprawling Operation Condor investigation. The judge listed Chilean military personnel and U.S. officials he intended to summon to testify, including SIM officers "Raúl Manesas and Jaime Ortiz," but the handful of interviews actually conducted were with eyewitnesses to the detentions and with Horman's and Teruggi's American friends.

The narrative of the film and the scenario created by Edmund Horman appeared to provide a template as the investigation progressed. In October 2002, Guzmán turned the case over to a colleague, Santiago Appeals Court Judge Jorge Zepeda, who could dedicate more time to the investigation. Zepeda quickly energized the probe. The family's Chilean lawyers also pushed the judge to structure his investigation around the newly released U.S. documents and the accusation of U.S. involvement. The first piece of evidence the judge recorded was Rafael González's affidavit in the civil suit against Henry Kissinger and others in 1979, in which he reaffirmed the truth of his statements alleging U.S. involvement in Horman's execution. After a few months, Zepeda ordered the detectives to bring González in for formal questioning.

Subsequently, Zepeda assigned detectives to try to track down the military personnel who had detained and executed Horman and Teruggi. It was a logical step in an effort to bring charges against the Chilean actors who made the decisions and carried out the crimes. But the investigation quickly turned in a different direction. In late 2003, Judge Zepeda formally charged González as an accomplice, and announced it to the press. From that point forward, the judge's attention, and coverage of the case, shifted almost entirely to the U.S actors and efforts to prove their guilt.

In 2011 Judge Zepeda announced murder charges against retired U.S. Naval officer Ray Davis and began extradition proceedings to bring him to Chile to face trial.[57] The court charged that Davis had provided information about both Horman and Teruggi to Chilean intelligence agents, that he had foreknowledge about their executions and did not prevent them "although he was in a position to do so given his coordination with Chilean agents." The charges against Davis echoed almost exactly the scenario created by Edmund Horman many years before, but for the first time they alleged involvement by U.S. officials in Teruggi's death as well.

The extradition documents did not specify what evidence was available to prove the charges but indicated the court had relied heavily on declassified U.S. documents. The court stated that Horman was killed because he knew too much about U.S. collaboration with the Chilean military in the 1973 coup. Davis was alleged to be running a surveillance program against Horman, Teruggi and other American leftists and conveying the information to the Chilean military. The judge cited U.S. documents showing Teruggi was under investigation by the FBI, but then asserted, without proof, that the FBI information, including his address in Chile, was also provided to Chilean agents. The FBI investigation of Teruggi, the court asserted, was "part of" (*se inserta en*) the secret surveillance activities in Chile conducted by Davis, as head of the U.S. MilGroup.

Zepeda's charges were explosive. It was the first time an official of the U.S. government had been formally accused of murdering U.S. citizens in Chile. In effect, the judge claimed to have evidence that U.S. government officials had participated directly in criminal activity in Chile and coordinated with the Chilean military in the mass repression after the coup. The *New York Times* story was headlined:

CHILE INDICTS EX-U.S. OFFICER IN 1973 KILLINGS

Other than references to already public declassified documents, the court did not specify what new proof it had obtained to prove the charges, such as that Davis had passed information about Horman and Teruggi to those who killed them.

Janis Teruggi Page, Frank's sister, expressed satisfaction but indicated more concrete evidence should be expected. In a statement, she said: "I, along with Joyce Horman, am looking forward to understanding the evidence behind these indictments. The fact that Judge Zepeda has spent considerable time investigating and evaluating these cases gives me hope that finally the truth will be revealed about their murders, and justice will be achieved."[58]

The judge also indicted Pedro Espinóza on murder charges, based on testimony that he was one of the officers in charge of interrogations at the Stadium and made the decisions about which prisoners lived and died.[59] Judge Zepeda issued his final verdict in January 2015, and it was ratified by the Chilean Supreme Court in July 2016. Pedro Espinóza was convicted of aggravated homicide, which the court described as a crime against humanity, and sentenced to a prison term of 15 years. Espinóza, a notorious human rights criminal, was already in prison on other charges. He had been the principal deputy to Colonel Manuel Contreras in DINA, and was a key figure in overseeing the assassination of Orlando Letelier in Washington, DC, in 1976. Rafael González was also convicted of complicity. Because of mitigating actions such as providing evidence, his sentence of three years was reduced to parole, allowing him to serve the sentence in his home.

Extradition proceedings in Davis's charges dragged on in Chile's bureaucracy for several years but were never formally presented to the United States. In a remarkable irony, Davis did not need to be extradited; he had been living in Chile for years, in a nursing home, unbeknownst to the court. The U.S. Embassy eventually established that he had died in Santiago in 2013 and informed the court. Zepeda removed Davis from the case but retained all of the so-called "established facts" about his alleged action in the final verdict.

The court also awarded compensatory damages to the Horman and Teruggi families, in the amounts of pesos $130,000,000 (approximately U.S. $200,000) and pesos $100,000,000 (U.S. $154,000), according to the exchange rate at the time.

· · · · ·

When I read about the verdict, and its historic finding of U.S. responsibility, I again took up the investigation I had begun in 2000. Many times in the past, fingers had been pointed at the U.S. government in the case—media articles in the 1970s, the Hauser book, the family's civil suit against Henry Kissinger, the film *Missing*—but always based on circumstances and presumptions emerging from the unseemly intimacy of American officials with agents of the dictatorship. Rafael González's statements seemed to be the closest thing to actual evidence, but in the 40 years since he made them no additional evidence had come to light to corroborate his alleged meeting with General Lutz, the unnamed American "CIA agent" and Horman himself.

Judge Zepeda's categorical findings about a U.S. role in the killings, ratified by Chile's highest court in 2016, seemed to promise that newly developed evidence had been found to finally prove the case and, in effect, to confirm what Edmund Horman had been saying all along. The totality of the evidence, I was told, could be found in the multivolume written court record of the case. I formally asked for access to the trial record, the so-called *Expediente*. Almost two years passed, but finally Judge Zepeda gave me permission to view the records. In November 2017 I spent more than three weeks at Zepeda's offices in the Supreme Court, with a research assistant and scanning equipment. I went through all 17 volumes, reading the evidence and copying the most relevant documents.[60]

I had expected to find solid proof of U.S. government responsibility in the murder of the two Americans, but I was disappointed. To be sure, the judge's record provided substantial evidence establishing that Horman and Teruggi were in the custody of the Chilean military when they were killed. Yet I found no evidence that was in any way conclusive proving the direct or indirect involvement by U.S. actors in the murders. The hundreds of pages of U.S. declassified documents cited by the judge was material I was already familiar with, and I knew it was not dispositive. There had to be more. I poured over the interviews of Chilean military personnel conducted by detectives and the judge. No one testified that any U.S. officials had coordinated with them about the military coup or about Horman and Teruggi. No one said Captain Davis or any other official had passed intelligence information to the Chilean military. On the contrary: some Chilean officials interviewed denied any such coordination or information exchange had taken place. No one said they knew about U.S. surveillance of American leftists in Chile. Suspicions abounded, but evidence was absent.

I interviewed Fabiola Letelier, the lawyer representing the Horman and Teruggi families. I had known Letelier since the 1970s when I lived in Chile and we were good friends. I had written a book about the assassination of her brother, Orlando Letelier. I asked her repeatedly to give me examples of evidence showing Davis's connection to the murders.

Her answer referenced Rafael González's statements about the scene in Lutz's office:

Lutz decides that he [Horman] knew too much and that's why they had to kill him. But the information received by Lutz came from the U.S. because Lutz as head of the Chilean police obviously kept a close relationship with American intelligence sources, with the CIA and other US intelligence agencies. So he receives the information that he (Horman) is a subversive and decides that he must be eliminated and he orders that.

I said I wanted to understand what evidence showed that relationship and exchange of information, and what specifically was Captain Davis's role in the murders. Without indicating a single piece of specific evidence, she answered: "I think that the Chilean courts clearly establish that there was coordination between both Chile and the US police, so it wasn't a single person, but rather a whole system between whom there was an agreement."[61]

Examining the court record, I found no evidence either for general coordination or individual responsibility by U.S. officials in the deaths of the two Americans. By any standard, be it probable cause, preponderance of evidence or simply the journalistic rule of reasonable verification of facts and sources, I found the case against Captain Ray Davis did not stand up to scrutiny. And I was not alone in my skepticism.

In 2018, I discussed the case with another appeals court judge, Mario Carroza, who is the judge in the much more complex investigation of Operation Condor, the six-country alliance to carry out repression and assassinations across borders.[62] He was familiar with the Horman-Teruggi case, and—more to the point—he also had to deal with similar legal challenges in establishing guilt in human rights crimes.

In Chile's thousands of human rights cases, victims are usually dead and unable to speak. The military perpetrators, especially the leaders, hide their actions behind the veil of secret orders, chain of command and the anonymity of large unit operations. Military officers have the option of not giving testimony to the court, and if they lie, as was clearly the case in many of the interviews I read, there are no consequences. Perjury is almost never prosecuted in Chile. Judge Carroza explained that it is extremely difficult to link officers directly to crimes they ordered or participated in. The courts in Chile must rely on the doctrine of *presuncion fundada* (grounded presumption), an assumption deemed to be reasonable based on other established evidence.

In our interview Judge Carroza discussed the issue of presumption, specifically in reference to the evidence of guilt for Captain Ray Davis:

DINGES: From what I see, the presumption in this case is very weak.

JUDGE CARROZA: Very weak.

DINGES: Very weak. To the point that journalistically I could not use the [evidence] in an article saying that he participated [in the killings].

JUDGE CARROZA: It is so weak that he could not be convicted. It would have been easier to convict Henry Kissinger [laughs].[63]

For me, it was a shock and extremely disconcerting to find myself in a situation of questioning the work and conclusions of a human rights case and its judge, Jorge Zepeda. In numerous other cases I have examined in detail, I have found the evidence solid and the conclusions warranted, even when standards of judicial proof differed from those in use in United States courts.

Several examples from the court record illustrate the weakness and flaws of the court's purported evidence. Perhaps the most serious accusation is that Ray Davis and other officials knew from the first moment that the Chileans had detained Horman and did nothing to stop them from killing him. Here is how the court supported that charge: "That, before the death of Charles Edmund Horman Lazar, already on the 17th of September of 1973, the United States Embassy informed the Department of State about the disappearance of Charles Edmund Horman Lazar—according to declassified document 04565252528Z—*at the very moments when the victim was still alive, in custody and being interrogated in the upper floors of the Ministry of Defense*" (emphasis added).[64]

In other words, according to the judge's statement, the U.S. Embassy knew on the day of his arrest, September 17, that Horman was in military custody but had not yet been executed. Cited as proof is a cable identified as "declassified document 04565252528Z." From those numbers, I was able to locate the document in question. It is the *unclassified* cable Santiago 4565.

Here is the text:

04565 251518Z
251456Z Sep 73
Unclas Santiago 4565
Subj: Amcit Missing in Chile
Ref: State 109977

Embassy informed that Horman missing since 17 Sept. But no firm info on his detention. Military authorities continue deny he held at National Stadium, which official detention center for all persons to be held more than overnight. Consul saw list of detainees as of 19 Sept and Horman's name did not appear as such or under any of several possible variants. Embassy continues try locate him and all other missing Amcits with full resources at its disposal. Congressional interest. Davis

Unclassified

First it should be noted that the message is dated September 25, 1973, and it was never secret. Horman was detained September 17, eight days before the date of the cable. His wife did not know he was missing until the next day, September 18, and friends called the Consulate around midday. At that point, according to morgue records, he was already dead. There is clearly nothing in the cable indicating that U.S. officials knew anything about Horman on September 17, much less that the Embassy informed the State Department about his arrest on that day. To the contrary, the cable, written eight days later, states the Embassy knew he was missing but had "no firm info on his detention."[65]

The court, it must be concluded, misread or misinterpreted the cable and used it incorrectly in an attempt to demonstrate foreknowledge of Horman's death. It should be noted that the judge does not cite *any other evidence* besides the cable to support the idea of foreknowledge, with the exception, of course, of the statements of González, later retracted, about the presence of a CIA agent.

· · · · ·

A second example of flawed use of evidence concerns the charge that Captain Davis was running a surveillance program against American leftists. The court said the investigation had established that Horman and Teruggi were executed based on derogatory information about them provided by U.S. officials to Chilean security forces. The verdict states this unequivocally:

> The action against the life of Charles Edmund Horman Lazar occurred due to the secret North American investigation regarding U.S. persons targeted by the activity of collection of data about what they were doing politically in the U.S. and in Chile; activity described by the State agents as 'subversive' both inside and outside the United States. . . .
>
> These findings are consistent with the declassified document . . . dated May 8, 1973, 'The MHCHAOS Program' . . . which refers to the surveillance, telephone interceptions, monitoring and espionage directed against journalists in this period . . . one of which areas of operational interest was 'Santiago.'
>
> Regarding the action against Frank Teruggi this activity was carried out by the US Military Intelligence Group, directed by the accused officer [Ray Davis] Commander of the Military Mission of the United States in Chile, with regard to political extremism, inside and outside the United States.
>
> The files on Frank Teruggi were delivered by the North American agents to the Intelligence Service of the Armed Forces General Staff [EMDN], under the leadership of General Augusto Lutz Urzúa.[66]

Regarding Horman, the intelligence information given to Chile was said to be about his work at Chile Films and his investigation of the Viaux-Schneider case. Evidence cited for this includes González's 2003 testimony in which he mentioned both topics for the first time,[67] and testimony by Joyce Horman saying she and Charles had decided not to destroy his notes on it because everything in it was already public. The "intelligence" the U.S. agents allegedly conveyed to Chile about Teruggi included the FBI report about his leftist activities with CAGLA in Chicago, his connection to the group in Germany giving aid to defecting U.S. soldiers, and his work with *FIN* in Chile. The information allegedly conveyed by Davis to General Lutz was the basis for detention orders against both men and led to their deaths, according to the court.

But there is no evidence in the court record to support the judge's conclusion. There is no testimony or document showing that Captain Davis or any other U.S. officials were conducting surveillance of Horman and Teruggi in Chile. Nor is there a single interview or document showing that Davis communicated derogatory information of any kind about them to Chilean officials. The only communication of any kind cited by the judge is that between Davis and Navy Captain Raúl Monsalve.[68] Monsalve testified that at the time of the coup he was the Navy's liaison officer with Davis. He testified that he provided Davis with a *salvoconducto*, a military pass to travel to Santiago from Valparaiso after the coup, and that Davis told him he had given a ride to Charles Horman.[69] Monsalve did not say Davis gave him any information about Horman, nor that he or Davis communicated anything about Horman to Lutz.

Judge Zepeda also cited a CIA program called CHAOS, an illegal operation that conducted domestic and international surveillance in the 1960s and 1970s. He introduced a declassified document on the program as one of the final pieces of evidence before closing his investigation.[70] The program is well known in U.S. literature about CIA covert activity. CHAOS was created in 1967 by President Lyndon Johnson to try to confirm his suspicion that the American antiwar movement was being orchestrated by the Soviet Union and other enemies. Among its operations, Americans with "existing extremist credentials" were tracked when they traveled abroad and some were recruited as agents. Santiago, Chile, was listed as one of 20 "areas of operational interest." The CIA created files on 7,200 U.S. citizens—a clear violation of the CIA charter, which forbade spying on Americans. The illegal program never found any significant foreign links to American antiwar leaders. The Nixon-Ford administrations continued the program, and it was finally canceled by President Carter.[71]

Beyond citing the MHCHAOS document and its mention of Santiago, Judge Zepeda does not establish any connection between CHAOS and Horman, Teruggi or any other Americans in Chile. Nor does he back up his assertion that Captain Davis was in charge of the program in Chile, or that the program was operating at all in Chile in 1973.

Zepeda summoned Peter Kornbluh, of the National Security Archive in Washington, DC, to provide expert testimony about the CHAOS document. Kornbluh had assisted the Horman and Teruggi families in obtaining U.S. documents under the Freedom of Information Act (FOIA) and had testified previously in the case. He is also a member of the board of directors of the Horman Truth Project set up by Joyce Horman. Kornbluh says he told the judge he was skeptical about the relevance of CHAOS to the case. "[Judge Zepeda] insinuated that Ray Davis was doing the spying on the Americans as part of this program. I said I did not believe the MHCHAOS document provided any relevant details on the Horman or

Teruggi case. For one thing, the program was run by the CIA and the FBI, and Captain Davis was U.S. Navy. The document, of course, does not refer in any way to surveillance of reporters in Chile." [72]

In the final analysis, Zepeda's case rested fundamentally on the uncorroborated testimony of Rafael González, whose name appears more than 100 times in the verdict. The judge's narrative of the case repeats González's story of the meeting in General Lutz's office and says González saw "a gringo who he thought was an agent of the CIA." Nowhere does the judge acknowledge that González had specifically denied the truth of that statement. The judge does not reference the five-page affidavit, also in evidence, in which González described how the fabrication came about, and acknowledges he created the false account using a newspaper article by William Shawcross. Judge Zepeda ascribes credibility to some of González's statements without regard to whether they were made before or after his retraction. González's statements in 1976 are the only source of the allegation that Horman was killed because "he knew too much." González did not repeat that part of his story in his testimony to Judge Zepeda; in fact, he again repudiated it. González is also the only witness to say a U.S. official knew Horman was about to be killed and did nothing to stop it, a statement that was also retracted. In the end, the judge appears to pick and choose parts of González's narrative that support the assumptions the judge eventually pronounces as fact.

By any objective measure, the evidence to support the controversial charges regarding the U.S. role cannot be found in the official record of Judge Zepeda's investigation. Nor is there any "secret evidence" that is not part of the record. Judge Zepeda's chief judicial assistant, Manuel Muñoz, assured me that the *Expediente* record was complete, nothing was withheld, and that all the evidence considered by the judge was in the pages before me.[73] I submitted to Muñoz a long list of questions for Judge Zepeda concerning the evidentiary issues raised here. The judge declined an interview and did not respond to the questions.

・ ・ ・ ・ ・

Pascale Bonnefoy and Peter Kornbluh have written extensively about the Horman and Teruggi cases and are among the small group of investigators familiar with the evidence. Kornbluh said he studied the 300-page *Sentencia* and briefed Joyce Horman about it. He told her it was flawed: "The judge's ruling in the Horman/Teruggi case is filled with speculative assertions and major evidentiary gaps—most notably the lack of any evidence of a connection or communication between U.S. officials in Chile and the Chilean military officers who determined and implemented the murders of Charles Horman and Frank Teruggi. Judge Zepeda has failed to solve the basic mystery of their deaths—why they were executed."[74]

Bonnefoy, whose chapter on the case in her book *Terrorismo de Estadio* has been frequently cited here, said she has seen no evidence to support the judge's key findings about the U.S. role in the murders. With regard to Ray Davis, she said, "Judge Zepeda is making many assumptions based on the role of Davis as part of the U.S. MilGroup and liaison to Chilean intelligence."[75]

In other aspects, however, the voluminous court investigation was valuable in my effort to reinvestigate the Horman and Teruggi murders. The court uncovered unique records from 1973 documenting the work of PICH Inspector Mario Rojas, who discovered government interference to prevent identification of Horman's body. The court also brought together eyewitness statements and documentary records that comprise the most complete historical record of the controversial cases.

Despite more than a decade of investigation, however, the court left a major gap. It failed to follow up on two key witnesses, former SIM officers Raúl Meneses and Jaime Ortiz. Their names, with a slight error in the spelling of Meneses, appear several times in various testimonies, including the diary of Ed Horman. Both Judge Guzmán and Judge Zepeda instructed detectives to find them and obtain their testimony. Inexplicably, although both men were alive and well and living in Santiago, the detectives were not able to find them. In a report to Judge Zepeda in 2005, detectives Jaime Carbone and Alberto Torres wrote: "Regarding the identity of Raúl Manesas and Jaime Ortiz, the court has been informed that it has not been possible to identify them, because further information regarding their identity is missing. It cannot be ruled out that these are false 'code names' used by 'agents' of the security agencies of the time."[76]

The judge did not insist. As pointed out above, Pascale Bonnefoy easily located both agents in 2016 and interviewed them. They are the only witnesses known to have identified and contacted the military personnel who carried out Horman's detention. One of the officers they talked to in 1973, Colonel Fernando Grant Pimentel, admitted he dispatched the military squad to detain Horman in his house in Vicuña Mackenna and named other soldiers involved. But when Grant testified to Judge Zepeda in 2005, he claimed to know nothing about the operation. Had Meneses and Ortiz testified, their statements could have been the basis for criminal charges against Grant, a high-ranking intelligence officer. Meneses and Ortiz also identified two other officers, Lieutenant Enzo Cadenasso and Lieutenant Colonel Roberto Soto Mackenney, as directly involved in the operation to detain Horman. But they also evaded charges. It was a lost opportunity to accomplish a measure of justice in the case.

PART IV Conclusions

In retrospect, the United States government should have applied maximum pressure to the Chilean Junta to find and punish the murderers. . . . That we did not do so was a major miscalculation. The Junta needed us more than we needed them. . . . Why was such pressure not brought to bear or perhaps not even considered? The answer is that the United States Government was anxious to see the post-Allende regime prosper.

STATE DEPARTMENT OFFICER JEFFREY DAVIDOW, writing in 1982

The record, including material released under FOI[A], indicates clearly a presumption that Horman (and Teruggi) were killed in Chilean custody. But we have held to a public line that we do not know what happened to Horman.

STATE DEPARTMENT OFFICER FRANK MCNEIL, 1987

18 The U.S. Role

The theory that the United States government had a role in the deaths of Horman and Teruggi rises and falls on the 1976 interview of Rafael González. His allegation that a purported CIA agent heard and approved the order to kill Horman has shaped the narrative until today. González retracted the statements, but that was decades later and received little notice. Inside the State Department in 1976, however, it is not an overstatement to say the González interview caused a veritable earthquake. Despite official denials by the CIA and State Department, some officials in the Latin America division considered the accusations to be entirely plausible. They knew well the Embassy's close embrace of the new military regime. To those officials, who were already disturbed by the junta's rampant human rights violations, the idea that the CIA or the U.S. military might have stumbled into a role in the murders of two Americans was not beyond imagining. Their actions led to an internal investigation that attempted to determine the true extent of the U.S. government role. The ensuing inquiry was replete with embarrassing details and conjecture about U.S. actions but the investigation found nothing to support González's incriminating statements. Nevertheless, the investigation was conducted in secret, and its results were hidden from the family and the public for more than two decades.

Two of the diplomats involved, Robert Steven and Rudy Fimbres, have appeared in our story before. A third, Robert Driscoll, the Chile desk officer, teamed up with Fimbres to compile the most potentially compromising facts and underline the devastating impact they could have for the U.S. government. They wrote a detailed memo to their boss, Harry Shlaudeman, chief of the Latin America division.

> Subject: Charles Horman case
> This case remains bothersome. The connotations for the Executive are not good. In the Hill, academic community, the press, and the Horman family the intimations are of negligence on our part, or worse, complicity in Horman's death. (While the focus is on Horman, the same applies to the case of Frank Teruggi.)
> We have the responsibility:
> —categorically to refute such innuendos in defense of U.S. officials;
> —to proceed against involved U.S. officials if this is warranted.
> Without further thorough investigation we are in a position to do neither. At the moment we do not have a coherent account of what happened (see attached "Gleanings.") That is why we believe we should continue to probe.
> Based on what we have, we are persuaded that:
> —The GOC [government of Chile] sought Horman and felt threatened enough to order his immediate execution. The GOC might have believed this American could be killed without negative fall-out from the USG [U.S. government].
> There is some circumstantial evidence to suggest:
> —*U.S. intelligence may have played an unfortunate part in Horman's death. At best, it was limited to providing or confirming information that helped motivate his murder by the GOC. At worst, U.S. intelligence was aware the GOC saw Horman in a rather serious light and U.S. officials did nothing to discourage the logical outcome of GOC paranoia.*[1] (Emphasis added)

The memo seemed to endorse the suspicions about a U.S. role Ed Horman had expressed, now enhanced by the recent statements of González. In a paragraph headed "CIA," the authors write that "[the agency's] lack of candor with us on other matters only heightens our suspicions," further stating: "We find it hard to believe that the Chileans did not check with [one or two words omitted] regarding two detained Americans when the GOC was checking with Horman's friends and neighbors regarding Horman's activities."

From context, it is clear the deleted words referred to the CIA or a CIA official. Their argument was that since the Chilean intelligence agents were known to have called Horman's friends to ask about him, it made sense that they would have called the CIA as well.

The memo ticks off various charges Chilean officials had leveled against Horman and Teruggi in communications with the U.S. government: that Horman and Teruggi were described as "radicals" and "subversives"; that Horman was linked to Chile Films and "Coco" Paredes; that Horman "knew too much." The longest section of the memo is devoted to what it calls "The González Connection," which recapitulates his role in locating Horman's body for shipping back to the United States in 1974, and his statements to the journalists in 1976. That the Chilean military killed the two men is never questioned, contradicting U.S. government statements at the time asserting that "no one knows" who detained them.

· · · · ·

The Fimbres-Driscoll memo and related documents remained secret and the Horman-Teruggi case lay dormant until the story was jarred back onto the front pages in 1999 when the Clinton administration released thousands of documents on Chile in a massive declassification ordered by President Bill Clinton following the detention of retired dictator General Pinochet during a visit to London. Hundreds of documents on the Horman-Teruggi case were part of the release, including the Fimbres-Driscoll memo and an accompanying investigative report, in addition to five FBI reports showing that Frank Teruggi had been under investigation in 1972 for his antiwar activism and connections to the group in Germany helping U.S. GIs to desert.

The documents were immediately interpreted as confirming a U.S. role in the murders. One of the first stories stated it as fact in the headline:[2]

CIA COMPLICITY IS PROVEN IN "MISSING" JOURNALIST'S MURDER

A later *New York Times* front-page story reproduced two versions of the memo, the one given to the family in 1980 with relevant sections blacked out and the fully declassified version including the paragraphs quoted above. The reporter, Diana Jean Shemo, used more careful phrasing: "Some of the documents make clear for the first time that the State Department concluded from almost the beginning that the Pinochet government had killed the men.... The investigators speculated, moreover, that the Chileans would not have done so without a green light from American intelligence."[3] The *Times* article quoted Rafael González's statement that Horman was executed because he "knew too much," and that the decision to kill him was made in the presence of a man he presumed to be an American.

The CIA and State Department issued statements repeating previous categorical denials of any role in the deaths. But tellingly, the State Department refused to answer questions or explain anything about the background of the 1976 documents, saying most of the officials involved had retired. My experience was similar. On two occasions, in 2016 and 2021, I contacted officials in the Latin America section of the State Department, informed them of my preliminary findings and requested a meeting to discuss the case. Despite follow-up calls, there was no response.

There is an important backstory to the memo. I have interviewed the two State Department signatories, Rudy Fimbres and Robert Driscoll. I also spent many hours in multiple interviews going over the case with Robert Steven, an Embassy political officer at the time of the coup. From my work as a reporter at the time, I knew that all three officers were dissenters regarding Chile. They were acutely aware of rampant human rights violations in Chile and braved the ire of their boss Henry Kissinger by insisting on filing reports documenting abuses. They were considered "human rightsy" inside the State Department, Fimbres said, but they persisted. As mid-level specialists in the Latin America section, they were not in a policy-making role, but they had some support among higher-ranking officers who dealt directly with Kissinger. Fimbres mentioned in particular Shlaudeman's deputy William Luers.

They were responsible for handling the fallout from González's spectacular statements and began to put together the facts of the case to try to make sense of what had happened. Fimbres came to be personally convinced the CIA was hiding something, but he lacked definitive proof. The memo on Horman and Teruggi was written as an exercise in dissent.[4] The strong language used in the memo was designed to make it difficult for Shlaudeman and Kissinger to ignore their recommendations.

"I was trying to smoke something out. We were trying to make the case for an investigation," Fimbres said. He said he had no additional evidence, other than González's statements and other facts laid out in his memo, almost all of which are now publicly available and included in this book.

A key question was the source of the Chilean military's information about Horman and Teruggi. Robert Steven had fielded calls in 1973 from Chilean officials and wondered how they got their information. He concluded that most of what the Chileans knew came from their own sources:

> This is one of the key points in the whole Horman-Teruggi episode. What they [Chilean officials] knew—and the implication is what they may have been told by the United States government or something. I believe that the Chilean intelligence were well aware of people like Horman and Teruggi, who were young Americans who came down there, whose sympathies were clearly with the Allende government—that they probably were known to have been in touch with people in the Cordones; that they probably were seen, you know, at meetings, taking notes, et cetera, et cetera. I never thought it necessarily meant that they actually had documentation that had been provided from somebody else. This was their own observations of these people....
> If the Chileans killed them because of information that they had developed about their activities in Chile, that's very different from killing them because of information provided by the U.S. government.[5]

Steven said he is also confident that there are no still-secret caches of documents. He was assigned to review State Department documents on the case to decide what to release under the Freedom of Information Act (FOIA) in 1999. "I've seen as much, I guess, as anybody has been allowed to see. Later I worked on declassifying papers and saw everything in the files."

The pressure campaign by the dissident officials was unorthodox and perhaps risky in Kissinger's State Department, but it got the intended result. Latin America chief Harry Shlaudeman approved the memo's recommendation to conduct an internal investigation. On Shlaudeman's orders, State Department lawyer Frederick Smith, Jr., carried out a "thorough examination of the Department's files . . . in view of the unresolved questions surrounding Horman's death and, particularly, the recent statements of Rafael Augustin González . . . implying that the USG (i.e. CIA) played a role in Horman's death (at the hands of the GOC)." The investigation encompassed Teruggi's case as well, about whose death "there exists an almost equal number of unresolved questions." The 26-page report, "Death in Chile of Charles Horman,"[6] was completed in December 1976. Smith gathered press reports, statements from friends and family of the two victims and materials from other sources, including the FBI and CIA. It is the most complete compilation of facts done at the time and for many years thereafter. Smith's report has been a fundamental document in the investigation in this book and has been frequently cited.

In the report, Smith eschews the more passionate language and speculation of the Fimbres memo. The report coolly dismantles the Chilean government's repeated and changing denials of responsibility and attempts to blame leftists for the deaths. The evidence shows the two Americans were "deliberately killed" by the military, and the Chilean disclaimers are of "dubious validity" and "difficult to credit." The accusations by González about the CIA were more difficult to dislodge, Smith wrote. It was a critical issue: "Apart from González's statements and accusations there is no evidence in the files that any element of the USG played a responsible role, directly or indirectly, in the death of Charles Horman."

Smith recommended that González, then still in the Italian Embassy, be interviewed to answer specific questions about the presumed American intelligence agent present at Horman's interrogation and about "any information furnished to Chilean intelligence (pre- or post-coup) by U.S. sources regarding Horman or Teruggi or other American citizens."

Smith's main recommendation involved the CIA: "That high-level inquiries be made of intelligence agencies, particularly the CIA, to try to ascertain to what extent, if any, actions may have been taken or information may have been furnished, formally or informally, to representatives of the forces that now constitute the GOC, either before or after the coup, that may have led the Junta to believe it could, without serious repercussions, kill Charles Horman and Frank Teruggi."[7]

Shlaudeman, Smith's boss, approved Smith's recommendation to interview González. But as far as is known, no "high-level inquiry" of the role of the CIA was ever conducted. In a memo to a top Kissinger deputy,

Philip Habib, Shlaudeman said González should be questioned about his allegation "that Horman was fingered by the CIA," but stated his own view that "the CIA was not involved in the Horman tragedy." The CIA and other U.S. government agencies issued a series of categorical denials at the time and in subsequent years.[8] On the specific issue of conveying derogatory information to Chilean authorities, Smith's report cited official CIA communications stating that "the agency did not at any time supply information concerning Horman (or Teruggi) to the Junta or to any of the Chilean security forces."

In addition, the CIA was required on several occasions to search its files and respond to specific questions about Horman and Teruggi. The denials of involvement were again categorical, and—significantly—they were issued both during the pro-Pinochet Nixon-Ford administration, when Henry Kissinger was overseeing all policy regarding Chile, and in the Carter administration, which distanced itself from Chile's military government because of human rights abuses.

Despite the provocative language in the Fimbres memo, neither the memo nor Smith's report uncovered any new evidence pointing to U.S. foreknowledge of the murders or of any other level of involvement. González's statements remained the sole evidence of any direct role by the U.S. government in the deaths. In a fresh interrogation by a U.S. official a few weeks later, in February 1977, González denied he had spoken about the presence of a CIA agent and about Horman being in Valparaiso—statements that were clearly part of the tape-recorded 1976 interview. Otherwise he repeated his basic story that he saw Horman in Lutz's office.[9]

As far as is known, the Smith investigation was by far the most serious effort to find the truth. It was also the final effort. Smith made clear that he considered his review of the files and material in the public record to be the beginning, not the end, of a thorough investigation. After the re-interview of Rafael González in early 1977, however, no further action was taken. And although the State Department would in later years refer to its "intensive" efforts to investigate the cases, it blocked the families from seeing the report and its evidence for more than two decades.

The Smith report was an honest effort. Had it been released at the time to the families or perhaps even confidentially to interested House members and senators, it likely would have provoked new pressure to continue the investigation. Its conclusion that the preponderance of evidence pointed to the Chilean military would have made it impossible for the Embassy to continue to plead agnosticism on the question.

Chile continued to stonewall. Several weeks after the González accusations were publicized, the Foreign Ministry sent a diplomatic note to the Embassy: "National authorities had exhausted [in 1973] all possible means of investigating and clarifying the circumstances that led to the death of [Horman]. No new facts about the situation have become available since then."[10] The Embassy, headed in 1976 by Ambassador David Popper, took the Chilean position at face value and ceased to press the matter. It was the pattern of passive acquiescence the Embassy had followed since the coup.

· · · · ·

Jeffrey Davidow, a junior officer in the political section, was bothered by what he saw and would recall the Embassy's passivity a few years later when he heard about the Costa-Gavras film *Missing* in 1982. He thought about saying something publicly at the time, but was talked out of it by another officer. He went on to a distinguished career in the foreign service, earning the rank of Career Ambassador, having served as ambassador in Venezuela, Mexico and Zambia. He was Assistant Secretary for Western Hemisphere Affairs, the top policy position for the Latin American region. After I interviewed him for this book, he mailed me a copy of what he wrote in 1982, which he described as a draft essay intended as an op-ed. Writing from his new post in Zimbabwe, he called the piece "Missing from 'Missing.'"[11]

In the essay, he disputed the movie's premise that the U.S. government overthrew Salvador Allende, writing: "There appears to have been no concentrated American attempt to overthrow Allende via a military coup, though the hostility of the U.S. government and multinational corporations undoubtedly added to Chile's economic malaise."

Nor does he believe, he writes, that U.S. officials "are capable of ordering the murder of an American citizen overseas and engaging in a successful massive coverup."

Those allegations, while presented with great emotional impact in the film, do not come to grips with what Davidow considers "the essential questions" raised by the Horman case:

> The real question to be looked at is: What is the appropriate role of the United States Government when it is logical to assume that a friendly government has murdered or abused an American citizen? Put another way, How far should the American Embassy go in placing pressure on a foreign state to find the assumed perpetrators and bring them to trial for appropriate punishment?
>
> [In the Horman case] the record shows that the U.S. embassy in Santiago repeatedly requested information from, and passed possible investigative leads to, the Chilean authorities in an effort to stimulate the desired Chilean investigation....
>
> But the Chileans stone-walled, contending that Horman (and Teruggi) might have been killed by leftists masquerading as government soldiers after their release from the improvised prison at the National Stadium. The Embassy's diplomatic notes were politely, if not quickly, answered, and, in effect, the matter was left to hang there.
>
> In retrospect, the United States government should have applied maximum pressure to the Chilean Junta to find and punish the murderers or suffer the consequences of a serious deterioration in its relations with the U.S.
>
> That we did not do so was a major miscalculation. The Junta needed us more than we needed them.... Pressure, the use of leverage, and veiled and unveiled threats might have had more success than the exchange of diplomatic notes, which, while sent in deadly earnest by Ambassador Davis and his staff, were undoubtedly treated as props in an elaborate charade by the Junta.
>
> Why was such pressure not brought to bear or perhaps not even considered? The answer is that the United States Government was anxious to see the post-Allende regime prosper. It sought to not embarrass the Junta or lend credence to its poor public image.... It would not serve the interest of the USG to further tarnish the Junta's reputation, which was already more blotch than escutcheon.

In diplomacy, he wrote, there are always reasons not to confront a friendly government. Pressure might be counterproductive; publicity on a controversial matter might torpedo congressional support for important legislation, such as the foreign aid bill. What is to be gained? He answered his own question: "The answer is that there most certainly is value for the family and for society in general to punish wrongdoers, and greater efforts should have been made on our part to do so."

One tragedy led to another. Having killed two U.S. citizens without consequences, Chile's dictatorship in 1976 sent assassins to Washington, DC, where they used a car bomb to kill a prominent exile leader, Orlando Letelier, and an American woman, Ronni Moffitt, who was riding with him on Massachusetts Avenue. Davidow linked the two crimes: "The same cast of characters which got away with the murders of Horman and Teruggi, Letelier and Moffitt are still running the Chilean show. When the 'tinto' [red wine] is of a particularly good vintage and abundantly served they must laugh up their sleeves at our lack of resolve."

Davidow's essay, read many years later, has the bracing impact of truth-telling long overdue. An honest investigation by the U.S. government, truly aimed at bringing the wrongdoers to justice, was all the families and friends ever asked. The unexplored leads for such an investigation were abundant.

19 Leads Not Followed

The now declassified record of U.S. actions amply demonstrates that no sustained investigation and even less pressure was brought to bear in the Horman-Teruggi case. Potentially fruitful leads were left unexplored.

In September 1973, the U.S. Embassy, fresh from the triumph of their Chilean allies over the leftist Allende government, was confronted with the deaths of two American citizens who happened to be leftists. Hundreds of leftists were being rounded up and many were executed, and the Embassy knew that. Officials made inquiries, as was their duty. Eyewitness evidence strongly indicated both men were in military custody when they died. There was no evidence contradicting those witnesses, but Chilean officials denied they had been held. Rather than proceeding from the most likely premise of military responsibility, the Embassy treated the military's denials as the most credible starting point.

Two men involved in the earliest stages of the Embassy inquiries acknowledged the strictures they were instructed to work from. Judd Kessler was the first official to hear a report that Horman had been killed by the military. As shown in earlier chapters, his information was ignored and withheld from the family. In a 1977 interview, he offered a kind of explanation. "The posture of the Embassy at that time was," he said, "we'd gone to the government and asked for an explanation of where Horman was. So having the information wasn't a great deal of help in a way."[12] In other words, an unconfirmed report contradicting the government explanation was not useful. Instead of trying to confirm it, it was to be kept quiet. And that is what happened.

Consul Fred Purdy was kept busy for weeks dealing with the two missing Americans and their concerned families. He saw himself as doing his duty. But he also acknowledged the limits. His statement quoted earlier bears repeating: "We were told, fairly early on in the Horman part of it all, that we were not to ask personal questions or look behind the letter of what was told us."

Even as the Chilean junta's explanations changed, evaded and contradicted themselves, the U.S. official stance was to adhere to them. The Embassy posture during the Nixon and Ford administrations, sympathetic to the junta, was that it could not be known who killed Horman and Teruggi because the junta, the most obvious suspect, said their people did not do it.

The refusal to accuse Chile of the murders did not significantly change during the Democratic administration of Jimmy Carter. To be sure, some officials argued for a more candid expression of the known facts. Among them was Francis McNeil, of the State Department's Latin America bureau. He laid out the logic of his recommendation in a memo: "The record, including material released under FOI, indicates clearly a presumption that Horman (and Teruggi) were killed in Chilean custody. But we have held to a public line that we do not know what happened to Horman."[13]

The argument in favor of holding to that public line was that technically "we do not 'know' what happened," he said, and that the Chilean government would be unhappy "if we were to go public with our belief that Chilean security elements probably killed both Americans." He nevertheless recommended saying "something more pointed," at least to acknowledge publicly and to the families that the two victims were picked up by Chilean security forces and "there is evidence to suggest that they died while in custody."

But higher officials overruled even that limited statement pointing to the junta's responsibility. In a letter shortly thereafter to Ed Horman, replying to his request for the release of 100 documents still being withheld, State Department spokesman Hodding Carter held to the noncommittal posture:

> The Department deeply regrets the tragic death of your son, and has made a major effort to find out how and why he died. Many explanations have been offered, but despite that effort the facts have not been conclusively established. . . .
> The Chilean government has never given a satisfactory explanation for his death, and it is possible that we may never know why and how Charles was killed.[14]

As late as 1987, during the Reagan administration, that continued to be the official position. Senator Robert T. Stafford, Republican from Vermont, asked the State Department on behalf of a constituent about U.S. involvement in the coup and the disappearance of Charles Horman. The reply enunciated the still official position:

> Regarding Mr. Horman, records indicate that from the moment he disappeared the Department of State undertook intensive efforts to locate him and to learn the circumstances of his disappearance and death. Those efforts continued for eight years and included an internal investigation of the possibility that U.S. government officials might have condoned or failed to act effectively in Horman's disappearance and death. *No light was shed upon the circumstances of his death and little upon the circumstances of his disappearance*, and nothing was found to support the charge of complicity or negligence on the part of U.S. officials.[15] (Emphasis added)

In the light of what was known at the time, especially the findings in the Smith report, it was an astounding misrepresentation to say "no light" had been shed on the facts of what happened. That is a false statement, as is abundantly clear from reading this book. The "internal investigation" was undoubtedly a reference to Smith's work, which concluded the Chileans killed Horman and Teruggi. Yet the U.S. government, 14 years into the Pinochet dictatorship, was unwilling to state that conclusion in public. This was despite the fact that at the time other U.S. officials privy to the secret documents in State Department files knew the evidence of Chilean guilt and discussed it internally. Their superiors during four administrations refused to allow them to bring their reasonable conclusions about Chilean responsibility to public light.

The claim that U.S. officials undertook "intensive efforts" lasting eight years is a joke. More objectively one could say the claim clashes violently with known facts and the documentary record of inaction after 1976. With the exception of the Smith report, the Embassy investigation consisted almost exclusively of asking questions of Chilean officials and seeking their help. That might have been a reasonable approach in some countries, but it made little sense when the government being asked for help was in the midst of a campaign of mass killing and likely to be the guilty party. Edmund Horman has been proven right in his criticism of the sham "investigation" by U.S. Embassy officials. And his charge that there was a "coverup" by Embassy officials is at least partly correct: "Although their files show that they obtained a great deal of solid information, they [Embassy officials] made no cogent efforts to bring the Junta to book. Steps they might have taken if they had really wanted to resolve the matter can readily be [conceptualized]. It is obvious that efforts were being made to conceal the truth. The cover up continued."[16]

One can quibble with the word "cover-up." Horman's scenario, as shown earlier, includes the accusation that the U.S. officials were guilty of his son's murder and were covering it up. The evidence does not support that conclusion, but unquestionably it is fair to say that U.S. officials were "covering up" the evidence of their Chilean allies' guilt. The U.S. government did not abandon that stance until after the military government turned over power to elected civilians in 1990.

Following Ed Horman's lead, I would like to enumerate the investigative steps that could have been taken and leads that could have been followed, but were not. The common thread is that leads that pointed to the identification of the perpetrators of the crime were not followed up.

MICHAEL TOWNLEY KNEW THE IDENTITY OF TERUGGI'S KILLERS

This item is completely new. I encountered the story in a secret document declassified as part of the Horman-Teruggi collection. It has apparently gone unnoticed until this writing. Michael Townley, a young American expatriate living in Chile, was one of the assassins sent to

Washington in 1976 to murder Orlando Letelier. During the Allende government he participated in violent and nonviolent actions in concert with the extreme right-wing group Patria y Libertad. One of those actions, an attack in March 1973 on an electric power station in Concepcion, resulted in the death of a man who happened to be on the scene. Townley fled to Argentina and then to Miami. After the coup, he returned to Chile using a false passport, eager to get a job in the junta's new security apparatus.

Townley had been a frequent visitor to the Embassy and was friends with several political officers. Arriving in mid-October, he called Jeff Davidow, who was one of his Embassy contacts, and offered to provide information about the military government.[17] He told Davidow in a second call that he had information about one of the murdered Americans. He said he had landed a job in Army Intelligence (SIM), which was hiring Patria y Libertad militants as civilian operatives. At the intelligence agency "he had spoken to a Chilean who worked with SIM since 1971 and who claimed to have witnessed the slaying of Frank Teruggi." Townley was trying to establish a relationship with the Embassy as a friendly source inside the military, Davidow said. The tip on Teruggi was an example of the kind of information Townley could provide that presumably would be of interest to U.S. officials. He had arrived in Chile on October 18, the very day Horman was finally identified, and the case was much discussed both in the press and in Embassy circles. As we have seen, SIM was not only aware but deeply involved in the Horman and Teruggi operations. An experienced SIM operative told Townley what he knew about the killing of a fellow American. Davidow recorded Townley's information in a memorandum to the files dated December 12, 1973 (a document that is still secret). When Townley was identified in 1978 as the alleged assassin of Letelier, the Embassy reviewed its files about Townley and the Davidow information surfaced. In an interview, Davidow said his memo circulated inside the political section and he assumed it reached the ambassador, but no one ever asked about it. Nothing was done to follow up on the information. Townley served five years in prison and is living in the United States under a new identity provided by the Witness Protection program of the Justice Department. In an indirect email exchange, Townley said he doesn't remember "ever saying anything about Teruggi."[18]

If there indeed had been an active ongoing investigation to identify the murderers, as Embassy officials claimed, information identifying an eyewitness to Teruggi's death would have been a major lead. But Townley's tip appears to have been ignored, and the information is not referenced in any other files of the cases. The cable on Townley was part of the ongoing Letelier assassination investigation and was addressed to the Legal Attaché in Buenos Aires—Robert Scherrer—who was a lead investigator in the Letelier case. But the killings of two Americans in Chile were not part of his assignment and he did not act on the information.[19]

FAILURE TO FOLLOW UP WITH RAÚL MENESES AND JAIME ORTIZ

The most consequential missed opportunity to find the truth of Horman's disappearance was the failure to remain in contact with the two SIM investigators who evaded official obstacles and succeeded in identifying Horman's body. Meneses and Ortiz personally told Ed Horman that his son had been executed in the Stadium. Although they worked for the institution that was among the prime suspects in the murders, Meneses and Ortiz won the confidence and praise of Ed Horman, and in his diary they appeared several times in a helpful role. They also were referenced in official Foreign Ministry notes and in the Lutz report. A November 1973 Embassy draft letter includes the names among possible leads for follow-up.[20] Yet U.S. officials made no effort in late 1973 to debrief them or to ask Chilean authorities for their reports.

There was a second opportunity to get their full story, but that too was botched. The story of that incident is told here for the first time.

Meneses surfaced again in March 1987. He called the Embassy in Santiago and arranged a meeting with political officer David Dreher, who documented the meetings in a series of memos and cables. Meneses introduced himself as "a former military intelligence officer involved in the Charles Horman investigation," according to Dreher: "He says he knows who ordered the killing of Horman and that some of those people are currently top officials. . . . He was extremely critical of our role in 1973, saying we did next to nothing to aid Mr. Horman (the father). He was especially critical of some consular officers."[21]

The context of the meeting was, again, the Orlando Letelier assassination case. A member of the assassination team, Chilean officer Armando Fernández Larios, had turned himself in to U.S. officials in Santiago and had been given asylum in exchange for his testimony. Meneses compared himself to the highly publicized case, and said he also deserved help because of his information on the death of a U.S. citizen.

Dreher said that Meneses looked desperate and down on his luck. He was taller than average, with a military bearing, but "harried looking." He brought his wife, who was younger and had a new baby, to one of the meetings. Dreher said he thought Meneses was telling a credible story, but other officials were suspicious because he clearly wanted to leverage his story about Horman to gain entrance to the United States.[22]

Meneses said he was one of two SIM officials assigned to investigate the Horman case. He provided many more details than he had told to Ed Horman in 1973. The first name he mentioned got Dreher's attention. He said Horman was seized by intelligence units acting on information from Meneses's unit chief at the time, Hugo Salas Wenzel. In 1987 Colonel Salas Wenzel was director of CNI, the brutal intelligence and security service, and considered the mastermind of an operation that had killed more than a dozen militants.[23]

According to Meneses, Horman was taken to the National Stadium, and there, "he was considered a foreigner/extremist and the order was given to execute him." The kill order came from another notorious officer well known to the Embassy: Pedro Espinóza, by then a colonel, was under indictment for the Letelier murder. Meneses said Espinóza was "the person at the Stadium who made the decision on who was to die." Meneses said the Horman killing may have been a mistake. "Horman was a leftist but not a radical extremist and therefore his death was an injustice," he said.

Meneses said he had filed a report to SIM on his investigation, but it had been destroyed, and the government issued a statement claiming Horman had been killed by the left, which he called "a whitewash." Pressed by Dreher about a possible U.S. role, Meneses said, "To his knowledge, no U.S. official played any role in the death of Charles Horman since he was dead before anyone in the Embassy would have known of his detention." Nevertheless, several paragraphs referring to Meneses's criticisms of US officials are redacted from the documents.

Dreher met three times with Meneses, who seemed increasingly desperate to get out of Chile. In a cable on June 16, the Embassy evaluated Meneses's statements and his credibility. It concluded that his story generally corresponded to the "limited information in U.S. files" and added new information to explain the fact that some of the clothes found with Horman's body were different from those his wife said he was wearing.[24] Nevertheless, the Embassy was worried he might be a plant by the Chilean intelligence agency to create a provocation in the midst of the intense maneuvering in Chile about the Letelier case and Fernández Larios's apprehension. Dreher's superiors consulted with Washington and the decision was made, according to Dreher, that "the information he had to offer was not significant enough to get back in touch with him." The lead was dropped.

The memos about this incident were released in 1999 among other documents, but Meneses's name was blacked out and the texts were so heavily redacted their significance was not recognized. In 2015, however, several hundred new documents on Chile were released. Among them I discovered a cable about a Chilean officer who offered the Embassy information about Horman, and it revealed the officer's name without redaction, but spelled Manesas.[25] With the name, I was able to confirm that the man who spoke to Dreher in 1987 was the same person who helped Ed Horman in 1973. Horman mentioned both officers in his diary of his time in Chile, and both Raúl Meneses (spelled Manesas) and Jaime Ortiz were named in the Hauser book *Missing*. I then interviewed Dreher about his meetings with Meneses. Even with the various spellings of Meneses, it was relatively easy to find both men in Chile. As noted before, journalist Pascale Bonnefoy interviewed them both in 2016.

When Meneses offered his testimony in 1987, he was met with suspicion and indecision by the State Department and ultimately dropped out of sight until contacted 19 years later by Bonnefoy. Judges Guzmán and Zepeda also had the two men's names, from Hauser's book, but failed to locate them to summon them to court.

In early 2024, Meneses and Ortiz were summoned to testify in a related civil case. The family of General Augusto Lutz charged that the death of the former intelligence chief in 1974 following routine medical procedures may have been a murder orchestrated by the Pinochet government. Lawyers for the family located Meneses and Ortiz after reading the 2023 Spanish edition of this book. Meneses testified before Judge Paola Plaza on March 28, 2024. He ratified his and Sergeant Ortiz's investigation of Horman's killing, and added a few new details. He said he and Ortiz received an "Information Search Order" from their superiors in SIM and were specifically authorized to meet with Horman's father and wife to tell them the body had been identified in the morgue. He again named the three officers directly involved in Horman's detention, but all were deceased. In an interview with Olga Lutz, General Lutz's daughter, who brought the suit about her father's suspicious death, Meneses said he was uncomfortable being cast as a "hero" because of his successful investigation in the Horman case. He said he and Jaime Ortiz "were only fulfilling a mission assigned to them by the Army." He added that before the military coup there was a "good environment" in his intelligence unit and respect for all political tendencies. He said some of the soldiers were socialists and he himself had voted for Salvador Allende.[26]

THE FBI WAS NEVER CALLED FOR HELP

Diplomats are not investigators, and it showed. Professional help was available but not enlisted. FBI special agent Robert Scherrer was the legal attaché in Buenos Aires, with jurisdiction for criminal matters involving U.S. interests in several countries, including Chile. Arriving in 1972, he developed a reputation as a top investigator and intelligence operative, rivaling even the CIA.[27] He successfully investigated cases of kidnapped U.S. businessmen and several terrorist killings of American citizens in Argentina. He is credited with developing major leads in the assassination of Orlando Letelier in 1976, demonstrating that Chile's secret police DINA had carried out the crime. As a professional criminal investigator with established liaison relationships with Chile's Investigative Police (PICH), he was equipped to oversee a systematic probe, including following up on the obvious leads listed here that were otherwise ignored. He was also experienced in protecting vulnerable witnesses, a major concern in post-coup Chile.

Neither Scherrer nor any other FBI personnel were assigned to investigate the deaths of the two Americans. Indeed, the only FBI action in the case was to obtain Horman's fingerprints from his Air National Guard file and send them to Chile. An experienced FBI investigator like Scherrer would have been especially effective in unraveling the monthlong delay in identifying Horman's fingerprints. Yet Fred Purdy, the consul, was the only Embassy official who dealt in any way with the fingerprint issue. Once Horman was identified, with the help of the two Chilean intelligence officers, Purdy dropped the matter. It fell to an enterprising detective, Mario Rojas, to discover there had been interference by a Foreign Ministry official and a morgue secretary, which caused some or all of the delay. The long delay, in clear deviation from standard morgue and Civil Registry procedure, was an obvious example of Chilean government action that likely resulted from consciousness of guilt—in other words, the default explanation for such an action is that the officials who did it knew they were covering up a crime.

No U.S. investigator attempted to talk to PICH Inspector Rojas or to intersect with his agency's ongoing investigation. Such collaboration might have been fruitful. PICH had been put on the case by General Oscar Bonilla, the Interior Minister. Bonilla was a rival to Pinochet and, although an early leader in organizing the coup, he was known to be trying to stop or minimize the brutality. Rojas investigated at the Vicuña Mackenna scene, the morgue and fingerprint bureaus and the CIM (Comando de Institutos Militares), which launched the operation to detain Horman. He was in contact with Ed Horman and Fred Purdy during his investigation, but no U.S. official ever tried to follow up with him about what he knew. Judge Zepeda unearthed Rojas's reports from 1973, including the report on official interference with the fingerprint process, but Rojas had died by then and was never interviewed.

CONCEALING OF JUDD KESSLER'S INFORMATION

Embassy officer Kessler, based on information from Enrique Sandoval, was the first to report to the Embassy that Horman had been executed.

The information was provided at great risk by Sandoval's brother, Nelson, a Carabinero officer working in the Stadium. A proper approach and guarantee of U.S. protection could have led to his testimony. Sandoval's information was second-hand, but there was no reasonable excuse to ignore it. Yet no one from the Embassy contacted either Sandoval to obtain more details. Needless to say, Consul Purdy's decision to withhold Kessler's information completely from Joyce and Ed Horman was inexcusable and irreparably damaged the family's trust in the Embassy. Sandoval's information was transmitted a second time to the Embassy, through Ford Foundation official Lovell Jarvis, likewise without follow-up.

STADIUM EYEWITNESSES

Chile's Civil Registry office appears to have handled Frank Teruggi's case according to standard bureaucratic procedures, and he was identified within a few days. Consul Purdy nevertheless delayed notification to the Teruggi family for almost another week because the Chilean government had said that he was still alive, and Purdy did not want to contradict them. Months later, the family was informed that several eyewitnesses had seen and talked with Teruggi in the Stadium around the time of his death. The names of two of the eyewitnesses, Andre Van Lancker and Victor Eduardo Velastín Rodriguez, were revealed to Teruggi's father in 1975 and 1977, respectively. Both were living in Europe. No U.S. investigator attempted to interview either man about what they witnessed. Both had information that could have led to the possible identification of Teruggi's torturers, and Michael Townley had the name of the executioner himself. Likewise, no one contacted the Communist Party official, Gladys Marín, who at great risk had arranged for the eyewitnesses' information to be delivered to Teruggi's father during his visit in 1974. Van Lancker, Velastín and Marín have since died.

MILITARY OPERATIONS

The experienced U.S. military officers in Chile, MilGroup commander Davis and Defense Attaché Hon, understood how military operations are organized, and were well versed in military after-action reporting systems. They knew what questions to ask to get the details of an operation at a particular time and address. Memoranda from Hon indicate he and a subordinate embarked on this line of questions with top Chilean officers. Apparently rebuffed, however, the U.S. officers simply dropped the matter. Their passive reaction signaled to the Chileans that the Americans would not push back against stonewall tactics.

· · · · ·

A journalist's investigation like this one is never definitive, no matter how carefully it is conducted. The new evidence and conclusions presented here can and should lead to official reckoning with the sanction and resources of the courts and other government institutions. I have attempted to provide a complete picture of the political activities of Charles Horman and Frank Teruggi in Chile and the United States. My conclusions about the U.S. role differ significantly from the narrative presented in the film *Missing* and widely accepted thereafter. Some may still hold the view that U.S. officials caused or approved the murders. I only ask that they consider the evidence to the contrary presented here and take into account my detailed analysis of the unsupported assumptions in the Chilean court case and its flawed use of evidence.

The United States government was a principal actor in the tragic events of the 1970s in the Southern Cone, not only in Chile, but in Argentina, Uruguay, Bolivia and Paraguay. Those countries, especially Chile and Argentina, have made extraordinary efforts to investigate the human rights crimes of that period. Their primary aim has been to bring a measure of truth and justice to the victims and their families, but also to expose the political dynamics that enabled the massive use of torture and the tactic of disappearance. The United States has remained aloof from any similar calls for investigation of its own role in those events.

An investigation such as this one can bring a measure of justice by exposing the truth of what happened, but it cannot bring the guilty parties to account. Nothing short of a U.S. version of a Commission of Truth and Reconciliation, sanctioned and sponsored by the U.S. government, with power to compel testimony and documentation from the CIA and the U.S.

military, and with participation of victims and their representatives, will be able to put to rest the unresolved questions about the relationships of U.S. and Chilean actors after the coup. Only such an authoritative commission can overcome the persistent lack of credibility U.S. agencies have earned by their past record of obfuscation. State Department officer Frederick Smith called for "high level inquiries" in 1976, but his recommendation was ignored. An independent inquiry with no information off limits is not an unreasonable demand for a democracy founded on principles of equal justice and transparency. If South Africa and the countries of South America can do it, there is no reason it cannot be done in the United States as a way of coming to a final reckoning with the sometimes tragic collateral damage of the Cold War.

Frank Teruggi and Charles Horman were idealistic, talented and morally committed Americans who joined their destiny to a country they had come to love. They were not passive observers so much as partisans engaged in what they, and many other Americans, saw as a Chilean movement to a better future, an experiment that if successful in Chile could be a model for other poor countries and perhaps even for the United States. Socialism and democracy were the two poles Salvador Allende established for his experiment. They were goals worth fighting for.

Frank and Charlie did not intend to give their lives in the struggle they embraced, but that is what happened. Of the dozens of foreigners and hundreds of Chileans killed by the Chilean military in September 1973, they were the only Americans. Their families, especially Joyce Horman and the foundation she created, have been relentless in seeking justice and demanding a clarification of the U.S. role. Moreover, they leveraged the high profile of the two well-known American victims to focus a powerful spotlight on the injustices done to thousands of others who were caught up in the same vortex of violence and official impunity. Unrelenting pressure by Ed and Joyce Horman and by Frank Teruggi, Sr., and Janis Teruggi Page played a significant role in the strengthening of public policies in support of human rights. I hope they will find this book an important contribution to that truth-seeking process and a rectification of the historical record.

Charlie and Frank were internationalists, and they are in the noble ranks of so many others who traveled to another country to support and experience a revolution grander than themselves. The cause of Chile did not invent international solidarity nor were its foreign supporters the first to come away in defeat and disillusionment. Like the international *brigadistas* who defended Spain, the Americans who experienced Allende's Chile, even in its defeat, never forgot and never regretted, and came away changed for a lifetime.

Speaking for myself, Chile is a great love, and what happened there was a great wound in our hearts.

Acknowledging a Legacy

Most of the veterans of the Chile experience only intensified their activism on behalf of Chile on their return to the United States after the coup. Steve Volk, an informal leader of the *FIN* group, continued to reflect on the impact of Chile as a professor of Latin American studies. At the time of the 50th anniversary of the coup, he wrote: "There is little question that the Chile solidarity movement—the upsurge of activity that rose immediately following the 1973 coup and continued to grow over the following decade and beyond—was the most successful international solidarity movement since the Spanish Civil War in the 1930s, both in the US and worldwide."[1]

Chile was the catalyst for "an entire political apparatus devoted to human rights protections" that arose around the many conflicts and civil wars elsewhere in Latin America, especially in 1980s Central America, Volk added.[2] Americans who had been in Chile created organizations to advocate for human rights and cut off U.S. aid to the Pinochet dictatorship. One of Horman's friends in Santiago, Bob High, led the activist group Non-Intervention in Chile, which had been founded by another Chile veteran, Eric Leenson. Joseph Eldridge, a Methodist minister working with other religious activists at the time of the coup, founded the Washington Office on Latin America to channel congressional opposition to Pinochet. WOLA remains a mainstay of human rights advocacy in the United States. The deaths of Horman and Teruggi mobilized early intense interest among key congressmen, such as Representatives Michael Harrington and Ed Koch and Senators Jacob Javits and Ted Kennedy, who were joined by

Representatives Don Fraser, Tom Harkin, George Miller and Toby Moffett to create a phalanx of establishment activism to dispute the legitimacy of authoritarian regimes throughout Latin America. There is a long and respectable list of books, articles, and memoirs by the American veterans about Chile and the region. I can't help but think that Charles Horman and Frank Teruggi, both prolific writers, would have made major contributions to the bibliography of Chile and human rights.

Their legacy as men of conscience in the fight for justice has not been forgotten. In 2018 the University of Chile awarded Frank Teruggi a posthumous degree in Economics, together with other students whose careers were cut short by the repression. In 50th Anniversary events in 2023, Chile's president Gabriel Boric inaugurated a plaque honoring Charles Horman and other journalists killed during the dictatorship.

In writing this book, I came to admire Edmund Horman for his intelligence, persistence and grit. I was challenged by his many writings in which he tried to puzzle out the truth in the midst of great uncertainty and the conviction he was being deceived. He saw the deception and the contradictions in the official story fed him by the Chilean government and U.S. officials, and he systematically mapped out what he didn't know and needed to know. My intention in this reinvestigation of the case was to answer Ed Horman's questions by marshaling the massive documentation finally available. I hope he would have looked at the new evidence, as he scrutinized so incisively the pieces of the puzzle he had at the time, and say, perhaps, now we are closer to the truth.

Joyce Horman, in a series of email exchanges as the book was in the final editing process, offered helpful comments on the manuscript. I have made clarifying changes in the text in several places in response to some of her concerns. I am grateful for her thoughtful suggestions. Her input does not imply agreement with all of the conclusions of the book.

This has been a work of collaboration. Pascale Bonnefoy and Peter Kornbluh contributed major pieces of original investigation in our common determination to arrive at the facts of what happened. Carlos Osorio tracked down key documents in the declassified collection. Marcelo Montecino, master photographer, contributed photos from the time of the coup and made old snapshots come to life for the photo section. Maga Miranda and Carolina Rojas helped scan the many hundreds of pages from the Chilean court's official record. This book could not have been written without them.

So many people who experienced those years in Chile, many of them friends of Charlie and Frank, helped me by sharing their memories and their questions. I am confident they know what I mean by the title of this book. My greatest thanks to Steve Volk, David Hathaway, Roger Burbach, Pat Flynn, Mishy Lesser, Marc Cooper and Linda Wine among the Americans. Among the Chilenos, my

ACKNOWLEDGING A LEGACY   221

thanks to Ximena Andrade, Sergio Trabucco, Guillermo Orrego, Pedro Alejandro Matta, Alejandro Duhalde and Andres Ajens. Janis Teruggi generously shared letters and photographs from her brother. They were indispensable. Thank you Janis. Gigi Mohn Purdy shared her husband's unfinished manuscript for a book on Chile and the Horman-Teruggi case; Don Lenzer and Mark Harris had preserved a trove of Horman's letters and private writings and passed them on. My sincere thanks. Also among those who deserve thanks are two sources who requested anonymity for personal reasons. Pascale Bonnefoy, Peter Kornbluh and Steve Volk read the manuscript and made substantive and invaluable suggestions. Thank you so much.

My old friend Frank Manitzas was the first to investigate the killings in Chile, even before he made history by interviewing Rafael González. Manitzas kept meticulous notes and preserved documents from that time, and his daughter Elena Manitzas generously shared that material with me after Frank's death in 2017. His near verbatim notes of interviews conducted in October and November 1973 were an invaluable primary source. Thank you. Robert Steven has helped me on all my books on the dictatorships. I hope he doesn't mind my saying he was a beacon of human rights enlightenment in the U.S. Embassy and the State Department, while never compromising an iota of his professionalism. A career of thanks to him. Likewise, Jeffrey Davidow searched his files and showed me a unique window of conscience in an Embassy unwilling to pressure an anticommunist ally. Thank you. With a nod to our mutual friend Saul Landau, thanks to filmmaker and Chilenophile Dick Pearce, who insisted on nothing less than a true portrayal of his friend's political commitment. At an early point in this investigation I had the support of RetroReport; my thanks to executive producer Kyra Darnton and co-founder Larry Cholette. Thanks also to Dr. Jim Hook. You had my back. My editors at Penguin Random House/Chile, Aldo Perán and Melanie Josch, commissioned this project and rushed it into print in Spanish translation for the 50th Anniversary of the coup. Mil gracias a los dos. The English version appears more than a year later, giving me time to incorporate important new interviews and source materials, such as the collection of 40 letters from Charles Horman to his friend Don Lenzer. My thanks to Enrique Ochoa-Kaup of the University of California Press for his support and editor's eye, and to copyeditor Catherine Osborne for her meticulous scrutiny of my sourcing.

My wife Carolina Kenrick read many portions of the book when I needed a reality check. We met in Chile 50 years ago, and with love in our hearts we built a true Chilean–North American family, with our children's families and grandchildren now in Santiago, California and Maryland. My love to Tomás, Sebastian and Camila and to your wonderful children, Hazel, Max, Wyatt, Leonor and Lucas.

Sources and Methods

A work of investigative journalism like this one aims to discover the fact-based truth of an important issue, to the extent that is possible, by examining the primary sources, interviewing protagonists, and meticulously reading the documentary record. "Read everything," was the instruction from my onetime guide, journalist Izzy Stone, many years ago as I was learning the craft of investigation. In the narrative of the book, I have refrained from too much explanation of my methods and analysis of the sources that underlie my conclusions. I will endeavor to do that here.

There is a limited literature on the Horman-Teruggi case, although it is frequently mentioned briefly in books on the Allende government and the military dictatorship. Four books provide original research or personal accounts on the case: Thomas Hauser, *The Execution of Charles Horman: An American Sacrifice* (Harcourt Brace Jovanovich, 1978; renamed *Missing* in 1982); Nathaniel Davis, *Last Two Years of Salvador Allende* (Cornell University Press, 1985), 367–382; Peter Kornbluh, *The Pinochet File: A Declassified Dossier on Atrocity and Accountability* (The New Press, 2003; revised ed., 2013); and Pascale Bonnefoy, *Terrorismo de Estadio: Prisioneros de Guerra en un Campo de Deportes*, 2nd expanded ed. (Editorial Latinoamericana, 2016).

Hauser's book was the basis for the 1982 Costa-Gavras film *Missing*. The author presents the story of Charles Horman according to accounts of the Horman family and friends, interviews with U.S. officials and U.S. documents obtained by Ed Horman at the time (many of them highly redacted). The book is investigative in format but advocates unabashedly for the thesis that Horman "was executed with the foreknowledge of American Embassy officials in Santiago because he stumbled upon evidence of United States involvement in the Chilean coup." Teruggi's killing is covered in a short chapter.

Nathaniel Davis was the U.S. ambassador in Chile at the time of the coup and the killing of the Americans. His book is a gripping account of the coup and the aftermath, which he portrays as the unfortunate but inevitable result of the troubled and divided government of the Marxist president. He defends his efforts to find out what happened to the two Americans. He repeats the U.S. government position at the time, that it is unknown who killed them, noting that Chilean authorities "never satisfactorily explained" what happened. Davis was one of several U.S. officials who brought a libel suit against the Costa-Gavras movie *Missing*, alleging defamation.

Kornbluh's 2003 work is a comprehensive survey of U.S. declassified documents on the Allende and Pinochet eras. In a long chapter on the case, "American Casualties," the author reproduces 13 pages of recently declassified documents, including the so-called Fimbres memo, which appeared at the time to bolster the thesis of U.S. responsibility. Kornbluh provides a thorough survey of the facts of the case in the light of the declassifications. He criticizes the U.S. government for withholding information from the Horman family and for failing to conduct a serious investigation. Among other documented actions, he writes that the State Department "deliberately hid" the most provocative elements of the Fimbres memo until its release in 1999. The chapter is framed by Rafael González's 1976 accusations that a CIA agent was present at Horman's interrogation. González's recantation of his story is mentioned, without further detail, in the 2013 revised edition. Kornbluh's chapter does not attempt a conclusion about the question of possible U.S. complicity in the murders.

Kornbluh directs the Chile Documentation Project at the National Security Archive, which has supported my investigations and where I serve as a senior fellow. His knowledge of the case and mastery of the documentation were an invaluable contribution to my work on the Horman-Teruggi case. He was also a member of the board of the Horman Truth Project, the nonprofit organization set up by Joyce Horman to advocate for further investigation of her husband's murder. Interviewed for this book, which he has read in manuscript, he said he supports its findings about the U.S. role: "After a half century of investigations and judicial proceedings, no hard, documentary evidence has emerged to suggest U.S. foreknowledge of, or participation in, the Chilean military's decision to murder these two American citizens.... Nor does the historical record, as it has advanced over these decades, indicate the existence of such evidence in the few files that remain secret from the time of the coup." Based on his reading of the record, he considers the U.S. failure to fully investigate the murders a case of "malicious negligence" and disregard for the truth.

Bonnefoy, a journalist, was the first to conduct a serious investigation of the case in Chile. She used not only the U.S. declassified documents but had access to some of the evidence presented in the Chilean court case. Most significantly, she worked with the author to identify and interview two Army intelligence officers who conducted an investigation of the case and were willing to talk about it. Her chapter "Los Gringos" contains important investigative advances on both Horman and Teruggi, but does not conclude either way about the question of U.S. involvement.

In the present work, perhaps the most important finding is that the theory of U.S. involvement in Horman's murder, advocated by Hauser's book and the movie *Missing*, was factually wrong. I also found that some of the conclusions of the Chilean Court investigation, which went beyond the book and movie to allege U.S. responsibility for Teruggi's killing, were deeply flawed.

All of those accounts rely heavily on the 1976 statements of Chilean agent Rafael González, in his interview from the Italian embassy with reporters Joanne Omang, Frank Manitzas and Rudolph Rauch. González said outright that Horman was executed "because he knew too much, and this was done between the CIA and local authorities." González later retracted that statement, saying he invented the false story about a CIA person in the room when Horman's fate was determined. In my investigation, based on a close reading of all of González's statements over the years, I conclude that the retraction should be given much greater credence than his 1976 accusations of CIA involvement. Without González's 1976 charge of a CIA presence and his portrayal of Horman as the man "who knew too much," the entire edifice of U.S. involvement in the murders falls to the ground. Other evidence put forward in the book crumbles into pure speculation as well—for example, that Horman learned something about U.S. participation in the 1973 military coup and that Horman's ride with a U.S. officer from Valparaiso to Santiago was linked to his death.

So it is critical that I explain why I give credence to González's retraction and not to his original statements.

I have examined an exhaustive assemblage of his statements and writings, including transcripts and notes of the journalists' recorded interviews, conducted on June 7, 8 and 11, 1976; three interviews with U.S. Embassy officials that took place June 8, 1973, and January 24 and 31, 1977 (the latter two also recorded); a sworn affidavit by González submitted to the U.S. District Court for the District of Columbia in the wrongful death suit by Joyce Horman against Henry Kissinger and others; a five-page retraction written in November 2001, in which González describes how and why he invented the story of the CIA agent; a 17-page document written after his arrest and testimony; and Chilean court documents containing González's testimony to the court after his arrest in May 2003. In addition, I conducted email exchanges with González in 2016 and 2024, in which he answered my questions at length and with seeming forthrightness. There are other materials by and about González in my possession, but the ones cited above form the basis of my investigation.

González is a complicated but clearly very intelligent person who worked undercover as an intelligence agent for many years. In his writings he betrays fervent antisemitic sentiments, identifying people frequently as belonging to Jewish lodges. As I write in chapter 14, "The Making of the 'Man Who Knew Too Much,'" González says he was forced by Italian diplomats to invent the story about the CIA agent. The diplomats, according to González, were leftists and wanted him to implicate the CIA in Horman's murder "so that as a result sectors in the United States would pressure [the U.S. government] to withdraw all support from the military government."[1]

In our email correspondence, starting in July 2016 after his sentencing to three years of home confinement, he said he wanted the truth to come out: "Although I have already been convicted, I am hopeful that your investigation can identify the real perpetrators of Horman's death, and, if not legally, at least morally my reputation will not be associated with this crime."[2]

In a more recent exchange, I asked González to confirm he used a 1974 *London Times* article to make up his story. His reply:

> I confirm to you that I read William Shawcross' article when it was given to me at the Italian Foreign Ministry [Embassy], that I followed the instructions I was given to use it for the story I was to tell the Washington Post reporters, and that Gen. Lutz did not say Horman knew too much.
>
> I have never recanted being in Gen. Lutz's office. The things I have recanted are on the five pages [the 2001 retraction statement].

By admitting that he had seen Horman in Lutz's office—the one part of his 1976 statement that has never wavered—González had linked himself to Horman's detention, and in effect provided a piece of key evidence Judge Zepeda used to convict him as an accessory (*complice*) to the crime. In that version of his story, there is no American present and Lutz orders Horman to be deported, not executed. In evaluating González's credibility, this was an important detail. In recanting his story about the CIA but retaining the incriminating detail about his own presence, González in effect was testifying "against interest," which I consider a strong sign he was telling the truth.

There were other early signs he was wavering from the statements in the 1976 press interview about the CIA and Lutz. As described in chapter 19, González's statements to the press led to an internal State Department investigation, documented in the Fimbres memo (August 25) and the Frederick Smith report (December 1976). González's statements were part of the "circumstantial evidence" that, according to the Fimbres memo, suggested "U.S. intelligence may have played an unfortunate part in Horman's death." The upshot of the report was an order for a top U.S. Embassy official, Deputy Chief of Mission Charles Stout, to interview González according to a detailed questionnaire. In that interview, over two days on January 24 and 31, 1977, González gave evasive answers and backed away from his charge that a CIA officer was present when a Chilean intelligence officer ordered Horman's execution. He also denied that he knew anything about Horman having been brought to Santiago from Valparaiso. Those and other answers contradicted what he had said on tape to Omang and Manitzas six months before. The transcripts of those interviews, which tended to discredit González's story, were not declassified until 1999.

Finally allowed to leave Chile safely in 1978, González was contacted by Ed Horman and flown to New York in January 1979, for the purpose of testifying in the ongoing lawsuit the family had brought against Henry Kissinger and other U.S. officials. González claims he told Horman that his story about the CIA and Lutz was an invention, but that he didn't want to interfere with Horman's legal efforts.[3] Instead of testifying, he presented a sworn affidavit saying all the statements in the interview with Omang and Manitzas "were made by me and are true." He went into even more detail about the alleged CIA agent's clothing and shoes, which led him to believe the man was an American. He also said the transcript of his interview with Stout was false and inaccurate.

From the time of the New York visit in 1979 to 2001, González remained silent, returning to Chile after democracy was restored in 1990 and living quietly. In 2000, however, he read about the U.S. documents that had been declassified and the opening of Judge Guzmán's Estadio Nacional trial in Chile. He decided to finally come forward with the truth:

> A criminal complaint had been filed in Chile regarding the death of Horman and it was reasonable to assume that I would be called to testify. In order to make an orderly statement of the facts, I drafted those five pages and showed them to a couple of people.
> First of all, I must say that the most comfortable thing for me would have been to continue repeating the lies I was forced to tell at the Italian Embassy. On the other hand, it was obvious that there were many people who did not want me to say something that would seem to exonerate American officials from responsibility for his death. But I do not claim that such responsibility did not exist, I only say that I myself do not know that, and that if I said it, it was under duress.[4]

In another email, he further explained the motives he ascribed to the Italian diplomats: "The people who forced me to talk to the press in the Italian Foreign Ministry wanted the U.S. government to appear to be involved in the overthrow of Allende, in the death of people and among them, in a particularly sensitive way for the American public, one of their own fellow citizens, so that U.S. support for Chile would become untenable and the Pinochet government would lose its main ally."[5]

Given that González has reversed himself twice since his original statements about Horman and the CIA, it is impossible to say categorically when he is telling the truth. My considered judgment is that his retraction is much more likely to be true than the story implicating the CIA. It deserves more credence, among other reasons, because no other evidence has emerged over the past 50 years to corroborate the story he recanted. He provides a key verifiable detail that is persuasive: he explains that he used the article in the *London Times* to build his story about Horman, about whom he knew nothing, when he claims to have met him in Lutz's office in 1973.

I do not believe there is evidence that González had anything to do with Horman's execution. But his retelling, which exonerates both himself and Lutz, does not explain the inexorable fact that Horman was executed within a few hours of González's supposedly innocent encounter with him in the intelligence chief's office. Whatever the details of the retelling, the bottom line is that Horman was in the custody of the Chilean military at the time he was killed. And González's repudiation of his 1976 statement removes any connection between U.S. officials in Chile and the murder of one or two American citizens.

Likewise, statements by González cannot be used to support the idea that Horman's experiences in Valparaiso, whatever they were, provided the motive for U.S. officials to arrange to kill him. The "man who knew too much" was an invention.

Ignoring González's recantation, Judge Zepeda attempted to build his case on the official connections between the U.S. Military Group, headed by Captain Ray Davis, and Chilean military leaders in the Defense Ministry before and after the coup. Those liaisons were well known and part of longstanding procedures governing the military-to-military relationship. Zepeda alleges, but fails to provide any evidence, that Captain Davis communicated his desire to have Horman detained and acquiesced in his execution. The judge simply presumes that the existing liaison contacts would have been used to communicate such intentions and desires regarding Horman.

My method in analyzing the court case was to compare the evidence cited in the 277-page verdict (*Sentencia*) with the actual evidence found in the court record (*Expediente*). I found not a single instance of U.S.-Chilean communication regarding a request to detain Horman or any other American. Direct evidence is also absent to support the charge that U.S. officials, led by Davis, conducted surveillance on Horman, Teruggi and other American leftists.

The argument has been made, including in recent email exchanges with Joyce Horman, that it is possible that still hidden evidence in U.S. or Chilean documents might prove U.S. involvement in the murders. Yet in multiple declassifications spanning many administrations, no hint that such documents exist has come to light. It was argued at one point in Chile, by one of the attorneys for the families, that the proof for Zepeda's conclusions might be found in a secret section of the court record that has never been disclosed.[6] As I write in chapter 17, I checked with Zepeda's chief assistant, who assured me that no such secret evidence exists, and that the totality of Zepeda's evidence is included in the record made available to me.

The mere absence of such evidence cannot be used to argue that such evidence must exist. Or, as I tell my students in teaching the techniques of investigative reporting, "The absence of evidence is not evidence of absent evidence."

PRINCIPAL SOURCES USED IN MY INVESTIGATION

Publicly Available Document Collections

U.S. government declassified documents regarding Chile and Argentina, released 1999–2016. U.S. government documents, unless otherwise indicated, are from Department of State declassified collections, including four binders of U.S. documents released to the families in 1999. I have accessed many other documents about the case using the State Department "Virtual Reading Room" and search engine of more than 400,000 U.S. declassified documents at https://foia.state.gov/Search/Search.aspx. The documents include the Horman-Teruggi documents, which are a subset of the Chile Collection (also referred to by the State Department as the "Chile Declassification Project").

Notable documents:

R. V. Fimbres, R. S. Driscoll, W. V. Robertson, State Department memo, "Charles Horman Case," August 25, 1976, secret (Chile Project), with attachment "Gleanings."

Frederick Smith, Jr., "Death in Chile of Charles Horman," State Department memo, with a cover memo dated December 29, 1976. Twenty-six-page report ordered by Assistant Secretary of State for Latin America Harry W. Shlaudeman, in response to the Fimbres memo. Smith concludes with a high degree of certainty that the Chilean military killed Horman and Teruggi, although the State Department officially continued for more than a decade to say that no one knew what had happened.

"FBI investigation: Memorandum, To Acting Director FBI, from Legat Bonn, Subject Frank Teruggi, SM-Sub, October 15, 1972." This is the most extensive of five FBI documents describing its investigation of Teruggi, who was already in Chile.

Santiago 4565, "Amcit Missing in Chile," September 25, 1973. Cable cited by Judge Zepeda to demonstrate, erroneously, that the U.S. Embassy knew of Horman's arrest and reported it to Washington on the day it occurred, thus showing foreknowledge of his death. Actually the cable gives the correct date of Horman's detention but was written eight days after the fact. The document was difficult to locate among the declassified documents because the judge identified it only with a 12-digit document code that had two incorrect digits. Thanks to Carlos Osorio of the National Security Archive for finding the document.

Santiago 1596, "Letelier/Moffit case: Embassy file on Michael Vernon Townley," March 8, 1978. Cable summarizing files in Santiago Embassy on

Townley, who was being investigated for the murder of Orlando Letelier. One of the memos cites Townley as telling an Embassy officer, Jeff Davidow, that he had spoken to a Chilean operative who witnessed Teruggi's killing. Fifty years later, Townley told the author he didn't remember the exchange.

Santiago 2440, April 3, 1987, "Letelier Case: Mariana Callejas Calls on Political Section April 3, 1987." This cable revealed the name of Sergeant Raúl Meneses (spelled Manesas), who offered information on the Horman case to Embassy officer David Dreher. The name is redacted in all other declassified documents. But having the name in one document unlocked his identity in the other documents, and allowed me to connect the person who approached the Embassy in 1987 with the two Chilean intelligence officers who met with Horman's father and ultimately identified his son's body.

Private Papers

Joyce Horman and Edmund Horman Papers, Benson Latin American Collection, University of Texas at Austin, https://txarchives.org/utlac/finding_aids/00271.xml. Correspondence of Edmund Horman, legal filings from lawsuit against Henry Kissinger and other U.S. officials, press clippings. The papers contain very little material on Charles Horman and his time in Chile. Memos written by Edmund Horman, such as those found in the Manitzas Papers, do not appear in this collection.

Unpublished Documents

Charles Horman, 40 letters to Don Lenzer, provided by Lenzer.

Frank Teruggi, 30 letters to his family and sister, provided by Janis Teruggi Page.

Frank Manitzas, "American Murder: The Story Behind the Murder of a New Yorker," unpublished manuscript. Also titled "An American Murder in Chile."

Manitzas Papers: Papers of reporter Frank Manitzas provided by his family. Notes of interviews conducted in Chile in September–November 1973 and other contemporary materials, memoranda and correspondence by Edmund Horman, correspondence with Frank Teruggi, Sr. Manitzas visited the abandoned Horman house several times and retrieved papers left behind, including a letter written by Horman to his wife on the day of his kidnapping.

Jorge Reyes, "Testimony of Jorge Reyes" and "Avenue of the Americas: The Story of a Film and Its Shooting," April 14, 2018. The documents can be located at https://nanopdf.com/download/read-the-testimony-of-jorge-reyes-in-format_pdf.

Edmund Horman, "The View after Three Years," unpublished manuscript dated December 22, 1976. In Manitzas Papers.

Chilean Court Case

"Causa 2182-98 por el sequestro y homicidio de Frank Teruggi y Charles Horman" (Episodio Estadio Nacional) [Case 2182-98 regarding the kidnapping and murder of Frank Teruggi and Charles Horman (National Stadium Episode)], in the Santiago Court of Appeals, referred to here as the "Chilean court case." The case was opened by Judge Juan Guzmán Tapia, who began taking testimony on Horman in December 2000. Judge Jorge Zepeda Arancibia took over the case in October 2002, and issued his verdict (*Sentencia*) in January 2015. I was given access to the complete court record (*Expediente*), which consists of 17 volumes of numbered pages of testimony, documentary evidence and court filings, with a total of 6,976 pages. I scanned approximately 1,500 pages and obtained about 1,000 other pages that had already been digitized.

Notable documents:

Verdict (*Sentencia*), issued January 15, 2015, 277 pages. The verdict contains a selected list of evidence and near verbatim transcriptions of the testimony of some of the witnesses that are considered most important by the judge. There are telling exceptions: the judge includes a transcript of Rafael González's 1976 interview with journalists Joanne Omang of the *Washington Post* and Frank Manitzas of CBS, but he omits González's retraction to the court in 2003. Judge Zepeda makes no mention in the verdict of González's five-page written statement explaining in detail how he fabricated the story.

Judges Guzmán and Zepeda summoned a long list of Chilean and U.S. witnesses, many of whom were brought from the United States to testify. Among them were Joyce Horman, Terry Simon, Janis Teruggi Page, Steven Volk, David Hathaway, Frank Manitzas, Fred Purdy, Costa-Gavras, many of the eyewitnesses to the detentions, Lluis Mestres, Nelson and Enrique Sandoval, Pascale Bonnefoy and Peter Kornbluh. Multiple military officers who had served under Pinochet were called to testify, including some of those identified in this book as directly involved in Horman's and Teruggi's detentions. None of them acknowledged knowing anything about the two Americans except what they read in the press after their deaths. Several officers who served in Chilean intelligence agencies testified, including the former head of Naval Intelligence Raúl Monsalve, who acknowledged his professional liaison relationship with U.S. officers, including Ray Davis. But none of them provided any information supporting the charge that Davis or anyone else asked them to detain Horman or Teruggi. Although former MilGroup commander Davis was living in Chile after his retirement, the court did not know that and sought his extradition from the United States. He died in Chile a few years before the court's verdict was issued.

The court record contains hundreds of U.S. declassified documents, which are cited in support of the charges that U.S. officials surveilled Americans and acquiesced in the murders. I have analyzed those and many other relevant U.S. documents and did not find any such support, as shown in the book.

I found it uncomfortable to rebut and refute the investigative sources, methods and findings of a Chilean court. Chile's courts, since the restoration of democracy, have done monumental work in human rights cases, including the prosecution by Judge Guzmán of General Pinochet himself. Other cases I have examined—of the Letelier assassination in Washington, or the Operation Condor case—have been rigorous and their conclusions carefully drawn. As I have shown, that was not true of Judge Zepeda after he took over the Estadio Nacional case from Judge Guzmán and immediately focused it on the testimony of Rafael González and his allegations of U.S. involvement in the murders.

First-Hand Accounts

Joyce Horman:

Joyce Horman statement, November 10, 1973, 31 pages. The signed document, written after her return to the United States, begins, "To the best of my recollection, the following statements are true." A somewhat revised copy of the statement was entered into evidence in the court case in 2000. A more complete copy from the 1970s was found in the Manitzas Papers.

I consulted many of Horman's other statements made over the years, both to the Chilean court and elsewhere. We had one interview, of several hours, in 2016. In email exchanges in 2023 and 2024, in which she reviewed the manuscript and made comments, she provided several other substantive details about her husband.

Terry Simon:

Simon kept notes of her experiences in Chile when she was visiting Charles and Joyce Horman. In the fearful days after his disappearance, she got the help of Steven Volk to transcribe her recollections and notes. Volk called the transcribed notes the "Chapstick Papers," because they were hidden inside an empty chapstick tube and smuggled out of Chile in Volk's luggage.

Another set of handwritten notes by Volk apparently remained in Chile. It is described as "Brief chronology of events from Thurs. Sept. 13 to Wed Sept 19. (Terry Simon and Charles Horman's trip to Viña and return). Told by TS [Terry Simon]." I found the original, written on yellow lined paper, in the Frank Manitzas Papers. Although neither Simon nor Volk remember preparing the notes, Volk verified it is in his handwriting. I consider the document to be authentic, for the following reasons: It was found in Manitzas's papers together with other documents from September and October 1973; and the document contains details about activities with Charles Horman that were known only to Terry Simon, and that she describes later in another interview. One example (of several): in the handwritten document she says that on September 14, she and Charles "take a walk on the beach to dump some literature but are met by someone from hotel and decide against it." Simon recounted the same incident, repeating the same and additional details, in Hauser, *Execution*, 79. The document is factually consistent with Simon's other statements from the time and with her testimony to the Chilean court. In addition, none of the facts in the handwritten account differ from accounts of the same events by Joyce Horman, Lluis Mestres and Frank Manitzas, all of whom are mentioned.

Simon also wrote about her experience in *Senior Scholastic*, the magazine where she worked in New York City: "An American Girl in Chile's Revolution," December 6, 1973.

Books and Reports

Salvador Allende, *Salvador Allende: Palabra y Acción* (Fondo de Cultura Económica Chile, 2020). Contains Allende's speeches in 1973, including his final address on September 11.

Antony Beevor, *Battle for Spain: The Spanish Civil War, 1936–1939* (Phoenix, 2004).

Simon Collier and William F. Sater, *A History of Chile, 1808–2002* (Cambridge University Press, 2004).

Pamela Constable and Arturo Valenzuela, *A Nation of Enemies: Chile under Pinochet* (Norton, 1991).

Covert Action in Chile, 1963–1973: Staff Report of the Select Committee to Study Governmental Operations with Respect to Intelligence Activities, December 18, 1975. The investigation was led by Sen. Frank Church, Idaho, and is commonly referred to as the Church Committee Report.

John Dinges, *Los Años del Condor: Operaciones Internacionales de Asesinato en el Cono Sur* (Penguin Random House, 2021). This is the expanded edition of my 2004 book, *The Condor Years: How Pinochet and His Allies Brought Terrorism to Three Continents* (The New Press, 2004).

John Dinges and Saul Landau, *Assassination on Embassy Row* (Pantheon, 1980; Open Road, 2014).

El Caso Schneider: Operación Alfa (Editorial Quimantu, October 1972). The book, published around the time Charles Horman was researching the kidnapping of General Schneider, contains court documents, testimony and photos.

Franck Gaudichaud, *Chile 1970–1973: Mil dias que estremecieron el mundo; Poder popular, cordones industriales y socialismo durante el gobierno de Salvador Allende* (LOM, 2016).

Mónica González, *La Conjura: Los Mil y un Dias del Golpe* (Ediciones B, 2000).

Tanya Harmer, *Allende's Chile and the Inter-American Cold War* (UBC Press, 2011).

Informe de la Comisión Nacional de Verdad y Reconciliación (CNVR), 3 vols., published in 1991. Also known as the Rettig Commission Report. The commission's data has been updated as recently as 2021.

International Commission of Jurists, "The Application in Latin America of International Declarations and Conventions Relating to Asylum," September 1975. Documents the situation of political refugees in Chile before and after the coup.

Memoria Viva, accessed at https://memoriaviva.com. The site compiles human rights cases using information from the Rettig Report, other official sources and press reports.

Jefferson Morley, *Scorpion's Dance: The President, the Spymaster, and Watergate* (St. Martin's, 2022).

Dolores Mujica, *Cordones Industriales: Cronología Comentada* (Ediciones Museo Obrero Luis Emilio Recabarran, 2013).

Pablo Neruda, *Spain in Our Hearts—España en el Corazón*, dual-language edition (New Directions, 2005). Neruda wrote most of the poems in this searing account of the Spanish Civil War in 1936.

Paul E. Sigmund, *The Overthrow of Allende and the Politics of Chile, 1964–1976* (University of Pittsburgh Press, 1977).

Steve J. Stern, *Remembering Pinochet's Chile* (Duke, 2004). The book contains a valuable critical survey of original sources about the Allende period and the coup.

Sergio Trabucco Ponce, *Con los ojos abiertos: El Nuevo Cine chileno y el movimiento de Nuevo Cine latinoamericano* (LOM, 2016). The book describes the making of Pablo de la Barra's *Queridos Compañeros* and Jorge Reyes's, *Avenue of the Americas*, based on Charles Horman's research and script.

Tim Weiner, *Legacy of Ashes: The History of the CIA* (Doubleday, 2007).

Books on Political Movements of the 1960s

Todd Gitlin, *The Sixties: Years of Hope, Days of Rage* (Bantam, 1993).

Milton Viorst, *Fire in the Streets: America in the 1960s* (Simon and Schuster, Touchstone, 1979).

Press Articles with Original Research

Jack Anderson, "Memos Bare ITT for Chile Coup," *Washington Post*, March 21, 1972.

Lewis H. Diuguid, "The Man Who Knew Too Much," *Washington Post*, June 20, 1976.

FIN, "Collision Course: Chile Before the Coup," *NACLA's Latin America & Empire Report*, October 1973. NACLA credits Frank Teruggi as part of the *FIN* collective that authored the article.

Kevin Hall, "Chilean Spy Recants Story of CIA's Link to Slain U.S. Citizen," *Inquirer*, February 18, 2004. Hall's article, one of the few about González's retraction, quotes his son Sergio González saying his father "falsely implicated the CIA" out of fear for his life.

Godfrey Hodgson and William Shawcross, "Destabilisation," *Sunday Times*, October 27, 1974. Rafael González, in recanting his 1976 charge alleging CIA involvement, says he used this article to obtain details about Charles Horman and to borrow the phrase "the man who knew too much."

Paul Hoeffel, "Murder Chilean Style," *Attenzione*, July/August 1982. A profile of Frank Teruggi.

Marvine Howe, "2 Americans Slain in Chile: The Unanswered Questions," *New York Times*, November 19, 1973.

Jim Moscou, "Declassified Documents Reveal Washington May Have Given Clearance to the Execution of Charles Horman," *Editor and Publisher*, October 16, 1999. The first article on the declassified Fimbres memo. The story about the document did not gain traction until it appeared in a longer story in the *New York Times* several months later.

Joanne Omang, "Chilean Charges General Ordered American's Death," *Washington Post*, June 10, 1976. Based on interview with Rafael González.

Diana Jean Schemo, "U.S. Victims of Chile's Coup: The Uncensored File," *New York Times*, February 13, 2000. Schemo's report cover an array of the most important documents released on the Horman-Teruggi case, including the Fimbres memo.

Norman Stockwell, "A 41-Year Saga: Seeking the Truth in the Death of Frank Teruggi," *Tico Times*, October 17, 2014. A shorter version appeared in the *Progressive* as "The Other 9/11: Seeking the Truth about Frank Teruggi," September 12, 2014.

Writings by Americans in Chile at the Time

Peter Andreas, *Rebel Mother: My Childhood Chasing the Revolution* (Simon and Schuster, 2017). The author's mother, Carol Andreas, was a friend and a passionate supporter of the cause of women's rights in the Chilean revolution.

Hope Boylston, *Hay Locos* (Kaye Productions, 2011). A memoir.

Roger Burbach, *Fractured Utopias: A Personal Odyssey with History* (Freedom Voices, 2017).

Marc Cooper, *Pinochet and Me: A Chilean Anti-Memoir* (Verso, 2001).

Fred Purdy, untitled manuscript, 1991. Purdy lists several potential titles, including "*Found*: The Sequel to *Missing*" and "The Road to Chile and Unwanted Celebrity—How Fred Purdy Became a Public Figure and Didn't Like It." Provided by his widow, Gigi Purdy.

Films

Avenue of the Americas, 1975, produced by Jorge Reyes and Walter Locke. Charles Horman wrote the original script.

Battle of Chile, produced by Patricio Guzmán, portrays with extensive original footage the three years of the Allende government and the military coup.

Campamento, 1972, filmed at Nueva la Habana, a radicalized squatter community in Santiago, by Richard Pearce.

Missing, 1982, directed by Costa-Gavras, staring Sissy Spacek as Joyce Horman (called Beth in the film), and Jack Lemmon as Ed Horman. https://www.boxofficemojo.com/release/rl3714221569/weekend/.

Que Hacer, 1972, directed by Saul Landau, Nina Serrano and Jorge Ruiz. Available on YouTube. Dick Pearce and Pablo de la Barra were members of the crew, among other friends of Charles Horman.

Queridos Compañeros, 1977, directed by Pablo de la Barra. A scene in the movie was filmed at the Hormans' house on Paul Harris Street.

Interviews

Andres Ajens, 2016
Fernando "Marcelo" Alarcón, 2018
Marco Antonio Alvarez, 2016
Ximena Andrade, 2017
Ramon Barceló, 2018
Jim Beckett, 2016
Andy Scott Berman, 2002
Carlos Beust, 2018
Karen Bixler, 2002
Simon Blattner, 2018
Shepherd Bliss, 2000
Pascale Bonnefoy, 2016
Hope Boylston, 2018
Marco Bravo, 2017
Roger Burbach, 2000
Manuel Cabieses, 2017
Stephanie Campbell Graham, 2016
Judge Mario Carroza, 2018
René Castro, 2018

Lance Compa, 2000
Marc Cooper, 2024
Carter Cornick, 2016
Sergio Corvalan, 2017
Jeff Davidow, 2023
Pablo de la Barra, 2016
Howard Denike, 2002
Jack Devine, 2001
David Dreher, 2016
Janet Duecy, 2016
Joe Eldridge, 2016
Pat Fagen, 2022
Rudy Fimbres, 2000
Goeff Fox, 2018
Esther "Cuqui" Fuentes, 2017
Sandro Gaete, 2017, 2018
Frank Gaudichaud, 2017
Christopher Goldschmidt, 2018
Trevor Greenwood, 2023
Mark Harris, 2023
David L. Hathaway, 2023
Lief Hedman, 2016
Manuel Hidalgo, 2017
Paul Hoeffel, 2016
Joyce Horman, 2016
Milton Jamail, 2024
Larry Jans, 2016
Lovell Jarvis, 2024
Diana Kay, 2016
Karen Kerschen, 2016
Judd Kessler, 2016
Peter Kornbluh, 2016
Rafael Kreis, 2018
Don Lenzer, 2023, 2024
Mishy Lesser, 2016, 2024
Fabiola Letelier, 2016
Walter Locke, 2016
Barbara Margolis, 2016
Pedro Matta, 2018
Manuel Muñoz, 2017
Olga Muñoz, 2018
Sergio "Cochín" Muñoz, 2018

Guillermo "Memo" Orrego, 2018
Janis Teruggi Page, 2016
Celsa Parrau, 2018
Andrés Pascal Allende, 2000
Richard Pearce, 2016, 2023
Darío Pulgar, 2016
Fred Purdy, 2006
Gigi Purdy, 2018
Rudolph "Ru" Rauch, 2023
Liliana Salazar, 2017
Jan Sandquist, 2016
Paulo Santos Lopes, 2017
Adam Schesch, 2016
Robert Steven, 2000, 2016
Harry Straholz, 2000
Roberto Thieme, 1979, 2007
Joe Thome, 2016
Sergio Trabucco, 2021
Paulina Vidal, 2017
Steve Volk, 2000, 2018
Max Watts, 2001
William Whitaker, 2019
Linda Wine, 2024
Anonymous: Two interviewees requested anonymity for personal reasons.

Email communication only:
Rafael González, 2016, 2024
Terry Ann Simon, 2024
Kyle Steenland, 2024
Michael Townley, 2024
Andy Zimbalist, 2024

Notes of interviews conducted by other journalists:
By Pascale Bonnefoy with Raúl Meneses, Jaime Ortiz, May 2016 (typed notes).
By Maria Olga Lutz with Raúl Meneses, May 2024.
By Frank Manitzas (handwritten notes in reporter's notebook) with Warwick Armstrong, Ray Davis, Joyce Horman, Dr. Julio Núñez, Lluis Mestres, Fred Purdy, October–November 1973.
By Norman Stockwell with Shepherd Bliss, 2014 (transcript).

Notes

INTRODUCTION

1. Antony Beevor, *Battle for Spain: The Spanish Civil War, 1936-1939* (Phoenix, 2004), 177ff; interview with Patricia Fagen. Joyce Horman is a member of the honorary board of the Abraham Lincoln Brigade Association, according to Executive Director Mark Wallem.

2. Translation by Mark Eisner, in *The Essential Neruda: Selected Poems*, edited by Mark Eisner (City Lights Books, 2004), shortened and slightly revised by the author. The full volume is Pablo Neruda, *Spain in Our Hearts—España en el Corazón*, dual-language edition (New Directions, 2005).

3. Saul Friedman, "U.S. in 'War' at Home?," *Des Moines Tribune*, September 5, 1970. The story cited Treasury Department and Senate reports documenting 3.1 bombings per day as of July 1970.

4. Todd Gitlin, *The Sixties: Years of Hope, Days of Rage* (Bantam, 1993), 401–412.

5. Cited in John Dinges and Saul Landau, *Assassination on Embassy Row* (Pantheon, 1980), 42. A 2014 revised edition is available in ebook and audio book from Open Road Media.

6. CIA order: Select Committee on Intelligence Activities, *Alleged Assassination Plots Involving Foreign Leaders: Interim Report*, 231.

7. See Tanya Harmer, *Allende's Chile and the Inter-American Cold War* (UBC Press, 2011), 5. Harmer suggests the coup was seen as a victory for U.S. opposition

to Allende and formalized a policy of seeking stronger ties to the military in other countries, especially Brazil, which had overthrown a leftist government in 1964. In the Southern Cone, she writes, U.S. representatives "assisted local rightwing dictators and enabled counterrevolutionary military elites to take power in the few countries where they were not already in control. . . . [T]he Southern Cone became a historically significant grouping as a result of what happened."

8. Dinges and Landau, *Assassination on Embassy Row*.

9. Saul Landau and John Dinges, "The Truth Behind 'Missing,'" *Inquiry*, April 12, 1982.

10. Examples of publications that treat the charge of U.S. involvement as essentially proven by the Fimbres memo include Patrice McSherry, *Predatory States: Operation Condor and Covert War in Latin America* (Rowman and Littlefield, 2005), 83–88; and Margaret Power, "The U.S. Movement in Solidarity with Chile in the 1970s," *Latin American Perspectives* 36, no. 6 (November 2009). Most books on Chile that describe the case portray the issue as disputed or unresolved. Among them: Pamela Constable and Arturo Valenzuela, *A Nation of Enemies: Chile under Pinochet* (Norton, 1991); Steve J. Stern, *Remembering Pinochet's Chile* (Duke, 2004), 173; Heraldo Muñoz, *The Dictator's Shadow* (Basic Books, 2008), 90–92 (quoting Fimbres memo).

11. State Department memo: "Charles Horman Case," from R. V. Fimbres, R. S. Driscoll, W. V. Robertson, August 25, 1976, secret (Chile Project), with attachment "Gleanings." FBI investigation: Memorandum, To Acting Director FBI, from Legat Bonn, Subject Frank Teruggi, SM-Sub, October 15, 1972. These and other documents will be explored in detail in subsequent chapters, especially chapters 2, 13 and 18. "Chile Project" is the State Department's name for the systematic declassifications of documents on human rights in Chile, ordered by the Clinton Administration and carried out in a series of tranches in 1999–2016, and all declassified U.S. government documents cited in this book can be found here unless otherwise noted.

12. In a recent example with parallels to the Chile case, in 2022 the Justice Department opened an investigation into the killing of Palestinian American journalist Shireen Abu Akleh in West Bank territory occupied by Israel. See Patrick Kingsley, "U.S. Investigating Killing of Al Jazeera Journalist in West Bank, Israel Says," *New York Times*, November 22, 2022. Abu Akleh was wearing a flak jacket marked "Press" when she was shot in the head by an Israeli soldier. Israel claimed Palestinian militants had killed her, then conceded it was an Israeli soldier, but refused to conduct a criminal investigation.

PART I. ROADS TO THE REVOLUTION

1. Harvard years: Email exchanges with classmates at Leverett Hall. The "gentle manner" comment is from Robert Mnookin.

2. Louisiana: Unpublished writing by Charles Horman, provided by Mark Harris. "Boy" was a demeaning term used in the South for Black men.

3. Experience with King Broadcasting: interviews with Mark Harris, Trevor Greenwood and Richard Pearce.

4. Interview with Mark Harris.

5. Letter to Lenzer, December 1970, from Owatonna, MN. Tolstoy quote: Unpublished writings by Horman.

6. Chicago demonstrations: Unpublished writings by Horman; Charles Horman, "TV: Daley's Hour," *The Nation*, October 7, 1968. The piece was a critical review of a documentary film about the incidents produced by the office of Chicago Mayor Richard Daley.

7. CHAOS and COINTELPRO: Frank J. Donner, *The Age of Surveillance* (Vintage, 1981), 162–167; Todd Gitlin, *The Sixties: Years of Hope, Days of Rage* (Bantam, 1993), 378.

8. Letters to Mark Harris; interview with Don Lenzer; Charles Horman, "Public Television: The Producers Organize," *The Nation*, May 19, 1969.

9. Organizing efforts: Unpublished writings by Horman. He names as organizers of the Media Project Alan Young of Liberation News Service; Mike Locker of NACLA; and Mike Nolan, whose apartment hosted the meeting.

10. Email exchange with Joyce Horman.

11. Interview with Pablo de la Barra.

12. Letter to Don Lenzer, approximate date April 13, 1971. In undated letters to Lenzer dates are approximated from partial postmarks and internal references.

13. Freire's most notable work was *Pedagogy of the Oppressed* (1970), which described a literacy training method designed to liberate poor people to take charge of their own destiny. German psychologist Erich Fromm also lived in Cuernavaca and lectured occasionally at CIDOC. He wrote the introduction to one of Illich's books, *Celebration of Awareness: A Call for Institutional Revolution* (Penguin, 1973). Illich called for the "deschooling" of society and opposed compulsory education. Horman was attracted to the idea, writing to a friend he met at Cuernavaca that he wanted to create an open university project emulating CIDOC in the United States. Letter to Milton Jamail, May 3, 1971. At CIDOC virtually anybody could teach a course, since Illich refused to impose limits or requirements, much less teaching credentials or grades.

14. In addition to Mishy Lesser, these included Linda Wine and Janet Duecy. Cuernavaca: Interviews with Mishy Lesser, Richard Pearce, Milton Jamail, Linda Wine, in addition to my personal experience. Letter to Don Lenzer, approximate date May 13, 1971. After completing my degree work at Stanford I returned to Cuernavaca a second time, in October 1972.

15. Interview with Milton Jamail.

16. Letter to Don Lenzer, July 8, 1971.

17. Letter to Don Lenzer, November 25, 1971.

18. Travel through South America: Letters to Lenzer, May 17, 1971, June 19, 1971; Joyce Horman statement, November 10, 1973, after returning to the United States. Copy entered into evidence in Causa 2182-98 por el sequestro y homicidio de Frank Teruggi y Charles Horman, in the Chilean Appeals Court (hereafter referred to as "Chilean court case").

19. Among the few media profiles of Teruggi are: Paul Hoeffel, "Murder Chilean Style," *Attenzione*, July/August 1982; Norman Stockwell, "The Other 9/11: Seeking the Truth about Frank Teruggi," *The Progressive*, September 12, 2014; a longer version of Stockwell's piece, "A 41-Year Saga: Seeking the Truth in the Death of Frank Teruggi," *Tico Times*, October 17, 2014; and Janis Teruggi Page, "Did US Intelligence Help Pinochet's Junta Murder My Brother?," *Mother Jones*, September 21, 2013.

20. St. George's College was one of Chile's most progressive private schools, integrating working-class children on scholarships with the sons of affluent families able to pay the tuition. Several priests were arrested by the military after the coup. The award-winning movie *Machuca* (2004), directed by Andres Wood, told a coming-of-age story of students grappling with class discrimination and reacting to the violent takeover of the school by the military in 1973.

21. Biographical information on Teruggi: interviews and correspondence with Janis Teruggi Page, Shepherd Bliss and Roger Burbach. Page is quoted in Stockwell, "41-Year Saga," 2014.

22. Stockwell, "41-Year Saga," 2014. The picture of Teruggi appeared in the February 13, 1968, edition of the *Pasadena Star-News*.

23. Sworn statement in Alameda County, CA, from Michael Couzens, no date, provided to the author.

24. Interviews with Shepherd Bliss, Andy Scott Berman, Max Watts (aka Thomas Schwaetzer), and Karen Bixler, the Heidelberg activist in charge of copying and distributing 100 copies of the RITA newsletter *FighT bAck*. Berman gave a detailed account of RITA activities in an email to Janis Page, shared with the author by both Berman and Page.

25. Two FBI agents who served in the 1970s explained the markings and their meaning in interviews. FBI Director J. Edgar Hoover, a hardline anticommunist who ordered widespread surveillance of antiwar activists, died in May 1972, but surveillance of peaceful activists continued for several years.

26. FBI documents: Memorandum, To Acting Director FBI, from Legat Bonn, Subject Frank Teruggi, SM-Sub, October 15, 1972; Letterhead Memorandum (LHM), Department of Justice FBI, title [redacted], October 25, 1972; Memorandum, To Acting Director FBI, from Legat Bonn, Subject [redacted] SM-Subversive, November 28, 1972; Letterhead Memorandum (LHM), Department of Justice FBI, Chicago, Illinois, Frank Teruggi, December 14, 1972; Memorandum, To Acting Director FBI, from SAC Chicago, subject Frank Teruggi, SM-Subversive, December 14, 1972.

27. Letter addressed to Vince, Jerry, Guillermo, Nancy, Shep, Ed Sunshine, Elba, Carmen, Grant, Reri, etc, from Santiago, Chile, January 14, 1972.

28. Interview with Mishy Lesser.

29. Volunteer work: Interviews with Carlos Beust, Paulina Vidal, and Esther "Cuqui" Fuentes, who was also a participant. Letters from Teruggi to his parents, sister Janis, and friends. Janis Page provided copies of 30 letters from Chile, dated January 1972 to August 1973.

30. Allende's inaugural address is quoted in Paul E. Sigmund, *The Overthrow of Allende and the Politics of Chile, 1964-1976* (University of Pittsburgh Press, 1977), 130.

31. Economic policies: Sigmund, *The Overthrow of Allende*, 134-137.

32. Inflation stood at 22 percent, compared to 36 percent in the last year of the previous government. Former president Eduardo Frei, on seeing the success of Allende's policies, wrote a "stern letter" to his economic advisers, asking why they hadn't implemented a similar populist success during his government. See Daniel Mansuy, *Salvador Allende: La Izquierda Chilena y la Unidad Popular* (Taurus, 2023).

33. Simon Collier and William F. Sater, *A History of Chile, 1808-2002* (Cambridge University Press, 2004), 330.

34. Teruggi letter: April 30, 1972. Work at CESO: Interviews with Ramon Barceló, CESO fellow Patricia Fagen, Sergio Muñoz, and Diana Kay. Barceló quotation is from his court statement. Diana Kay remembered Teruggi's attendance in Hinkelammert's course

35. *El Mercurio*, January 16, 1973. The description of *FIN* quoted here was prepared for the 40th anniversary of the coup and presented at a dinner of the Horman Truth Project in 2013. It is cited in Stockwell, "41-Year Saga," 2014. The formation and membership of *FIN* were detailed in interviews with Steven Volk, Stephanie Campbell, and David Hathaway, among others from the group.

36. Letter to Don Lenzer, June 19, 1972.

37. Letters to Don Lenzer, June 19 and July 12, 1972.

38. Paul Harris house: interview with Janet Duecy. Money on hand and computer job: Joyce Horman, statement in Chilean court case, April 8, 2009.

39. *The Sunshine Grabber*: Copy with text and illustrations accessed at HormanTruth.org. Interviews with Joyce Horman, March 21, 2016, and Pablo de la Barra.

40. Schneider case: *El Caso Schneider: Operación Alfa* (Editorial Quimantú). The book is undated but the introduction is dated October 1972. The book includes a 50-page excerpt of the text of the verdict of the military court. In an interview, Joyce Horman said her husband was investigating the case "in the court records." U.S. involvement in the plot was revealed in *Covert Action in Chile, 1963-1973: Staff Report of the Select Committee to Study Governmental Operations with Respect to Intelligence Activities*, December 18, 1975. The

committee investigation was led by Sen. Frank Church, Idaho, and will be referred to hereafter as the Church Committee Report.

41. Letter to Don Lenzer, November 6, 1972.

42. Letter to Don Lenzer, December 12, 1972.

43. Film project: interview with Walter Locke; letter to Don Lenzer, December 12, 1972. Armstrong's comment is from Manitzas, "An American Murder in Chile," 22, unpublished manuscript, in Manitzas Papers.

44. Reyes is quoted in Sergio Trabucco Ponce, *Con los ojos abiertos: El Nuevo Cine chileno y el movimiento de Nuevo Cine latinoamericano* (LOM, 2016), 314–315. Reyes's film experience and street vendor avocation: p. 359.

45. Chile Films quotas: interviews and emails with filmmakers Dario Pulgar and Sergio Trabucco.

46. PICH stands for Policia de Investigaciones de Chile. The acronym was changed to PDI in the 2000s.

47. Hernán Cortés house: letter from Olga Muñoz to Janis Teruggi Page; interview with Fernando Alarcón.

48. Political affiliations: Interviews with Lance Compa, Olga Muñoz, Fernando Alarcón, David Hathaway, Janis Teruggi Page.

49. Economic crisis: Collier and Sater, *A History of Chile*, 333–337; Sigmund, *Overthrow of Allende*, 234–237. On copper price manipulation, Nixon commented, "Cutting the stockpile would hurt Chile and also save on the budget," in a meeting on November 6, 1973, recorded in "Memorandum of Conversation of a Meeting of the National Security Council," *Foreign Relations of the United States* (FRUS), 1969–1976, vol. 21, document 173. Election analysis is in Sigmund, *Overthrow of Allende*, 198–200; and Collier and Sater, *A History of Chile*, 351.

50. Allende statement on weapons: cited in Franck Gaudichaud, *Chile 1970–1973: Mil dias que estremecieron el mundo* (LOM, 2016), 318.

51. Allende call to arms: Sigmund, *Overthrow of Allende*, 215.

52. Teruggi's final letters, July 10, July 17, August 19, August 21, 1973.

53. The article was published after the coup as "Collision Course: Chile Before the Coup," *NACLA's Latin America & Empire Report*, October 1973. The article is credited to *FIN*, "a research and publishing group of North Americans in Santiago." Teruggi is the only author mentioned by name, in a note saying, "NACLA mourns the death of Frank Teruggi.... He died after the coup at the hands of the Pinochet junta." A shorter *FIN* article along the same lines appeared in the leftist weekly *The Guardian* a week before the coup.

54. Teruggi's final letters, July 10, July, 17, August 19 (about reading Trotsky) and August 21, 1973.

55. Letter to Don Lenzer, May 2, 1973.

56. Letter to Don Lenzer, March 29, 1973. Marc Cooper, a journalist but not part of the *FIN* group, said he attended several of the sessions but found them overly doctrinaire.

57. Leninism: Letter to Don Lenzer, May 2, 1973. Volunteer work: Letter to Don Lenzer, November 6, 1972.

58. Horman guarding: Armstrong interview with Frank Manitzas, October 1973. In "American Murder," 6, Manitzas writes: "In the turbulent months that followed, Horman was known to have worked briefly helping some pro-Allende construction unions guard a new housing area. Many were armed, but not Horman." The construction site on Cuarto Centenario Avenue was about a mile from Horman's house.

59. Letter to Don Lenzer, March 15, 1973. Horman expressed his misgivings about his accomplishments in several letters to Lenzer, including September 16, 1972.

60. Agenda in New York: Lluis Mestres, declaration in Chilean court case, April 6, 2004. Mestres's testimony referred to the film with Locke and the *Sunshine Grabber* project.

61. Thomas Hauser, *The Execution of Charles Horman: An American Sacrifice* (Harcourt Brace Jovanovich, 1978), 44–47.

62. Interviews with Don Lenzer, 2024.

63. It was Pearce's second visit: he had been part of the crew shooting the 1972 independent film *Que Hacer*, directed by Saul Landau, Nina Serrano and Jorge Ruiz.

64. Interviews and email exchanges with Dick Pearce, 2016 and 2023.

65. Interview with Jerry Cotts, 2024.

66. Weekend at beach house: interview with Simon Blattner, August 26, 2018. Begged to stay: Hauser, *Execution of Charles Horman*, 48.

67. Conversation about film: Interview with Walter Locke, May 17, 2016. Hauser's book says little about Horman's political activism. The New York trip was to see family. Hauser describes Horman as buying jeans, going to movies, eating hamburgers and shopping during his time in New York. "In between he raised money for a film he was planning on the transition to socialism under Allende." An unnamed "friend who contributed," said Horman, "made me understand what the social revolution in Chile was all about" (*Execution*, 45–48).

68. Arrived happy: Lluis Mestres, declaration in Chilean court case, April 6, 2004.

69. Email exchange with Joyce Horman, May 31, 2024, and April 27, 2024. The quotation is from the May 31 note. She said his use of the word "friends" indicated the request did not come directly from factory workers, because he would not have used that word to refer to workers. She learned about the fundraising for worker defense years later from their friends Dick Pearce and Don Lenzer, who had given Horman money.

70. Weapons manufacture: interview with Celsa Parrau. See also John Dinges, *Los Años del Condor: Operaciones Internacionales de Asesinato en el Cono*

Sur (Penguin Random House, 2021), 93. Uruguayan and Chilean leaders of the guerrilla alliance JCR (Junta Coordinadora Revolucionaria), which also included Bolivian and Argentine revolutionaries, told me about the weapons manufacture by "MIR technicians." They said the manufacturing operation was moved to Argentina before the Chilean coup. Drills at Chile Films: email exchange with Sergio Trabucco, a Chile Films employee.

71. Terrorist bombings: Sigmund, *Overthrow of Allende*, 228, and interviews with Roberto Thieme, the Patria y Libertad leader who carried out many of the bombing attacks.

72. MIR Central Force activities: interviews with Fernando Alarcón, Olga Muñoz and David Hathaway; interview with Andrés Pascal Allende, cited in *The Condor Years*.

73. Photos of ships: interviews with Carlos Beust and Paulo Santos. Horman had gone to Valparaiso with Walter Locke earlier in the year as part of the film project.

74. Navy revolt: The leaders of three parties confirmed the meetings in publications and interviews after the coup. MIR leader Andrés Pascal Allende described successful MIR activities to recruit both Naval and Army personnel in the weeks and months before the coup, in a 2000 interview cited in *The Condor Years*.

75. Interview with David Hathaway.

76. The black market rate for dollars was wildly fluctuating and hard to pin down around the time of the coup. U.S. Consul Fred Purdy, in an unpublished memoir obtained by the author, wrote that the rate was 3,000 escudo to $1, which declined to E 850 immediately after the coup. Prices for ordinary living expenses were amazingly low for those with access to dollars. In my case, I agreed to pay my landlord in dollars, at a rate of $50 a month, for a large house in Ñuñoa.

77. Dr. Núñez attended patients in the house, which according to Lluis Mestres included women seeking abortions—a procedure that was illegal in Chile but subject to lax enforcement. See court statements by Ariela Angelica Vecchi, Lluis Mestres and Joyce Horman.

78. None of his writings from September have surfaced. In an email exchange, Joyce Horman said, "I am not aware of any notes that he was writing in Valparaiso and Viña."

79. Email exchanges with Joyce Horman.

80. Trip to Viña: Statements and notes of Terry Simon (see Sources and Methods). No notes written by Charles Horman from the time have ever surfaced.

81. Coup events: Collier and Sater, *History of Chile*, 357; Sigmund, *Overthrow of Allende*, 242. The CIA had information that the Navy was prepared to act alone, with the support of the rightist civilian group Patria y Libertad. U.S. intelligence had advance notice of this possible scenario. The President's Daily Brief of

September 8 reported, "There are also indications that naval officers could be planning joint anti-government actions with militant civilian opponents. The far-rightist Fatherland and Freedom Movement has been blocking roads." In the first report to President Nixon the morning of September 11, intelligence briefers said, "In Chile, plans by navy officers to trigger military action reportedly have support of some key army units." It is perhaps notable that on the early morning of the coup U.S. intelligence was still uncertain if General Pinochet and the Army were fully on board. CIA, President's Daily Brief, September 8 and September 11, 1973. In fact, Pinochet, who had not been previously involved in coup preparations, met with Army, Navy and Air Force coup plotters over the weekend and gave his definitive approval on Sunday, September 9. See Monica González, *La Conjura: Los Mil y un Dias del Golpe* (Ediciones B, 2000), 303–326.

82. Interviews with Salazar, Santos, Vidal and Beust.

83. Allende's address: *Salvador Allende: Palabra y Acción* (Fondo de Cultura Económica Chile, 2020). Allende spoke to his followers five times between his arrival at La Moneda at 7:55 a.m. and his 9:10 a.m. farewell address.

84. Interview with Fernando Alarcón.

85. Interviews with Steve Volk and other *FIN* members; interviews with Carlos Beust and Paulo Santos.

86. Estimate from International Commission of Jurists, "The Application in Latin America of International Declarations and Conventions Relating to Asylum," September 1975. The vast majority of refugees were from Brazil, Bolivia, Uruguay, Paraguay and Argentina, which with Chile would later establish the Condor military alliance.

87. Military warning: *La Tercera*, September 16, 1973.

88. De la Barra set up Producciones Americana (PROA) to produce his film *Queridos Compañeros*, about MIR. De la Barra emphasized in our interview that the Hormans' animation project was completely separate from PROA, which operated out of his studio in downtown Santiago. He said the Hormans were "dear friends" (*queridos amigos*), and he probably would have done anything he could to help them, but he remembers nothing about the *Sunshine Grabber* project. "I was working in my company, they were working in their company.... They set up a company to make animated films, I had my company set up to make my film."

89. Simon's conversations with Creter, Ryan and Frauenfelder are recounted in Terry Simon, "Chapstick Papers," September 1973.

90. Creter remarks amplified: Simon, "An American Girl in Chile's Revolution." In Simon's statement of April 4, 1974, she renders it as "Creter explained that he was in Chile to do a job with the Navy."

91. Simon, "Chapstick Papers," September 1973.

92. Marvine Howe, "2 Americans Slain in Chile: The Unanswered Questions," *New York Times*, November 19, 1973. Howe attributes the statement to Joyce

Horman, who said she based it on information provided by her husband before his death and that "this was a reference to the coup." In her first statement after returning to the United States, however, she referred to Creter but did not put his statement in the context of the coup. See also the statement of Joyce Horman, November 10, 1973. Hauser quotes the statement exactly as rendered in the Howe article (*Execution*, 55, 235).

93. Navy statements about Creter: U.S. Navy Fort Amador Panama, cable November 23, 1973, "Interview with Art Creter"; Captain Ray E. Davis, letter to Commander in Chief U.S. Southern Command, January 14, 1975, "Case of Charles Horman." Davis says after reading the *New York Times* article, he "personally (at the ambassador's residence) advised Marvine Howe of the detailed technical aspect of Creeter's [sic] visit and about her inappropriate suggestion that Art Creeter's job was connected in any way with the coup of 11 September." The only part of the exchange quoted in the *New York Times* that he denied was the part about his work being "done." In an interview with author Thomas Hauser, he stated his work in Chile involved "repair of fire extinguishers on board Chilean vessels" and had "barely got off the ground" (*Execution*, 236).

94. Horman and Simon's activities with Ryan are in Simon, "Chapstick Papers," September 1973; and Simon, "Brief Chronology," November 1973. Ryan's description of the activities is in Department of Defense, "Resume of involvement of Navy mission members, Valparaiso, Chile, and COMUSMILGRP in Santiago in regards Charles Horman case . . .," prepared in December 1973 (labeled SC093); and Department of Defense, letter from Lt. Col. P.J. Ryan to Fred Purdy, U.S. Consul, October 8, 1974 (labeled SC120). *Esmeralda*: Stacie Jonas and Sarah Anderson, "This Tall Ship Has a Brutal, Bloody History: *La Esmeralda*," *Baltimore Sun*, June 18, 2000.

95. Incorrect intelligence reports: for example, a CIA Intelligence Information Report, September 22, 1973, said 500 people had been killed in the attack on La Legua and overall 3,000 to 5,000 killed in the country, according to CIA sources. The killings in the early weeks were carefully documented years later by the human rights investigation first published in 1991 as *Informe de la Comisión Nacional de Verdad y Reconciliación* (hereafter CNVR), the so-called Rettig Commission Report.

96. Simon, "Chapstick Papers," and Davis, Undated chronology September 14–September 29, 1973. Davis's account of the ride is in two memoranda. The first document is untitled, September 30, 1973; the second is "Memorandum of Record 1 Oct 1973, Captain Davis-Mrs. Horman." The two memoranda are a detailed chronology of Davis's contacts with Charles Horman, Terry Simon and Joyce Horman, from September 14 to October 1, 1973.

97. Factories near Horman's house: Formerly the American-owned ITT, Standard Electric was the main manufacturer of telephones and switching equipment. After the revelations of ITT and CIA intervention in the 1970 elec-

tion, the factory was one of the first to be expropriated. Interviews with Guillermo Orrego, October 2018. Events at Textile Progreso were recounted by Orrego, and in a published interview with the factory's controller, Heriberto Medina, "El Tesonero Tejido de la Memoria," February 26, 2016, https://formasdellamar.wordpress.com/tag/textil-progreso.

98. Fighting at Sumar and La Legua: Gaudichaud, *Chile 1970-1973*, 390-391; and interviews with Orrego.

99. Gaudichaud, *Chile 1970-1973*, 391.

100. MIR's arms caches: interview with Andrés Pascal Allende. New details of the Cuban shipments were revealed in Tanya Harmer, *Allende's Chile and the Inter-American Cold War* (UBC Press, 2011), 232-234. In interviews with Harmer, Cuban intelligence officer Ulises Estrada discussed the details of the shipments and the Chileans' ultimate failure to distribute the weapons. GAP means "Grupo de Amigos Personales."

101. Simon, "An American Girl in Chile's Revolution."

102. Joyce Horman, November 10, 1973, statement; Mestres testimony, June 4, 2004, Chilean court case; interview with Manitzas, October 1973; Manitzas, "American Murder," 8. The idea that Horman was frightened by the meetings with officers in Viña and Valparaiso does not appear in contemporaneous statements. In statements much later, after the public narrative linking the Viña events to Horman's death was well established, both Joyce Horman and Mestres added that that Charles Horman expressed fear about what happened with the American officers. In an interview with the author in 2016, for example, Joyce said her husband was "terrified by Ray Davis," and "saw evil in his eyes."

103. Handwritten notes described as "Brief chronology of events from Thurs. Sept. 13 to Wed Sept 19 (Terry Simon and Charles Horman's trip to Viña and return). Told by TS [Terry Simon]," in Manitzas Papers, hereafter "Simon handwritten chronology." Steve Volk confirmed the handwriting is his, although neither he nor Simon remember preparing the handwritten notes. Major details in the notes coincide with testimony by Simon, Joyce Horman and Lluis Mestres, and there are no factual contradictions between the notes and those accounts. Simon remembers some of the details differently 50 years later. She said Bob High and Mestres were not at the house when they arrived. But both Joyce Horman and Mestres, in their testimony, confirm Mestres's presence. High was a friend of the Hormans who had been a frequent visitor at their previous house on Paul Harris Street.

104. Keeping books and papers: Manitzas interview with Joyce Horman, October 1973 (Manitzas Papers); Manitzas, "American Murder," 8-10.

105. Meeting with film crew: Jorge Reyes, "Testimony of Jorge Reyes" and "Avenue of the Americas: The Story of a Film and Its Shooting," April 14, 2018, https://nanopdf.com/download/read-the-testimony-of-jorge-reyes-in-format_pdf. Reyes writes that he and Horman met in the UNCTAD cafeteria on Alameda

near the Catholic University. More likely they met somewhere nearby, since after the coup the military government immediately occupied the UNCTAD conference center and eventually converted an adjoining building, Edificio Diego Portales, into the headquarters for the military junta.

106. Chile Films raid: Hubner's account is quoted in two articles: Daniel Zegers, "Cuando el Golpe llegó a Chile Films," *El Dinamo*, September 13, 2011; and Jaime Alexis Quintana, "El Golpe al Cine Chileno," *La Nacion*, September 12, 2004. The mass execution of Paredes and others is documented by CNVR, Tomo 1, 133, and in Memoria Viva, https://memoriaviva.com, which puts the number of those killed at 27. The false report on Paredes was published in *El Mercurio*, September 14, 1973.

107. Alejandro de la Barra and his wife, Ana Maria Puga, lived clandestinely under assumed identities for more than a year. DINA agents shot and killed them in December 1974 in an ambush at a childcare center where they went to pick up their young child. See https://memoriaviva.com/nuevaweb/ejecutados-politicos/ejecutados-politicos-d/de-la-barra-villarroel-alejandro.

108. Raid on de la Barra's studio and use of Horman house: interview with de la Barra. The address of his studio (*productora*) was Calle Constitución 88.13.

PART II. THE SEARCH

1. *El Mercurio*, September 17, 1973.
2. The most complete account of activities in the National Stadium is Pascale Bonnefoy, *Terrorismo de Estadio: Prisioneros de guerra en un campo de deportes*, 2nd expanded ed. (Editorial Latinoamericana, 2016). Espinóza's role is mentioned there and in U.S. documents describing the statements to an Embassy officer by former SIM operative Raúl Meneses. See David Dreher, memo to DCM, April 20, 1987.
3. CAJSI system: Bonnefoy, *Terrorismo de Estadio*, 22–23.
4. The Red Cross estimate is cited in *Informe de la Comisión Nacional de Verdad y Reconciliación* (hereafter CNVR), vol. 1 (1996), 128. Death tolls could not be reliably determined until years after the events. Data from official investigative commissions, updated as of 2019, show that 416 people were killed in the first six days, before people were called back to work on September 17, including about 25 members of the military.
5. Elecmetal arrests: CNVR, vol. 1, 157; Memoria Viva, citing resumen.cl, August 12, 2021. The victims were identified as Augusto Andino Alcayaga Aldunate (president of the employees unión), José Rosa Devia Devia, José Maldonado Fuentes, Miguel Alberto Fernández Cuevas, his brother Juan Dagoberto Fernández Cuevas, and Francisco Flores Flores. Cruces escaped into exile and eventually returned to Chile, but has been reluctant to speak publicly. Historian

Dolores Mujica, in *Cordones Industriales: Cronología Comentada* (Ediciones Museo Obrero Luis Emilio Recabarran, 2013), says she was able to locate him and confirms that he was among the union leaders detained that day. Raids at other factories: *El Mercurio*, September 18, 1973.

6. Joyce Horman statement, November 10, 1973.

7. Encounter with Manitzas: Simon handwritten chronology; Manitzas, "American Murder"; Simon testimony, July 17, 2001, Chilean court case. Later press reports that Horman and Simon asked for protection or asylum in the Embassy and were refused are not borne out in contemporary accounts by Simon and Manitzas. After one such report in 1974, a State Department official called Simon at her home in New York. She repeated that officials at the Embassy and Consulate were not helpful in finding a flight, but she denied she had asked for asylum or refuge. "No, there was no need for either of us to seek political asylum," the official quoted her as saying (Arnold Isaacs, "Charge that Embassy Denied Asylum to Charles Horman," March 8, 1974, Department of State).

8. Consulate visit: Simon handwritten chronology; Simon testimony, July 17, 2001, Chilean court case.

9. Horman's intention to write: Mestres testimony, Chilean court case. Final writing: letter to Joyce, in Manitzas Papers. Manitzas said he obtained it during one of his visits to the abandoned Horman house in the weeks after his disappearance. He sent it to Ed and Joyce, who said she had not seen it before. The note clearly was written at the house the afternoon of September 17. The first sentence says: "Tried to phone out here a few times but I guess the doctor and his wife were out all day." See also Manitzas, "American Murder," 21.

10. Horman's detention: Eyewitness testimony by Ariela Vecchi (Mrs. Núñez), November 9, 2003; Mireya Guerra (Vecchi's friend, who reported what she saw to Vecchi); and neighbors in nearby apartments: Leticia Frias (December 1, 2003), Victoria Osorio and her husband, Jorge Rodriguez (December 4, 2003), Chilean court case; PICH Report 16, December 15, 2003. Terry Simon's handwritten chronology (Manitzas Papers), says she and Horman spoke to Mrs. Núñez on Sunday and she said that Carabineros had come to the house on Saturday and said "they might want to take it over for a police HQ."

11. Military information: Raúl Meneses, statements to Embassy officer David Dreher, 1987; interviews with Raúl Meneses and Jaime Ortiz by Pascale Bonnefoy, 2016.

12. Calls from SIM: Testimony of Isabella Rastello (October 18, 2004), Chilean court case; statement of Mario Carvajal to the U.S. consulate, September 18, 1973; account of call to Warwick Armstrong and his actions, Santiago 5668, "Senator Javits interest in Horman Case," November 18, 1973; and a summary of the events involving the calls in Frederick Smith, "Death in Chile of Charles Horman," State Department memo, December 1976, 3. The memorandum is a 26-page, meticulously documented report on the case prepared at the

instruction of Assistant Secretary of State for Latin America Harry W. Shlaudeman.

13. Joyce Horman statement, November 10, 1973; testimony, July 10, 2002, Chilean court case; testimony of Lluis Mestres, April 6, 2004, Chilean court case; interview with Manitzas, October 1973. Joyce Horman said three people "from a neighboring lot" came to speak to them and told them the military had come three times the night before, and that they should leave immediately. Mestres says they also talked to the landlord as well as to a neighbor, a woman, who said the military had detained Charles.

14. Stay at Heliette Saint Jean house: Joyce Horman testimony, July 10, 2002, Chilean court case.

15. Interview with David Hathaway, February 14, 2023.

16. Helpful but abrupt: Interview with anonymous. The comment about his idea of democracy is from her testimony in the Chilean court case. Teruggi's friend Steve Volk was one of those who thought Frank's sometimes brash manner might have been a factor in what happened. "I could see him pissing off an investigating officer, saying something stupid, assuming as we all did that we had certain immunity" as Americans (interview, May 20, 2016).

17. Teruggi and Hathaway arrest and subsequent events: "Statement made by David Hathaway on the Disappearance of Frank Teruggi in Chile," September 30, 1973 (transcription of tape recording); David Hathaway testimony, July 7, 2001, Chilean court case; letter from Hathaway to Charles Anderson, Department of State, January 23, 1974; interview with Hathaway.

18. The six were later identified as Óscar Ernesto Pizarro Vicencio (2828), Aerolite government controller (*interventor*); Miguel Hernán Arancibia Castillo (2829), Aerolite union member; Ernesto Vásquez Godoy (2830), MIR, adviser to Pizarro; Nelson Gonzalo Durán Castillo (2831), former Marine corpsman, 22 years old; Frank Randall Teruggi Bombatch (2832); and Guillermo Osvaldo Vallejos Ferdinand (2833), adviser to Pizarro.

19. Bodies at morgue: SML Libro Transfer, the handwritten log book recording all incoming bodies, at the Santiago Servicio Medico Legal, aka the Morgue, photographic copy in possession of author; Database ArchivosChile.com, which combines SML data from the "Transfer" book, autopsies and other SML records with the human rights database of the CNVR, available at https://archivoschile.com/ejecuciones-chile-1973.

20. Accounts of torture: Gladys Marín, statement delivered to Frank Teruggi, Sr., during his visit in Chile February 1974. Copy in Spanish and English translation included among U.S. declassified documents. Marín, who in democracy became head of the Chilean Communist Party, said the students who spoke to her did not recognize the name Teruggi, but were sure the name of the fellow student they spoke to was "Frank" and that he said he was North American. She says

she conveyed the information "indirectly" (*en forma indirecta*) to the Catholic Church in early October 1973.

21. Frank Teruggi, Sr., letter to Frank Manitzas, November 4, 1975, Manitzas Papers. The letter said Velastín was a former director of a La Florida school, and had been a candidate for governor of Los Andes province. Teruggi had been told Velastín was in exile in Sweden, but was not able to locate him. Victor Velastín Rodriguez, identified as "professor," is listed as a detainee in the National Stadium in Manuel Contreras, *La Verdad Historica: El Ejercito Guerrillero* (Ediciones Encina, 2000). Teruggi's letter spells the name "Velestin Rodrigues." I reached Velastín's daughter in 2023. She said he had died in Chile more than a decade earlier.

22. Van Lancker affidavit, "Subject: Frank Teruggi, U.S. Citizen," November 4, 1975.

23. "No capacity": Viron P. Vaky, Analytical Summary of Options Paper for NSC Discussion, November 3, 1970, FRUS, vol. E-16, document 34. U.S. plan: Kissinger describes the plan he favored in a memo to Nixon, Kissinger, Memorandum for the President, November 5, 1970. Nixon approved Kissinger's preferred policy option the next day.

24. CIA cable [General Pinochet's Views on Allende], September 27, 1972, reproduced in Peter Kornbluh, *The Pinochet File: A Declassified Dossier on Atrocity and Accountability* (The New Press, 2003), 144–145.

25. Transcript of a telephone conversation between the President's Assistant for National Security Affairs (Kissinger) and President Nixon, September 16, 1973, FRUS, vol. 21, document 357.

26. Santiago 4154, Gen. Pinochet's Request for Meeting with MilGp Officer, September 12, 1973, FRUS, vol. 21, document 350.

27. Foreign prisoners: Database compiled by the author and summarized in John Dinges, *Los Años del Condor: Operaciones Internacionales de Asesinato en el Cono Sur* (Penguin Random House, 2021), 15 and annex 5. Foreign interrogators: Bonnefoy, *Terrorismo de Estadio*, 174–175.

28. Asylees in embassies and safe houses: Comision Interamericana de Derechos Humanos, *Informe sobre la situación de los derechos humanos en Chile, 1974, Cap. 13,* http://www.cidh.org/countryrep/Chile74sp/Indice.htm. UNHCR, "Chile durante el régimen del general Pinochet," in *La situación de los refugiados en el mundo: Cincuenta años de acción humanitaria* (UNHCR, 2000).

29. Email exchange with Joyce Horman, August 10, 2023.

30. Embassy note: Diplomatic note No. 378, September 28, 1973. The note, which was not included in any of the collections of declassified documents on Chile, was obtained from the archives of the Chilean Foreign Ministry.

31. Lists and Consular access: Santiago 4339, September 17, 1973; Santiago 4442, September 20, 1973 (listing Horman); September 20 press briefing: transcript, State 187854, September 21, 1973 (FRUS, vol. E-16).

32. Access denied: Santiago 4442, "Detained or Missing U.S. Citizens in Chile," September 20, 1973, which names Horman, has the annotation "Consul unable visit in spite of repeated requests" in reference to Adam Schesch, a graduate student from the University of Wisconsin, whose status as a prisoner in the Stadium was confirmed by the junta. A similar notation of denial of access was attached to the name of Joseph Dougherty, a Maryknoll priest.

33. Santiago 4462, "Detained Americans," September 21, 1973.

34. State 187383, "Detained Americans," September 20, 1973.

35. Interview with Fred Purdy, 2007. Purdy said he was contacted in about 1990 by a former officer in Chilean military intelligence who was close to General Pinochet. The officer offered what amounted to a bribe if Purdy would say publicly that Michael Townley worked for the CIA. Purdy refused, because he did not know it to be true. After the encounter, he said, "I went home paranoid."

36. Anderson's CIA identity was confirmed many years ago to the author in interviews with FBI agents and Embassy officials, to whom it was well known. Anderson spoke to the *Washington Post* about the Horman-Teruggi case and his CIA identity is stated in the article: Vernon Loeb, "Files Raise Questions on Journalist's Death; Did U.S. Agents Finger American to Chile?," *Washington Post*, November 19, 2000.

37. Anderson's contacts: Santiago 6111, Secret-Noforn-Roger Channel, "González Allegations Re Horman Case," June 23, 1976. The cable from Ambassador Popper to Assistant Secretary Shlaudeman, protected with a high level of classification, recounts comments by Rafael González to U.S. Consul Brownell about Anderson. González claimed he had known Anderson socially since 1972 and was aware of his "dual role" as consular officer and CIA operative.

38. U.S. policy: Kornbluh, *The Pinochet File*, 201ff, documents this policy, which included coaching Chile's new ambassador to the United Nations in countering fierce international criticism of the new government.

39. Interview with Jeffrey Davidow, 2024.

40. Robert S. Steven, Oral History, August 3, 2001, Association for Diplomatic Studies and Training Foreign Affairs Oral History Project. The author had three long interviews with Steven in November 2000, and a fourth in August 2016; the quotation in the following paragraph is from the 2016 interview.

41. Minutes of a Meeting of the Washington Special Actions Group, September 14, 1973, FRUS, vol. 21, document 353.

42. Policia de Investigaciones de Chile. The acronym was changed to PDI, for Policia de Investigaciones, after the return to civilian government.

43. Accounts of U.S. action: Statements by Consul Purdy, Captain Davis, Colonel Hon. The State Department prepared several separate chronologies of actions taken with regard to Horman and Teruggi. The chronologies summarize information from individual statements and cables to and from the State Department. I checked the chronologies against the original statements and did not

find significant discrepancies. The most extensive official account is the 26-page analytical report by Frederick Smith, "Death in Chile of Charles Horman," State Department memo (hereafter "Smith report").

44. Purdy visit: "Chronology of Information Received and Actions Taken Concerning Welfare and Whereabouts in Chile of Charles Edmund Horman," updated version dated December 10, 1976. Purdy's personal account is in his unfinished and untitled memoir, dated 1991, provided by his wife, Gigi Mohn Purdy.

45. Testimony in Chilean court case, PDI report 16.

46. Cable: Santiago 4442, "Detained or Missing US Citizens in Chile," September 20, 1973. Besides Horman, the detained Americans listed were Mohamed Aicha Abeid, a laboratory technician from Texas later determined to be a Kuwaiti citizen; Carol Rich Andreas, from Kansas; Joseph Dougherty and Francis Flynn, both Maryknoll priests; Schesch and Garrett, with the note "Still detained at National Stadium and Consul unable visit in spite of repeated attempts"; Carol Nezzo, a Methodist Church worker who was detained with the two priests; and Julius Wool, no information. Koch speech: reported in cable, October 1, 1973.

47. The Civil Registry's fingerprint department actually sent an official report (number 22,445) to the morgue the previous day, Monday, September 24, the same day Volk reported him missing. The report identified Teruggi and 22 other deceased persons. The document was obtained by Archivos Chile in 2011 using Chile's access to information law. See Archivos Chile, "Registro Civil: Identidades cruzadas, cuerpos sin nombre," https://archivoschile.com/registro-civil.

48. Fingerprint identification and subsequent false statements: Santiago 4588, September 25, 1973; Santiago 4594, September 26, 1973; Santiago 4638, September 27, 1973. DOS, Chronology of Information Relevant to Frank Randall Teruggi (primarily from Santiago and State Telegrams), October 5, 1973.

49. Interview with David Hathaway.

50. Identification of Teruggi: Fred Purdy, Chronology of Teruggi case, September 24–October 29, 1973; Volk statement to CNVR, December 3, 1990, and interview with author; CIA, Telegram from the Station in Chile, Santiago, November 24, 1973, in FRUS, vol. E-11, part 2, document 154.

51. Submission of Horman fingerprint record: This key fact is contained in two reports to the Minister of Interior by PDI detective Mario Rojas, October 20 and 21, 1973, in Chilean court case, 1899–1903.

52. Enrique Sandoval deposition in Horman v. Kissinger, January 24, 1979; testimony in Chilean court case by Enrique Sandoval and Nelson Sandoval, 3381–3385. Affidavit by Judd L. Kessler in Horman v. Kissinger, November 30, 1987; interview with Judd Kessler. Purdy testimony in Chilean court case, 0976 and 1382, May 10, 2002. Joyce Horman statement, November 10, 1973.

53. The plot, in which Valenzuela's group worked together with a group led by retired General Roberto Viaux, resulted in the murder of Army Commander

General Rene Schneider. A new investigative account of the CIA's involvement in the plan to kidnap General Schneider is Jefferson Morley, *Scorpion's Dance: The President, the Spymaster and Watergate* (St. Martin's, 2022), 132-138.

54. Joyce Horman describes the contact with Valenzuela in her November 10, 1973, statement, an early copy of which was obtained from the Manitzas Papers. A somewhat modified version of the statement was submitted to the Chilean court in approximately 2001. Colonel Hon quotes Carvajal in Memorandum for the Record, "Efforts to Locate Charles Edmund Horman," October 4, 1973 (hereafter "Hon memorandum"). De la Barra's political party: Interview with *Últimas Noticias*, September 11, 2023, https://www.youtube.com/watch?v=t1KF0qXzcKA.

55. Memorándum reservado No. 3560/6, del Jefe del Estado Mayor de la Defensa Nacional al Ministerio de Relaciones Exteriores, 24 de septiembre 1973, Chilean court case.

56. Hon memorandum, October 4, 1973. Much the same information about actions by U.S. Embassy personnel is summarized in a handwritten chronology attached to a January 23, 1976, memorandum, INR Roger Kirk to INR/DDC Verne Jennings.

57. According to Urrutia, Morel presented the questions to General Brady, in charge of the countrywide CAJSI command, and General Sergio Arrellano, commander of *Agrupación Centro*, the Central Army Group, which operated in the Vicuña Mackenna area (Col. Carlos E. Urrutia, memorandum for the record, "Status of US Citizen," September 29, 1973, declassified U.S. documents).

58. Morel response: Urrutia memorandum.

59. Names on lists: "Chronology of Mission Activities in Teruggi Case," September 24–27, 1973, prepared by the Consulate, which states that neither Hathaway nor Teruggi appeared on any list inspected as of September 24. Another document, "Chronology of Teruggi Case," prepared by Vice-Consul James Anderson, points out the discrepancy of the lists. Such chronologies were maintained and updated by Embassy officers as late as late 1976.

60. Anderson investigation: Memorandum for the Record: Charles Edmund Horman, October 1, 1973. Anderson visited both 4126 Vicuña Mackenna and 2575 Hernán Cortés (Horman's and Teruggi's homes, respectively) to interview neighbors and take inventory of the contents of the houses. He also went to the two Carabinero stations nearest Horman's address, San Joaquin and Macul, where policemen said they knew nothing. He also interviewed Steven Volk about the Hormans, recorded in a second memorandum with same title and date: "Volk said that the Hormans are a very nice couple and apparently have a good family relationship, although both are rather independent. In the past she has gone on vacation alone, as has he. For example, Mr. Horman travelled to the U.S. alone during the month of August and returned to Chile early in September. On 10 September he travelled to Valparaiso with Miss Terry Simon, a friend who had returned to Chile from the U.S. with him."

61. Joyce Horman statement, November 10, 1973, copy found in Manitzas Papers.

62. Davis sent Colonel Ryan to obtain Hotel Miramar records and included the room number where Horman and Simon stayed in his reports. Horman said the most direct comment came from consular official Schaeffer, who "suggest[ed] that Charles was in hiding because he did not want to see me. I assured Mr. Schaeffer that this was impossible" (Joyce Horman statement, November 10, 1973). Horman's friend Lluis Mestres, in his 1973 interview with Frank Manitzas, said Joyce Horman told him about the conversation with Davis, quoting him saying the embassy officials assigned to investigate "might lose interest in the case . . . if they knew about him and Terry" sharing a room. A State Department chronology, January 1, 1976, which compiles previous Embassy reports, makes a similar allusion.

63. Ministry of Foreign Relations notes 15125 and 15126, October 3, 1973. The notes are found in the Chilean court case and in the declassified U.S. documents (Chile Project).

64. Horman letter to Charles Anderson, State Department, September 28, 1973.

65. Thomas Hauser, *The Execution of Charles Horman: An American Sacrifice* (Harcourt Brace Jovanovich, 1978), 144.

66. State Department document, October 3, 1973, listing telegrams received between September 26 and October 3, 1973, passed on to the Santiago Embassy. Signatories included Senator Frank Church of Idaho, Congressmen Ed Koch of New York, Edward Mezvinsky of Iowa, and Republican Jack Kemp from New York. Sixty-seven signatures were from the Motion Picture Editors Union of New York.

67. Ed Horman took careful notes and memorialized his visit in several documents. "Statement of Edmund C. Horman," February 28, 1974, and attached "Diary-Edmund Horman," 10 pages, documents entered in evidence in Chilean court case. Except as otherwise noted all description of Horman's trip is from these sources.

68. Purdy testimony, May 10, 2002, Chilean court case.

69. The FBI sent a photographic copy of Horman's prints in addition to numeric codes used in fingerprint identification. According to U.S. declassified documents, the prints arrived on October 2. The Embassy delivered the sets to the Foreign Ministry on October 3, and they were then conveyed to the Identifications Bureau of the Interior Ministry on October 6. The relevant documents, in the special collection regarding the Horman case, are SC026, SC026A, SC041, and SC041A, all dated between October 2 and October 9, 1973. There is no evidence any of the requested fingerprint checks were actually carried out.

70. Santiago 4992, "Conversation with Pinochet," October 12, 1973.

71. Col. W. M. Hon, Defense Attaché, Memorandum for the Records, October 16, 1973. Lutz reprised what was becoming the standard cover story: "His

theory is that Terruggi [sic] was picked up by his friends and ultimately disposed of. Gen. Lutz said they have knowledge that Terruggi was here in Chile to spread false rumors to the outside world relating to Chile and the situation. Concerning Charles Horman, Gen. Lutz said they have no record of Horman being detained or was ever in the National Stadium. His theory is that during this particular time of his disappearance groups of robbers or extremists dressed in soldier uniforms were making searches and robberies of houses known to be occupied by North-Americans and foreigners for the purpose of finding dollars or other saleable merchandise." The Smith report mentions the conversation with Lutz as taking place in person on October 15.

72. Statement of Edmund C. Horman and "Diary-Edmund Horman"; Pascale Bonnefoy interviews in 2016 with Meneses and Ortiz; John Dinges interview with David Dreher, July 7, 2016; Dreher declassified memos to file and cables about his three meetings with Raúl Meneses. These heavily redacted memos are dated March 3, April 20 and April 24, 1987. The cables are State 100094, April 3, 1987 (quoting Santiago 2440, dated April 2, 1987); Santiago 3059, "Reports on GOC Involvement in Death of Charles Horman," April 28, 1987; State 1465, "Reports on Death of Charles Horman," May 14, 1987; Santiago 4395, "Horman Case: Embassy Views on Credibility of Source," June 16, 1987. Meneses's name is redacted in all of these documents with the exception of State 100094, April 3, 1987 (quoting Santiago 2440, dated April 2, 1987). This key document, released in full in October 2015 and discovered by the author, unlocked Meneses's identity in all the other documents. Bonnefoy's interviews contain the detail that Pinochet gave the order to Lutz. Meneses gave a final interview, which was facilitated by the author, with the daughter of General Lutz, Olga Lutz, May 23, 2024.

73. The cable was from Foreign Minister Ismael Huerta, who spoke at the UN General Assembly on October 8 to defend the Chilean coup. It described the pressure generated by Horman's father among U.S. congress members, and recommended maximum speed in finding the body. See Bonnefoy, *Terrorismo de Estadio*, 208.

74. The Army's Escuela Militar—Military Academy—is the equivalent of West Point Military Academy in the United States and has a large campus on Americo Vespucio Avenue in Las Condes. Some prisoners, mostly high-profile leaders of the Popular Unity, were held at the facility.

75. Department III was commanded by Lt. Colonel Roberto Soto Mackenney, who was deposed by Judge Zepeda in 2003. He acknowledged being chief of Department III Operations, but denied any knowledge of Horman or any other detentions. At the time of Soto's testimony, Judge Zepeda knew nothing about the version of events from Meneses and Ortiz, whom he had been unable to locate; he was told they were probably false names.

76. Horman diary. The officers' names, with the same misspelling of "Manesas," are cited in Hauser's 1978 book *Execution* (170). In other entries in the diary, Horman gives the men's correct first names: Raúl and Jaime. According to Horman, the two SIM officers' second visit was the next day, October 17. See also Horman, letter to Senator William Fulbright, October 25, 1973; Meneses interview with Maria Olga Lutz Herrera and Rodrigo Lledó, her lawyer, May 23, 2024. In the interview Meneses confirmed his unit was assigned to the search for weapons in Cordones factories before the coup, adding that the only weapons they found were *"linchacos"*—devices used in martial arts consisting of two wooden clubs connected by a short chain. The weapon is also called nunchaku.

77. Interview with Jarvis; Ed Horman's diary. Jarvis's source was Mark Dolgin, an officer in the Canadian embassy. Dolgin got the information from Enrique Sandoval, the same source who had talked to Embassy officer Judd Kessler two weeks earlier. Dolgin said Sandoval had contacted him after seeing no action from the Embassy.

78. Meneses interview with Bonnefoy.

79. Purdy fingerprint check: Santiago 5128, "Apparent Verification of Identity in Case of Charles Edmund Horman," October 19, 1973. Purdy reported that the fingerprint card taken at the morgue contained an error in the numeric classification for the little finger of the left hand, "3 instead of 2." He reported that the error "may—repeat—may have been the reason for failure of identification when check for identification first made." The mistake was technical and not sufficient to account for the failure to identify Horman based on the other fingerprints. But later U.S. documents (for example, Edmund Muskie, In Camera Affidavit and Claim of Privilege by the Secretary of State, submitted in case 77-1748, July 16, 1980) referred to Purdy's statement as justification for the one-month delay in identifying Horman's body in the morgue.

80. Pascale Bonnefoy and John Dinges, *Burocracia de la Muerte*, "El agujero negro de las fiscalías militares" (2011), https://archivoschile.com/investigaciones/burocracia-de-la-muerte and https://archivoschile.com/fiscalias-militares. Our investigation established that the Fiscalia Militar did not open a criminal investigation in a single case of a person arriving at the morgue with gunshot wounds from September 11 to the end of the year.

81. Commission on Truth and Reconciliation, list of victims as updated in 2019. Spreadsheet in author's files.

82. Bonnefoy and Dinges, Burocracia de la Muerte, "Registro Civil," https://archivoschile.com/registro-civil. Using the morgue log book "Transfer" for the September–December 1973 period, Archivos Chile confirmed that more than 500 bodies entered the morgue as NN. All but 80 were identified by fingerprint checks with the Civil Registry database.

83. Joyce Horman, Declaration to PICH detective Mario Rojas, October 18, 1973, in Chilean court case, 1906–1907.

84. PICH detectives also interviewed Dr. Núñez, owner of Horman's rental home, according to Núñez's wife, Ariela Vecchi, in her testimony in Chilean court case.

85. Report to Chief of Department of Information (PDI), October 20, 1973, referencing Oficio No. 14, October 17, 1973, Santiago, signed Mario Rojas Chaves, Inspector, Grupo de Extranjeros [Unit for foreigners], Chilean court case, 1903–1904.

86. Rojas reports on interviews with Housset, November 22, 1973; and with Goycolea, November 29, 1973, Chilean court case 1985-86, and 1899-1902.

87. Purdy manuscript Chapter V, 15.

88. Among the indications that Horman's body was moved is the fact that two of Horman's friends, David Hathaway and Steve Volk, did not see him when they were taken to view bodies in the morgue on September 27 and October 2. Morgue records indicate Horman's body was interred in the General Cemetery on October 3. After his identification on October 18, Embassy officials were told the body was back in the morgue. Some time after that it was reinterred in a niche in the cemetery, where it was located in March 1974 and transported to the United States. The motivation behind these movements could not be learned, but they were unusual and atypical of morgue procedures.

89. Hon memorandum, October 4, 1973.

90. Memorandum, "Antecedents on Two Northamerican citizens' deceses" (sic), translation by the U.S. Embassy of memo in Spanish of "Antecedentes sobre fallecimiento de 2 ciudadanos norteamericanos," unsigned, attached to an Embassy memorandum for the records by Defense Attaché Col. W. M. Hon, November 2, 1973. Embassy reports attribute the report to General Lutz. Whether he authored it is not known, but it certainly was created under his authority as head of intelligence. For intelligibility, I have corrected the translation, including of the title (hereafter "Lutz memo").

91. Santiago 5391, "Continued Mission Activity in Horman and Teruggi Cases," November 2, 1973. The cable is signed by DCM Herbert Thompson, because Ambassador Davis had left the previous day.

92. FBI documents: Memorandum, To Acting Director FBI, from Legat Bonn, Subject Frank Teruggi, SM-Sub, October 15, 1972; Letterhead Memorandum (LHM), Department of Justice FBI, title [redacted], October 25, 1972; Memorandum, To Acting Director FBI, from Legat Bonn, Subject [redacted] SM-Subversive, November 28, 1972; Letterhead Memorandum (LHM), Department of Justice FBI, Chicago, Illinois, Frank Teruggi, December 14, 1972; Memorandum, To Acting Director FBI, from SAC Chicago, subject Frank Teruggi, SM-Subversive, December 14, 1972.

93. Interview with Robert Steven. Fimbres raised the issue in a long analytical memo, "The Charles Horman Case," August 25, 1976.

94. Guzmán conversation: Robert Steven to [DCM] Thompson, "Horman-Teruggi Cases," December 6, 1973.

95. Interview with Robert Steven.

96. Consul Purdy, for example, said he had received information portraying Horman as a dangerous leftist. According to Chilean detective Sandro Gaete, Purdy said Horman was "more than an activist" and was involved with MIR in connection with weapons. Gaete said he presumed Purdy got the information from Embassy "intelligence channels." Gaete and Judge Zepeda interviewed Purdy at his home in the early 2000s, but Gaete said they had not included the statement about weapons in the official account of the interview presented in evidence in the court case because Purdy made the comments "informally" (interview with Sandro Gaete, October 2018). Zepeda's presentation of the case in the final *Sentencia* (verdict) says almost nothing about political activities in Chile by Horman and Teruggi.

97. Intelligence information: The spokesman, probably Federico Willoughby, is quoted in Marvine Howe, "2 Americans Slain in Chile: The Unanswered Questions," *New York Times*, November 19, 1973. Bonilla's comment is cited in Memorandum of Conversation, General Oscar Bonilla, David Popper and Daniel Arzac, March 4, 1974. Bonilla told Popper he had met with Frank Teruggi, Sr., Teruggi's father, and promised to investigate.

98. *New York Times*, October 21, 1973; Ed Horman, handwritten notes in Manitzas Papers.

99. *New York Post*, October 23, 1973, story by Josh Friedman. Horman's conversation with Marshall is in her memo, "Horman and the New York Post," October 24, 1973.

100. Press guidance: State 212796, to Santiago Embassy, October 29, 1973, drafted by K[atharine] Marshall.

101. Ed Horman, letter to Sen. J. William Fulbright, October 25, 1973.

PART III. UNRAVELING THE TRUTH

1. "Victim's Father Is Bitter at U.S. Handling of Case," *New York Times*, November 19, 1973. In other coverage, Jack Anderson, in his "Washington Merry-Go-Round" column, criticized how Joyce and Ed Horman were treated in Santiago. The column was headed "Callous Consulate" and charged that the U.S. Embassy "ignored the disappearance and abuse of American citizens in order not to ruffle the epaulettes of the new Chilean junta" (*Washington Post*, November 17, 1973).

2. Marvine Howe, "2 Americans Slain in Chile: The Unanswered Questions," *New York Times*, November 19, 1973.

3. Early statements (1973 and 1974) by Simon and Joyce Horman clearly indicate that Charles was concerned and disgusted by the joyful enthusiasm about the coup he heard from the U.S. personnel in Valparaiso and Viña. But none of the early statements indicate that he and Simon learned something exclusive about the coup. That idea surfaces publicly for the first time in the *New York Times* article.

4. Godfrey Hodgson and William Shawcross, "Destabilisation: An Inquiry into Kissinger's Policy of Secret American Intervention in the Politics and Economy of Foreign Nations, and a Case Study of the Policy's First Big 'Victory'—the Destruction of Allende in Chile," *Sunday Times* (London), October 27, 1974.

5. The *Times* article bases its allegation of U.S.-Chilean coordination on an unpublished interview by journalist Marlise Simons with General Carlos Prats, quoting him as saying, "The real coordination and planning for the coup took place in Valparaiso." The *Times* reporters posit that Prats was referring to Captain Davis and Lt. Col. Ryan, who they say met secretly with coup plotters at the U.S. Naval Mission office in the port city. "General Prats said so in so many words," the authors write. Simons, in an email exchange with the author, said her interviews with Prats during his exile in Buenos Aires were intended for a book that was never written. In a 1977 article about Prats in the *Washington Post*, she says he discussed with "intensity . . . the U.S. military role in the months leading up to the coup. He admitted that he did not know all the details, but he harped on the fact that 'coordination and preparation for the coup' had taken place in the port of Valparaiso, where high Chilean Navy officials 'plotted directly with representatives at the U.S. Naval station.'" Prats was assassinated by agents of General Pinochet several weeks before the article appeared, on October 1. See Simons, "Diary of Murdered Chilean General Surfaces in Mexico," *Washington Post*, March 3, 1977. Historically, no evidence has surfaced to support the General's claim of U.S.-Chilean coordination on the coup. In his posthumous memoir, *Memorias de un Soldado* (Pehuen Editores, 1985), Prats does not say anything about U.S. Navy–Chilean coordination in the coup or refer in any way to the allegations he made in his conversations with Simons.

6. Transcript of interview with Rafael González Verdugo (later changed to Berdugo) in the Italian Embassy, Monday, June 7, 1976. The transcript, dated August 30, 1976, includes a second interview the next day, June 8. Copies of the interview transcripts are found in the Manitzas Papers, the Chilean court case and in U.S. declassified documents.

7. Joanne Omang, "Chilean Charges General Ordered American's Death," *Washington Post*, June 10, 1976.

8. Hodgson and Shawcross, "Destabilisation."

9. González retraction: Case 2182-98, 1852–1856, affidavit dated November 2001; 1842ff, Arrest order and statement to police, May 27, 2003; 2258ff, testimony before Judge Zepeda, Chilean court case. Transcripts of González's taped

interviews with U.S. officials after the interview with the journalists was published were released many years later. They show that González backed away from repeating his statement about an American or CIA officer being present, and denied other statements from the interview as well.

10. Juan Muñoz Alarcón, a leftist militant, became an informant at the time of the coup and infamously wore a hood with eye slots to hide his identity as he pointed out people for interrogation. He repented his action and gave a statement to the Comité Pro Paz, the ecumenical human rights organization set up by church leaders. Shortly thereafter he was killed by DINA, according to human rights records.

11. Tomaso De Vergottini, *Miguel Claro 1359: Recuerdos de un diplomatico italiano en Chile 1973-1975* (Editorial Atena, Santiago, 1991). De Vergottini says nothing about the González incident in his book. He died in 2008. The other diplomat, Silvia Meloni, died before 1991, according to Vergottini's book.

12. Quoted in Kevin Hall, "Chilean Spy Recants Story of CIA's Link to Slain U.S. Citizen," *Inquirer*, February 18, 2004.

13. Shawcross teamed up with veteran Latin American correspondent Peter Pringle for this story, which ran in the *Sunday Times*, June 13, 1976.

14. Hall, "Chilean Spy Recants Story of CIA's Link to Slain U.S. Citizen," features the interview with González's son Sergio, who said his father "falsely implicated the CIA" out of fear he would be expelled from his asylum in the Italian Embassy. A *New York Times* story said only that González had "changed his story," without giving details, after he was arrested by the Chilean judge. Actually González's affidavit retracting his charges was written two years before his arrest and testimony to Zepeda in May 2003.

15. González assignments: Pascale Bonnefoy, *Terrorismo de Estadio: Prisioneros de guerra en un campo de deportes*, 2nd expanded ed. (Editorial Latinoamericana, 2016), 211. González's background is described in, among other public sources, Manitzas, "American Murder." See also Bonnefoy, *Terrorismo de Estadio*, 211-217.

16. Memorandum of Conversation, "Teruggi and Horman cases," March 4, 1974.

17. Anderson, Memorandum for the Records, "Remains of Charles Horman," March 21, 1974.

18. Rauch interviewed González on June 11, in the Italian Embassy. But he said his editors at *Time* declined to publish it "because the information in it was thought to be of interest only to aficionados of the 1973 coup, not to the general public." Rauch sent a copy of the manuscript to Ed Horman explaining why it was not published, and it is located in the Horman Papers, Benson Library, University of Texas, Austin.

19. Differing versions: González spoke at length with Embassy officials on several occasions before and after his interview with Manitzas and Omang on

June 7. Interviews before that date concerned his visa situation, his son, and his desire to travel to the United States. He never mentioned Horman, but in a March 1976 interview he claimed to have documents linking the CIA to DINA operations against subversives. He was also interviewed on June 8 (the day after talking to the reporters), on June 11, June 22 and—in an hours-long session on tape—on January 24, 1977. The 1976 interviews are summarized in the Smith report, pp. 6–15. Transcripts of the June 8 and January 1977 interviews are among declassified documents: Airgram, Roger Channel, February 1, 1977, "Interview with Rafael González," with the 35-page transcript attached. Roger Channel is the most secure mode of encrypted communication between the U.S. embassy and the Department of State. The June 8 interview in which he repeats the phrase multiple times is Santiago 5663, June 11, 1976. His statements in the *Joyce Horman v. Henry Kissinger* suit are in an affidavit filed January 10, 1979.

20. The Supreme Court ratified Judge Zepeda's verdict in 2016, but increased González's sentence to three years' home confinement.

21. Ortiz statement: Bonnefoy, *Terrorismo de Estado*, 217. Ortiz says Horman, detained around 5:00 p.m., was taken to an Army operational facility (the School of Telecommunications) and then to the National Stadium. González says he saw him in the Defense Ministry, in another part of the city, around 6:00 p.m. That would have been a lot of territory to cover in an hour. The Defense Ministry in Central Santiago is about 2.6 miles from the Stadium, in Ñuñoa, and 2.3 miles from the Telecommunications School on Antonio Varas Street in Providencia. The Stadium and the Telecommunications facility are about 1.6 miles apart.

22. In González's statement to police, Chilean court case, 2109-2114, August 26, 2003, he states that two Army intelligence agents (*funcionarios*), whose last names he remembered as "Ortiz" and "Manesas," had a role in identifying Horman's fingerprints in the morgue. He cites Hauser's book as his source. Judge Zepeda ordered his investigators to locate the two agents, using the names from González but without checking Hauser's book or Ed Horman's diary, which contained their first names. The PDI detectives reported they were unable to find anyone by those names in Army rolls.

23. Interviews with Guillermo Osorio (union leader), Celsa Parrau ("Eleno" wing of the Socialist Party), Marco Bravo (MIR's Miguel Enriquez Foundation), Manuel Hidalgo (Socialist Party), and Rafael Kreis (Cordones historian). Osorio, Parrau (whose husband was part of the resistance at the *cordón*'s INDUMET factory and was later killed), and Hidalgo had direct knowledge of military preparations in the Cordones. Kreis, a writer, said he knew of fundraising efforts to buy weapons.

24. Dreher memo, April 20, 1987. Meneses interview, May 23, 2024. Salas was convicted and sentenced to life imprisonment in 2005 on charges he was the mastermind of a large-scale 1987 operation in which CNI agents rounded up and executed 12 members of the militant organization Manuel Rodriguez Patri-

otic Front, which was an offshoot of Chile's Communist Party. See Memoria Viva, https://memoriaviva.com/nuevaweb/criminales/criminales-s/salas-wentzel-hugo-ivan.

25. This van belonged to Janet Duecy. De la Barra says Charles Horman gave him the keys to the van. Duecy recalls that the van was for the use of whoever needed it, and that she left the van and the keys at the house when she returned to the United States for medical treatment in early September. De la Barra says that after the raid on his studio (chapter 7) he was trying to dispose of several pistols, some that had been used in production and some given to him by a Swedish journalist. He hid the pistols in the van and left it at the house of a friend, who was supposed to throw them in a river. Neighbors thought the van was suspicious, however, and called police, who found the guns. De la Barra turned himself in and tried to explain that the pistols were for film work, but police didn't believe him and he was held prisoner for two weeks. He said he does not remember the date, but his detention was probably in October. After his release he went into exile in Venezuela and finished the film there. This story is based on interviews with Pablo de la Barra and Janet Duecy.

26. For what it's worth, Rafael González said in an email exchange that in his opinion he considers the Chile Film connection the most likely motive for Horman's death. He made clear he was expressing his opinion based on what he learned about the case, not on his retracted claims made in 1976. He did not retract his claim that he had seen Horman in General Lutz's office in September 1973, and when he testified in the Chilean court case in 2003, he claimed for the first time that General Lutz mentioned Horman's connection to Chile Films and Eduardo Paredes.

27. Chile Films continued operating after the coup under military control. Carmen Bueno and Jorge Mueller, both clandestine MIR militants, were working on projects there at the time of their kidnapping by DINA agents in November 1974. Mueller had been assistant cameraman for Saul Landau and Nina Serrano's 1972 film *Que Hacer*; other Horman friends in the cast and crew included Dick Pearce, Pablo de la Barra and Elizabeth Farnsworth. My 1980 book *Assassination on Embassy Row*, co-authored with Saul Landau, is dedicated to Jorge Mueller.

28. Meneses to Dreher, Memorandum, April 20, 1987, and in Santiago 3059, Report on GOC involvement, April 28, 1987. Meneses made similar statements about Horman to Bonnefoy.

29. Edmund Horman, "The View after Three Years," unpublished manuscript dated December 22, 1976, 11, Manitzas Papers.

30. Bonnefoy interview with Meneses, May 27, 2016.

31. I have researched dozens of cases of victims of military violence and documented hundreds of others in less detail. In my books I describe many cases of seemingly arbitrary killing and irrational cruelty. See especially *Los Años del*

Condor: Operaciones Internacionales de Asesinato en el Cono Sur (Penguin Random House, 2021).

32. Letter to parents on Schneider: Hauser, *Execution*, 68.

33. *El Caso Schneider: Operación Alfa* (Editorial Quimantú, n.d.), 178–180.

34. ITT Papers: *New York Times*, July 3, 1972, and Jack Anderson, "Memos Bare ITT for Chile Coup," *Washington Post*, March 21, 1972.

35. Manitzas, "American Murder," 8; Manitzas interview with Lluis Mestres.

36. Manitzas, "American Murder," 10. Joyce said the same in her July 10, 2002 testimony in the Chilean court case. She said she and Charles looked over the Schneider-Viaux materials and notes, and "afterward we decided that the content of what we had was public and for that reason we did not destroy it."

37. Hauser, *Execution*, 228.

38. Edmund Horman, "The View after Three Years." Horman lists 80 documents provided by the State Department, with excerpts and his own notes.

39. Edmund Horman, "The View after Three Years," 14. The document in reference is described as CIA 12, June 12, 1976.

40. Edmund Horman, "The View after Three Years," 21–22.

41. Kessler, in an interview and in a statement in the *Horman v. Kissinger* civil suit, denied Sandoval told him about a dossier or said Horman was executed in the Stadium, but said only that he was dead. Sandoval's telling has never varied except to protect the identity of his brother Nelson. Pascale Bonnefoy interviewed Nelson Sandoval, leaving no doubt his information included both details. Ed Horman heard the report first from Ford Foundation officer Lovell Jarvis, then in person from Enrique Sandoval himself two years later.

42. Lewis H. Diuguid, "The Man Who Knew Too Much," *Washington Post*, June 20, 1976.

43. The source was John Tipton, a political officer in the Embassy from 1972 to 1976, Diuguid confirmed in an interview. Tipton, together with political officer Robert Steven, organized an effort to write a "dissent memo" calling attention to human rights violations in Chile in defiance of Henry Kissinger's instructions to downplay such concerns. Steven said he and Tipton were both convinced, based on conversations with Chilean officials, that the Chileans had files on Horman and Teruggi. He said Tipton was the unnamed source in Diuguid's story. From what Steven said, the files were Chilean, not necessarily CIA. Tipton's wife was a consular officer in Chile whose interactions with Terry Simon were criticized in Hauser's book.

44. Edmund Horman, "The View after Three Years," 22.

45. Thomas Hauser statement, August 5, 2014, Chilean court case; interview with Joyce Horman, 2016. Joyce Horman said Simon was Hauser's friend and Simon put him in touch with Ed Horman. Hauser said Simon introduced him to Joyce and Charles Horman at a dinner in 1971 in Berkeley, CA.

46. Hauser, *Execution*, 1, 255. With the success of the Horman book and movie Hauser would launch a writing career that included 30 books on boxing in addition to novels and other nonfiction works.

47. UPI, *San Francisco Examiner*, September 11, 1978.

48. The filmmaker's full name is Konstantinos "Kostas" Gavras. Costa-Gavras's *Missing* followed two previous films on similar political themes: *Z*, released in 1969, tells the fictionalized story based on real events in Greece, including a political assassination, after a military junta took power. *State of Siege* (1972) was filmed in Chile during the Allende government (and Joyce Horman was cast as an extra). It is set in Uruguay during the uprising of the urban guerrilla group Tupamaros, and involves the kidnapping and killing of a U.S. police officer conducting counterinsurgency training. The officer is based on a real person, Don Mitrione, a former Indiana police chief who was alleged to be teaching torture techniques.

49. *Missing* can be seen online at https://www.boxofficemojo.com/release/rl3714221569/weekend. González's name in the movie is rendered "Paris" in some accounts.

50. The Horman family attorneys were Ira Lowe, Rhonda Copelon, John W. Corwin, Nancy Stearns and Peter Weiss.

51. Edmund Muskie, In Camera Affidavit and Claim of Privilege by the Secretary of State, submitted in case 77-1748, July 16, 1980.

52. CIA denial: Summarized in State 056257, "Press Statement on the Movie 'Missing,'" March 3, 1982.

53. Lawyer's final motion: Memorandum in Support of Motion for Voluntary Dismissal without Prejudice, submitted in case 77-1748, December 10, 1980.

54. Memorandum and Order, case 77-1748, issued March 20, 1981.

55. The other officers named were: Colonel Victor Barría Barría, second in command of SIM (at the time of the killings); Colonel Jorge Espinóza, commander of the National Stadium prison camp; Navy Captain Ariel González Cornejo, head of the intelligence arm of the Armed Forces General Staff (EMDN); and Major Luis Contreras Prieto, who had informed Joyce Horman that SIM would contact her. No U.S. official was charged, although several, including Henry Kissinger, were listed as witnesses who would be summoned to testify. All of the defendants except Pedro Espinóza had died by the time a verdict was reached in 2016. The Horman and Teruggi cases added to an umbrella investigation, *Episodio Estadio Nacional* [National Stadium Episode], originally intended to include multiple killings associated with the Stadium.

56. Costa-Gavras testimony, October 15, 2002, Chilean court case, 1764ff.

57. Extradition filing in case 2182-98 (Estadio Nacional), Jorge Zepeda Arancibia, Ministro de Fuero, November 29, 2011.

58. Quoted in Pascale Bonnefoy, "Chile Indicts Ex-U.S. Officer in 1973 Killings," *New York Times*, November 29, 2011. Bonnefoy is the *Times*'s Chile correspondent (stringer).

59. Indictment of Pedro Espinóza: Auto acusatorio, case 2182-98 (Estadio Nacional), issued by Judge Jorge Zepeda Arancibia, Ministro de Fuero, June 16, 2016. Pedro Espinóza, a major in 1973, has often been confused with Colonel Jorge Espinóza, the officer in charge of administering the Estadio Nacional prison at the time. Jorge Espinóza testified to Zepeda and charges were not pursued. He denied knowing anything about torture or killings in the Stadium and repeated the standard line from the time of the junta that no mention of Horman could be found in Stadium records.

60. In Chile, human rights cases are adjudicated using a system of written submissions of evidence, depositions and pleadings. Witnesses appear before the judge but are not subject to cross-examination by defense counsel. The presiding judge (Ministro de Fuero) is equipped with broad powers to investigate, prosecute, indict, reach a verdict and sentence, subject to review by the Supreme Court. According to Chilean law, the official record, the *Expediente*, is secret until a sentence is issued, after which the presiding judge may grant access to outsiders, but is not required to do so. Each page in the *Expediente* is numbered—from the opening of the case on *fojas* 1 to the final appeals and the notification to the accused to begin serving their sentences on *fojas* 6976. I was able to scan approximately 1,500 pages and obtain an additional 1,000 pages of digital copies that the court had already provided to defense lawyers or as part of the extradition request.

61. Filmed interview with Fabiola Letelier, February 11, 2016.

62. See John Dinges, *Los Años del Condor: Operaciones Internacionales de Asesinato en el Cono Sur* (Penguin Random House, 2021). The Operation Condor alliance was founded in a meeting in 1975 in Chile. The cross-border operations resulted in approximately 384 deaths of exiles, mostly in Argentina, including 65 Chileans.

63. Interview with Carroza, April 30, 2018.

64. *Sentencia*, January 9, 2015, section II.A.12, pp. 156–166, Chilean court case.

65. The cable is Ambassador Davis's reply to State 190077, in which the State Department requested "status report ASAP" on Horman and ordering the Embassy to "redoubl[e] its efforts [to]locate Horman." The cable's identifying number, as cited by the court, was wrong in two digits, making it somewhat difficult to locate. The number cited, 04565252528Z, corresponds to the second line of the document "Page 01 Santia 04565 251518Z." The cable was released as part of several large collections of documents on Chile in 1999 and 2000. Following standard practice for State Department cables, the formula of numbers ending in "Z" indicates the day of the month and time expressed in Greenwich Mean Time

(also called Zulu or Z time). The codes allow the recipient to know exactly when it was transmitted. Both Santiago 4565 and State 190077 are reproduced in FRUS, 1969–1976, Volume XXI, Chile 1969–1973, 944–954. Thanks to Carlos Osorio of the National Security Archive for his work in locating the document.

66. *Sentencia*, January 9, 2015, sections II.A.14, II. B. 3, 4, pp. 156–166, Chilean court case.

67. After leaving Chile in 1978, González says he read the Church Committee Report and the Hauser book, which describe Horman's research on the case. In his testimony to Zepeda in 2003, after he had retracted his 1976 statements, he cited the Schneider research as a reason to make Horman disappear. But in that testimony, he also says that Lutz did not order Horman's execution, contradicting what he said in 1976. Rather, Lutz's comment about disappearance meant only that Horman should be expelled from Chile. In email exchanges with the author, González said he learned about Horman's research in the Schneider case from Hauser's book, not from any information he had in 1973.

68. Monsalve testimony, May 5, 2005, *Expediente, fojas* 3785–3788, and *Sentencia*, p. 191, Chilean court case.

69. Monsalve also said he gave the order to Rafael González to help the U.S. Consulate locate Horman's body in the cemetery in March 1974.

70. CIA, "The MHCHAOS Program," May 8, 1973. Zepeda cites the document in *Sentencia*, January 9, 2015, section II.A.14, p. 157, Chilean court case.

71. Tim Weiner, *Legacy of Ashes: The History of the CIA* (Doubleday, 2007), 285–288. CIA director Richard Helms reported to President Johnson in 1967 that the CIA had found no evidence linking the American left or Black activists to any foreign governments.

72. Interview with Peter Kornbluh. See also Kornbluh's highly regarded book, *The Pinochet File*, which has a chapter on the Horman-Teruggi cases and reproduces relevant U.S. documents.

73. Interview with Manuel Muñoz, November 17, 2017.

74. Interview with Peter Kornbluh, quoted in my 2017 paper, "What's Missing in 'Missing'? A Critical Examination of Flawed Evidence," presented at the Congress of the Latin American Studies Association in Lima, Peru, April 29, 2017.

75. Interview with Pascale Bonnefoy, quoted in "What's Missing in 'Missing'?"

76. PDI, Informe Policial, September 1, 2005, *Expediente*, pp. 4097–4103, Chilean court case.

PART IV. CONCLUSIONS

1. R. V. Fimbres, R. S. Driscoll, W. V. Robertson, State Department memo, "Charles Horman Case," August 25, 1976, secret (Chile Project), with attachment

"Gleanings." The results of the investigation were submitted in the 26-page Smith report and a cover memo dated December 29, 1976, also by Smith.

2. "U.S. Takes 20 Years to Acknowledge Its Involvement in the 'Horman Case': CIA Complicity Is Proven in 'Missing' Journalist's Murder" ["Estados Unidos tarda 20 años en reconocer su implicación en el 'caso Horman': Demostrada la complicidad de la CIA en el asesinato del periodista de 'Missing'"], *El País*, October 17, 1999. The first publication of the Fimbres memo was Jim Moscou, "Declassified Documents Reveal Washington May Have Given Clearance to the Execution of Charles Horman," *Editor and Publisher*, October 16, 1999.

3. Diana Jean Schemo, "U.S. Victims of Chile's Coup: The Uncensored File," *New York Times*, February 13, 2000.

4. Secretary of State Muskie, in refusing to release the memo to the *Horman v. Kissinger* litigation, characterized the memo and the ensuing investigation as part of a process in the State Department of "candid, 'devil's advocate' type of analysis" that resulted in an investigation and recommendations that were followed. But Muskie justified the continuing secrecy of the documents because "public disclosure of such opinions of a derogatory nature by career U.S. officials with respect to a foreign government could have a harmful effect on the conduct of foreign relations."

5. Robert Steven interviews and oral history.

6. Smith report. In a cover memo to Shlaudeman, Smith describes the scope of his investigation; a second memo discusses his recommendation to make a "high level approach" to the CIA and other intelligence agencies. A third memo on the report is from Shlaudeman to Undersecretary of State Philip Habib, in which he conveys and endorses Smith's recommendation. Habib was Kissinger's principal policy deputy at the top level of the State Department.

7. Smith report, 21.

8. U.S. categorical denials: All documents in declassified collection on Horman and Teruggi released in paper binders in 1999. CIA, October 25, 1975: Review of files shows no information that CIA assisted any entity in Chile in preparation of arrest lists. CIA, August 5, 1976: Says reference to "arrest lists" in Church Report, p. 38, may not be accurate, and denies "that 'arrest lists' ever existed at Santiago station." CIA, April 15, 1976: Answers the question on lists posed by Frank Teruggi, Sr., via Sen. Baker, saying that "Teruggi's name did not come to the attention of Santiago Station, according to its Chief at the time, until after the change of government in September of 1976." CIA, August 13, 1976: CIA counsel to Sen. Baker, saying there is one document in CIA files mentioning Teruggi, which was a "document provided to the CIA by a foreign liaison service," therefore exempt from disclosure.

July 16, 1980, Affidavit in U.S. District Court for the District of Columbia, Secretary of State Edmund Muskie, in Civil action 77-1748, Horman v. Henry

Kissinger et al. The suit was filed in 1977 and voluntarily withdrawn by plaintiffs March 20, 1981. Muskie refers to the Smith investigation and the Fimbres memo as follows: "The responsible State Department officials who investigated and considered this matter have found no evidence of involvement by any United States Government personnel in the disappearance and death of Charles Horman. Specifically, the State Department is not aware of any foreknowledge of or participation in Charles Horman's death by any United States Government personnel."

State 249067, September 3, 1982 (cable), press guidance for the release of *Missing*. It cites Muskie's affidavit in the civil suit and adds CIA director Stansfield Turner's testimony "that no evidence was found by the CIA to support the Horman's contention that agency personnel had advance knowledge of the abduction or of the subsequent death of Charles Horman."

9. "Interview with Rafael González," 35-page transcript of his January 24 and 31, 1977, interviews with Embassy officers Charles R. Stout and Joshiah H. Brownell, Airgram, Roger Channel, February 1, 1977. In email exchanges with the author, González vehemently denied he ever offered to work for the CIA. In the Spanish edition, I cited the Fimbres memo, in the Gleanings section, saying the CIA described González as a "rejected walk-in," a term indicating a person offering unsolicited cooperation with the CIA. González denied that characterization, saying his job before the coup including finding possible CIA agents and that he always had an antagonistic relationship with the CIA.

10. In note 173, June 14, 1976 (transmitted in cable Santiago 5745), the Embassy asked the Foreign Ministry to "investigate the assertions made by Mr. González and to inform the Embassy of the results." The Foreign Ministry replied with note 26, July 2, 1976 (transmitted in cable Santiago 6472, same date) saying that the Ministry's note 18557, December 12, 1973—two and a half years earlier—was the last word on the subject. The note also described González's statements as "irresponsible" and "absolutely false." Note 18557, in reply to detailed questions posed by the Embassy, provided only general answers and reiterated the military's cover story that leftists in stolen uniforms may have killed Horman and Teruggi.

11. Davidow unpublished op-ed: copy in author's possession, mailed by Ambassador Davidow, December 2023. Interview with Davidow.

12. Quoted in Paul Jacobs, "Chile: Their Blood and Ours, Too," *Newsday*, June 13, 1977.

13. McNeil to Ambassador Vaky, "Horman case," October 26, 1978. Another factor mentioned was that a candid statement might hurt the U.S. government's defense strategy in the ongoing *Horman v. Kissinger* litigation.

14. Hodding Carter, letter to Ed Horman, December 29, 1978.

15. Letter from State Department official J. Edward Fox to Senator Stafford, November 4, 1987.

16. Edmund Horman, "The View after Three Years," 22. The last word in the second sentence quoted was obscured in the document except for the letters "... alized." The meaning is clear from context.

17. Santiago 1596, "Letelier/Moffit case: Embassy file on Michael Vernon Townley," March 8, 1978. The cable summarizes 10 documents in Embassy files about Townley's activities and contacts with the Embassy.

18. Townley answer to author's query conveyed through a third party, June 23, 2024. Townley began to work for DINA in mid-1974, but he denied he worked for SIM at any time and said he did not recognize Davidow's name.

19. For Townley's role in the Letelier killing, see John Dinges and Saul Landau, *Assassination on Embassy Row* (Pantheon, 1980; Open Road, 2014), and John Dinges, *Los Años del Condor: Operaciones Internacionales de Asesinato en el Cono Sur* (Penguin Random House, 2021). In many hours of interviews, Scherrer never mentioned any work on the Horman-Teruggi case.

20. Santiago 5668, November 18, 1973, in which deputy chief of mission Herbert Thompson defended the Embassy's actions against severe criticisms by Ed Horman. The draft recommends follow-up interviews with several military intelligence officers: Majors Contreras Prieto and Salas Wenzel, and Sergeants Ortiz and Meneses, among others. There is no record that Thompson's recommendation was acted upon. A cable, Santiago 5668, November 16, 1973, based in part on Thompson's draft omits the names.

21. Meneses: Memo David Dreher to DCM, "Charles Horman Case," March 11, 1987. Santiago 2440, "Letelier Case: Mariana Callejas Calls on Political Section April 3, 1987," is the only document from this period in which Meneses (spelled Manesas) appears unredacted. Two other memos from Dreher to DCM are dated April 20 and April 24. The internal debate about whether to give Meneses protection and interview him is captured in a series of long cables, including Santiago 3059, "[blacked out] Reports on GOC involvement in death of Charles Horman, Asks Embassy for Asylum and Aid," April 28, 1987; and State 146544, "[blacked out] Reports on Death of Charles Horman," May 14, 1987. A four-page statement written by Meneses and given to Consular officer Jayne Kobliska has not been declassified.

22. Interview with David Dreher, July 26, 2016.

23. In 2005, Salas Wenzel was sentenced to life imprisonment for human rights crimes.

24. Meneses's account, as summarized by Dreher, is consistent in its major elements with what he had told Ed Horman, but differs in some details from his interview with Pascale Bonnefoy in 2016. Dreher's version says Horman was taken first to the Military School for interrogation and then to the Stadium. To Bonnefoy, in a taped interview, he and Ortiz say Horman's arrest was ordered by CAJSI, the operational command center headquartered in the Military School. The unit that carried out the detention was based at the Telecommunications

School, a military training facility. Those discrepancies might be accounted for by Dreher's own unfamiliarity with the military structures. In an interview, he acknowledged his Spanish was "not good" at that point and he had trouble understanding Meneses at times. In fact, Meneses told another U.S. official, Consul Jayne Kobliska, that Horman was taken first to the Military Institute Command, which is the same location on Antonio Varas Street as the Telecommunications School, not to the Military School.

25. Memo, David Dreher to DCM, "Charles Horman Case," March 11, 1987. Santiago 2440, "Letelier Case: Mariana Callejas Calls on Political Section April 3, 1987."

26. Meneses testimony, case 806-2017 in the Santiago Appeals Court, pages 1739–1742. Interview with Olga Lutz Herrera and lawyer Rodrigo Lledó, May 23, 2024. There is one discrepancy from the known record in his testimony. Recalling his investigation 51 years later, he said Horman's body had been found in the Mapocho River. The morgue log book recorded that Horman's body was found in the street.

27. This assessment of Scherrer's work is documented in my books *Assassination on Embassy Row* and *Los Años del Condor*.

ACKNOWLEDGING A LEGACY

1. Steve Volk, "Defending Human Rights and Democracy 50 years after the Chilean Coup d'état," U.S. Senate Office Building, September 18, 2023, unpublished remarks.

2. Volk was citing Kathryn Sikkink, "The Emergence, Evolution, and Effectiveness of the Latin American Human Rights Network," in Elizabeth Jelin and Eric Hershberg, eds., *Constructing Democracy: Human Rights, Citizenship, and Society in Latin America* (Westview Press, 1996), 63.

SOURCES AND METHODS

1. Rafael González, "El Caso Horman ('Missing')," a 14,000-word document in which González attempts to refute the evidence brought by Judge Zepeda linking him to Horman's detention. This is the only document not already cited in the main text of the book. It is undated but internal references place it in late 2004 or 2005. Much of the document, referring to his reasons for inventing the story of the CIA agent in Lutz's office, repeats sections of the 2001 Retraction document almost word for word.

2. Email exchange with Rafael González, July 23, 2016, and June 18, 2024.

3. González describes his stay with the Horman family in his 2001 retraction, in "El Caso Horman ('Missing')," and in an email of June 18, 2024: "In New York

I told Edmund Horman about the coerced statements and he told me that it would be a tremendous complication to his trial against Kissinger et al. if I disclosed it, to which I replied that I would remain silent, except if called to court."

4. Email from Rafael González, June 18, 2024.

5. Email from Rafael González, June 30, 2024.

6. Chilean attorney Fabiola Letelier suggested this in our recorded interview in 2016.

Index

Note: Locators followed by "n" refer to footnotes and locators followed by "n" with numbers refer to endnotes.

11 de Septiembre: Esa Semana (Allende Bussi), 62n

Abraham Lincoln Brigade, 2, 55, 218, 239n1
Abu Akleh, Shireen, 240n12
Aerolite factory, 93
Ajens, Andres, 221
Alarcón, Fernando, 41–42, 57–58, 63–64, 159
Alcayaga Aldunate, Augusto Andino, 250n5
"Alejandro." *See* Teruggi, Frank
Allende, Andrés Pascal, 32
Allende, Salvador, 1, 26; agrarian reform program, 31; CIA's covert actions against, 4–6, 38, 95–96; commitment to democracy, 30; death of, 62; enforcement of arms control law, 57; overthrow, 60; political and economic actions, 30–31; support of Latin American refugees, 1–2; and Tancazo, 44–47; and transportation strike (1972), 43–44; and Vietnam War, 3–4;
Allende Bussi, Isabel, 62n
Altamirano, Carlos, 57, 83

American Screw Company, 47
Andrade, Ximena, 221
Anderson, Jack, 38, 261n1
Anderson, James, 101, 151, 173; CIA identity, 254n36; in Horman-Teruggi case investigation, 106; lawsuit against, 177; release of Americans, 114
Andreas, Carol Rich, 255n46
Arancibia Castillo, Miguel Hernán, 252n18
Araya Peeters, Arturo, 56
Archivos Chile blog, 89n
Armstrong, Warwick, 40, 47, 87, 111
Arrellano, Sergio, 256n57
Association of Public Television Producers, 18
"Augusto." *See* Beust, Carlos
Avenue of the Americas (film), 40, 41n, 75

Baeza, Ernesto, 129
Barceló, Ramon, 32
Barría, Victor, 146, 267n55
Basso, Jorge Alberto, 30, 61.
The Battle of Chile (film), 76
Benavides (General), 123
Berman, Andy Scott, 27–28

275

Beust, Carlos, 30, 41–42, 61; recalling Teruggi and Horman's military ship photos, 58; searching for hideout after Chilean coup, 64–65
Bixler, Karen, 242n24
black market exchange, 29, 35, 48, 246n76
Blattner, Simon, 53–54
Bliss, Shepherd, 26–27, 28
BND. *See* Bundesnachrichtendienst
Bonilla, Oscar, 81, 151, 214; in Horman-Teruggi case, 105; statement in *El Mercurio* after Chilean coup, 81–82; statement on Teruggi's release, 137
Bonnefoy, Pascale, 111n, 122, 221, 225, 231, 250; contribution to Horman-Teruggi case, 190–91, 220; interview with Nelson Sandoval, 266n41; locating Meneses and Ortiz for interview, 191–92; Meneses's interview with, 212, 272n24
Boric, Gabriel, 220
Brady, Herman, 180
Bravo, Marco, 264n23
Brister, Judith, 34n, 75n
Brown, Bob, 36
Brownell, Joshiah H., 254n37, 271n9
Bullitt, Stimson, 15
Bundesnachrichtendienst (BND), 28
Burbach, Roger, 26, 220

Cadenasso, Enzo, 123, 192
CAGLA. *See* Chicago Area Group on Latin America
CAJSI. *See* Commandos of Area Jurisdiction of Interior Security
CalTech, 25
Campbell, Stephanie, 34n
Carbone, Jaime, 191
Carroza, Mario, 141, 185–86
Carter, Hodding, 206–7
Carter, Jimmy, 206
Carvajal, Mario, 87, 88
Carvajal, Patricio (Admiral), 160
Castro, Fidel, 2, 62n
cedulas (identity cards), 58
Celebration of Awareness: A Call for Institutional Revolution (Illich), 241n13
Central Intelligence Agency (CIA) 112, 114, 145, 148, 152, 168, 177, 195, 197–202, 225–28, 270n8; CHAOS program, 189; covert actions against Allende, 4–6, 38, 95–96, 96–97n; denials about providing Horman and Teruggi's information to Chile, 162; González's retraction affidavit, 149; involvement in Schneider's death, 165. *See also* Federal Bureau of Investigation (FBI)
Cerrutti, John, 114
CHAOS program, 17, 189
Chesterton, G. K., 145
Chicago Area Group on Latin America (CAGLA), 26, 135
Chile, 219; importance during Cold War, 3–4; Latin American refugees in, 1–2, 34–35; socialism *vs.* fascism in, 2–3; "socialist path" to development, 30; transportation strike (1972), 43–44. *See also* coup (1973)
Chilean government (post coup), 219; actions on Frank Teruggi's case, 215; consciousness of guilt, 214; coverup, 8, 129, 133–34, 136, 137, 155, 208; false report by Chilean Embassy, 107; policy to clear responsibility of, 139, 155–56; raising Cordones factor, 157; refusal of safe conduct pass to González, 147–48; shipping Horman's body to United States, 151; request for debt relief, 96; unanswered questions regarding Horman's execution, 137, 207
Chile Documentation Project at the National Security Archive, 224
Chile Films, 265n27; Army units attack on filming campus, 76; Horman's involvement in projects at, 39–41; Reyes email with Trabucco about, 41n; suspecting connection of Horman to, 159–60
Chile Project, 240n11
Chile's Investigative Police. *See* Policia de Investigaciones de Chile (PICH)
Chile with Poems and Guns (film), 75n
Cholette, Larry, 221
Christian Democratic Party, 39, 43
Christian Science Monitor newspaper, 18, 38
Church, Frank, 243n40, 257n66
CIDOC. *See* Intercultural Documentation Center
CIM. *See* Comando de Institutos Militares
Claro, Ricardo, 83
Clinton, Bill, 197
COINTELPRO, 17
Comando de Institutos Militares (CIM), 214
Comité Pro Paz, 263n10
Commandos of Area Jurisdiction of Interior Security (CAJSI), 82–83, 123, 180
Commission of Truth and Reconciliation. *See* National Commission of Truth and Reconciliation (CNVR)

INDEX 277

Commonweal publication, 18
communism, 4, 101, 157
Condor (Operation) 180–81, 268n62, 247n86
Contreras, Manuel, 183
Contreras Prieto, Luis, 122, 124, 267n55, 272n20
Cooper, Marc, 220, 244n56
copper mining in Chile, 30
Cordones Industriales, 42, 45, 52, 59, 61, 71, 83, 157–58, 161, 259n76
Costa-Gavras, 5, 37, 39, 146–47n, 180, 223, 224, 267n48. See also *Missing* (film)
Costas, Migueliño, 40, 41n
Cotts, Jerry, 50, 53–54
coup (1973), 1, 239n7, 247n81, 247n93; Araya Peeters's assassination, 56; arrival of bodies to Santiago morgue, 88–89; Bonilla's statement in *El Mercurio* after, 81–82; killing of foreigners after, 98; Patria y Libertad's role, 57; Pinochet's military rule after, 60–61, 63; Stafford's question about U.S. involvement in, 207; warning of pro-Allende Naval officers about, 58. See also Allende, Salvador; Horman-Teruggi case; Pinochet, Augusto
Couzens, Michael, 26
Covert Action in Chile report, 165
Creter, Arthur, 67–68, 144, 171, 173, 248n93
Cruces, Armando, 83–84, 250–51n5

"Daniel." See Santos, Paulo
"Daniela." See Virginia, Maria
Daley, Richard, 241n6
Darnton, Kyra, 221
Davidow, Jeffrey, 102–3, 193, 202, 221; link with Townley, 209; statement on Horman-Teruggi case, 202–4
Davis, Angela, 34
Davis, Nathaniel, 101, 104, 173, 224; actions to protect new Chilean junta, 155–56; lawsuit against, 177; libel suit by, 146; meeting with Ed Horman, 118; raising issue of disappeared Americans to Pinochet, 120; role in Horman-Teruggi case, 110–11, 119
Davis, Ray, 66–70, 100, 110, 144, 146–47n, 171, 173, 215–16, 228, 257n62; accusation in Horman-Teruggi case, 186, 191; connection with Chilean military, 101; flawed evidence against, 187–90; lawsuit against, 177; libel suit by, 146; ranking of, 101n; role in Horman-Teruggi case, 106, 110, 111–13, 115
de la Barra, Alejandro, 77, 250n107;
de la Barra, Pablo, 19, 22, 37, 77, 159, 265n27; about Hormans' animation project, 247n88; statement about pistols, 265n25
Democratic National Convention in Chicago: Horman's writing about, 17; Teruggi's participation in protest during, 25–26
dependency theory, 40
Des Moines Tribune newspaper, 4
Deutscher, Isaac, 22
Development Corporation in Chile, 31
De Vergottini, Tomaso, 149, 263n11
Devia Devia, José Rosa, 250n5
Díaz Estrada, Nicanor, 112
DINA. See Dirección de Inteligencia Nacional
Dinges, John, 6–8: investigation, 158, 168, 183–86, 198, 212, 246n76; personal history in Chile, 20, 44, 62–63, 72, 91n, 160, 165
Dirección de Inteligencia del Ejército (DINE). See Servicio de Inteligencia Militar (SIM)
Dirección de Inteligencia Nacional, 101, 122, 149, 152, 213, 264n19
Directorate of Army Intelligence. See Servicio de Inteligencia Militar (SIM)
Diuguid, Lewis, 170–71, 266n43
Dolgin, Mark, 111, 259n77
Dos Santos, Teotonio, 32
Dougherty, Joseph, 254n32, 255n46
Dreher, David, 121, 210–12, 251n11, 272–73n24
Driscoll, Robert: interviews regarding Horman-Teruggi case, 198–99; memo regarding Horman-Teruggi case, 195–97
Duecy, Janet, 22, 36–37, 48, 77, 265n25
Duhalde, Alejandro, 221
Durán Castillo, Nelson Gonzalo, 252n18

El Caso Schneider: Operación Alfa (Editorial Quimantú), 263
Eldridge, Joseph, 219
Elecmetal factory, 83
Elenos, 42, 45
El Mercurio newspaper, 5, 43, 81–82
EMDN. See Estado Mayor de la Defensa Nacional
Epley, Paul, 69
Escuela Militar (Military Academy), 123, 258n74

Esmeralda ship, 68
Espinóza, Jorge, 267n55, 268n59
Espinóza, Pedro, 82, 180, 182–83, 267n55; indictment of, 268n59
Estado Mayor de la Defensa Nacional (EMDN), 145, 151
execution. *See* motives, execution; United States (U.S.) involvement/role in execution
The Execution of Charles Horman: An American Sacrifice (Hauser), 146, 171–73, 223
Expediente (Horman-Teruggi case trial record), 184, 190, 268n60

Fagen, Patricia, 2
Farnsworth, Elizabeth, 265n27
Fatherland and Liberty. *See* Patria y Libertad
Federal Bureau of Investigation (FBI) 7, 9, 28, 120, 125, 130, 135–36, 182, 214, 242n25–26, 257n69; investigation on Teruggi, 162, 242n26; surveillance of "New Left" organizations, 17. *See also* Central Intelligence Agency (CIA)
FER. *See* Frente de Estudiantes Revolucionarios
Fernández Cuevas, Juan Dagoberto, 250n5
Fernández Cuevas, Miguel Alberto, 250n5
Fernández Larios, Armando, 211, 212
FighT bAck magazine, 27
Fimbres memo, 7, 195–97, 200, 201, 224, 226, 229, 240n10, 271n8; interviews with Fimbres and Driscoll, 198–99; interviews with Steven, 199; *New York Times* versions, 197–98; Smith's recommendations, 199–201. *See also* Horman-Teruggi case
fingerprints identification: of Horman, 119–20, 124–33, 175, 214, 257n69, 259n79; of Teruggi, 107–9
FIN. *See* *Fuente de Información Norteamericana*
Fitzgerald, Kathy, 34n
Flannery, Thomas, 178
Flores Flores, Francisco, 250n5
Flynn, Francis, 255n46
Flynn, Pat, 220
FOIA. *See* Freedom of Information Act
"Francisca." *See* Muñoz, Olga
Frank, Andre Gunder, 32, 40
Fraser, Don, 220
Frauenfelder, Roger, 68
Freedom of Information Act (FOIA), 189, 199
Frei, Eduardo, 31, 165, 243n32

Freire, Paulo, 20, 241n13
Frente de Estudiantes Revolucionarios (FER), 29, 61
Fromm, Erich, 241n13
Fuente de Información Norteamericana (FIN), 6, 33–34, 34n, 47
Fuentes, Esther "Cuqui," 61, 243n29
Fuerza Central (Central Force), 42, 57

Gaete, Sandro, 261n91
Garrett, Patricia, 106, 114, 255n46
Gavras, Konstantinos "Kostas." *See* Costa-Gavras
General Staff of National Defense. *See* Estado Mayor de la Defensa Nacional (EMDN)
González, Rafael, 141, 221, 254n37, 269n69, 271n10, 273n3; accusation of U.S. involvement in Horman's death, 145–47, 167, 224; asylum in Italian Embassy, 147, 149; character in *Missing* film, 174; Chilean court case, statement to, 264n22; conviction in Horman-Teruggi case, 183; Ed Horman's scenario based on statement, 169–72; Horman's detention and execution, statement on, 163–64, 226–27; interview with Manitzas, Omang and Rauch, 152–53; interview with Omang and Manitzas, 227; interview with *Washington Post*, 225; punishment for "self-serving" argument, 154; reason for Horman's death, statement on, 265n26; finding CIA agents, 271n9; retraction/recantation of accusations on U.S. role and General Lutz, 147–51, 153, 201, 226–28; source of information about Horman's knowledge about coup, 147; testimony to Zepeda, 269n67; U.S. Embassy officials, interviews with, 263–64n19; work in EMDN during Chilean coup, 151; working as intelligence agent, 226
González, Sergio, 149
González Cornejo, Ariel, 267n55
Goycolea Grez, Luis, 131, 132–33
GPM5. *See* Grupo Politico Militar
Gramsci, Antonio, 33
Grant Pimentel, Fernando, 123, 192
Greenwood, Trevor, 15
Grupo Politico Militar (GPM5), 61
Guerra, Mireya, 251n10
Guevara, Ernesto "Che", 32
Guijón, Patricio, 62
Guzmán, Juan, 180, 191; failure to find Meneses and Ortiz, 212–13; investigation

INDEX 279

against Pinochet, 180; investigation of Horman-Teruggi case, 180-81
Guzmán, Patricio, 76

Habib, Philip, 201, 270n6
Hamberg, Jill, 34n
Hampton, Fred, 4
Harkin, Tom, 220
Harmer, Tanya, 97n, 239-40n7
Harrington, Michael, 219
Harris, Mark, 15, 221; letter from Horman, 19; work with Horman, 15-16
Hathaway, David, 34n, 41, 75n, 119, 163, 220; application to join MIR, 42; connection with MIR, 159; detained by Chilean soldiers, 90-92, 107; identification of Horman's body, 260n88; questions about Teruggi's political activities, 92-93; release into Purdy's custody, 108, 114; statement about Teruggi's activities, 58; work in *Avenue of the Americas* film, 75n; work in MADEMSA, 60-61, 89-90
Hauser, Thomas, 118, 146, 165, 223, 266n45; *The Execution of Charles Horman*, 146, 171-73, 223; statement in Chilean court case, 266n45
Helms, Richard, 269n71
Henríquez, Juan, 106, 111-12
Hernández Croqueville, Maria Virginia, 41-42, 64; clandestine work for MIR's Political Committee, 57-58; move to safehouse after coup, 64-65
Herrera, Francisco, 112
Herrera, Sergio, 133
High, Bob, 219, 249n103
Hodgson, Godfrey, 144
Hon, William M., 101, 260n90; actions to protect new Chilean junta, 155-56; aware of military operations, 215; lawsuit against, 177; memorandum, 256n56; rank, 101n; receiving memorandum on Horman and Teruggi's case, 133; role in Horman-Teruggi case, 106, 111-12, 113, 120-21
Hook, Jim, 221
Hoover, J. Edgar, 17, 242n25
Horman, Charles Edmund, 1, 5, 89, 217-18; arrival to Vicuña Mackenna after coup, 71, 74-75; call to Walter Locke, 54; career in journalism, 15, 18; commitment to workers' movement, 47-48; connection with MIR, 158-59; conversation with American officers, 66-70; detained by Chilean soldiers, 85-86; Don Lenzer, request for money for weapons, 50-51; letters to, 16, 19-20, 22, 47, 48, 241n12; early life, 13; enforced disappearance of, 127-29; evidence of execution in Chilean military custody, 127-28, 137; film projects in Chile, 37-38; fingerprints identification, 119-20, 124-33, 175, 214, 257n69, 259n79; freelance assignments for newspapers, 38; friends in Chile, 19-22, 36-37; González's accusations about detention and execution of, 145-47; González's retraction of accusations on U.S. role, 147-51, 153, 201; graduation from Harvard, 15; honored by Chile's president, 220; internal dilemma between activism and observation, 18; involvement in Civil Rights Movement, 13-15; involvement in projects at Chile Films, 39-41; Jerry Cotts, request for money from, 53; journey to Chile, 22-23; Joyce Horman, letter to, 85; Joyce Horman, marriage with, 16; library of Marxist literature, 160-61; Mark Harris, letter to, 19; meeting with Locke and Reyes after coup, 75-76; political associations and actions, 8, 17-18; portrayal of Chileans, 36; preparation to leave Chile after coup, 84-85; protest at Democratic National Convention, writing about, 17; raising money for Cordones weapons, workers movement, 49-54; return to Santiago from New York, 55; Richard Pearce, request for money from, 51-52; sightseeing in Chile, 59-60; Simon Blattner, request for money from, 53-54; slandered as anti-American extremists, 133-37; Valparaiso experience, 66-70, 144-45; visit to parents in New York, 49-50; work with de la Barra's production house, 77; work with Mark Harris, 15-16
Horman, Edmund (Ed), 16, 117-18, 220; accusations against U.S. government, 137-39; Carter's letter to, 206-7; contradicted by U.S. government spokesperson, 138; documentation of Charles's case, 257n67; Hauser about, 118; meeting with Ambassador Davis, 119, 122; Meneses and Ortiz's revelation of Charles's execution, 210; Ortiz and Meneses's meeting with, 121-22, 124, 126, 138; search for Charles Horman, 119, 125; suspicions on U.S. Embassy officials, 164. *See also* Horman-Teruggi case; scenario of Edmund Horman

Horman, Elizabeth, 16, 49
Horman, Joyce, 16, 19, 55, 217, 220, 239n1, 249n103, 256n60; arrival in Chile, 36; caught out by curfew, 87; contact with Valenzuela, 256n54; Contreras Prieto's misinformation about Horman to, 122; film projects in Chile, 37–38; discovery of raid on house, 88; friendship with de la Barra, 19; lawsuit against Kissinger, 176–78, 225; Manitzas interview with, 165–66; preparation to leave Chile after coup, 84; Ray Davis, meeting with, 144; self-investigation for Charles Horman, 110, 112–15; sightseeing in Chile, 59–60; statement on Chilean court case, 252n13; statement on Horman-Teruggi case, 232; *Sunshine Grabber* animation project, 49; suspicions on U.S. Embassy officials, 164; U.S. Embassy's response on Horman's missing case to, 98
Horman-Teruggi case, 5, 216–17; analyzing method of court case, 228–29; Cadenasso acknowledges detention of Horman, 123; Chilean official's denial of eyewitness evidence, 205; concealing of Judd Kessler's information, 214–15; concealment of Charles Horman's body, 127–29; declassification of documents regarding, 197; distraction and deceiving by Chilean military in, 110–16; failure to follow up with Meneses and Ortiz, 210–13; identification process of bodies, 106–9; inaction of FBI officials, 213–14; lackluster approach of U.S. Embassy in, 102–3, 105; literature about, 223; military operations, 215–16; *New York Times* analytical stories on, 143–44; Ortiz and Meneses's contribution to, 121–26; Salas Wenzel's role in, 122–23; slandering as anti-American extremists, 133–37; sources in, 229–38; stadium eyewitnesses, 215; story of misplaced fingerprints, 124–33; Townley as witness of Teruggi's killers, 208–10. *See also* interrogations; trial in Chile
Horman v. Kissinger, 153, 176, 181, 225, 255n52, 266n41, 270n4, 271n13, 273–74n3
Housset Mera, Eliana, 131, 132–33
Howe, Marvine, 247–48n92, 248n93
Hubner, Douglas, 76
Huerta, Ismael, 258n73

Illich, Ivan, 20, 241n13
INDUMET factory: manufacture of weapons at, 57; resistance at, 72, 264n23
Innovation publication, 18
Intercultural Documentation Center (CIDOC), 20–21
interrogations: CAJSI for Santiago metropolitan area, 82–83; of Chilean prisoners, 82; with Elecmetal factory workers, 83; with Hathaway and Teruggi, 92; with Horman's friends and neighbors, 86–87; about killings of factory leaders, 84. *See also* Horman-Teruggi case; trial in Chile
"Ita." *See* Muñoz, Olga
"ITT Papers," 38, 165

Jamail, Milton, 21–22
Jaromir (Czech artist), 37
Jarvis, Lovell, 125, 215, 266n41
Javits, Jacob, 106, 118, 219
Johnson, Corki, 69
Johnson, Edward, 69
Johnson, Lyndon B., 17, 69, 189, 269n71
Josch, Melanie, 221
José "El Peláo," 42, 64–65

Kay, Diana, 243n34
Kemp, Jack, 257n66
Kennedy, Robert Francis, 16
Kennedy, Ted, 118, 120, 219
Kent State killings in United States, 4
Kessler, Judd, 119, 173, 205–6, 266n41; concealing Kessler's information by U.S. Embassy, 214–15; lawsuit against, 177; receiving information on Horman's death, 139; role in Horman-Teruggi case, 111; Sandoval's information about Charles's execution to, 170
King, Martin Luther, Jr., 16
Kissinger, Henry, 3, 244n43, 270n6; activities against Allende, 4–5; conversation with Nixon after Chilean coup, 96; support of new Chilean junta, 168; lawsuit against, 6, 146, 176–78, 225; listed as witness in Horman-Teruggi case, 267n55; Koch's letter regarding Horman's disappearance, 106
Kobliska, Jayne, 273n24
Koch, Edward, 106, 118, 219, 257n66
Kornbluh, Peter, 97n, 189–91, 220–21, 223–24, 231
"Kostas" Gavras, Konstantinos. *See* Costa-Gavras

INDEX

Krebs, Leslie, 34n, 39
Kreis, Rafael, 264n23
Kubisch, Jack B., 177

La Nacion newspaper, 47
Landau, Saul, 7, 221
latifundios, 31
"Leda," 42, 64–65
Leenson, Eric, 219
Lemmon, Jack, 174
Lenin, Vladimir, 33, 39
Lenzer, Don, 15, 50, 221; Horman asks him for money for weapons, 50–51; Horman's letters to, 16, 19–20, 22, 36, 39, 47–48, 241n13; about Horman's politics, 17–18; work in *Avenue of the Americas* film, 75n
Lepie, Jon, 34n
Lerner, Michael, 22
Lesser, Mishy, 21, 28–29, 33, 34, 34n, 220
Letelier, Fabiola, 184–85, 274n6
Letelier, Orlando, 7, 183, 204
Lledó, Rodrigo, 259n76, 273n26
Liliana Salazar, 61
Locke, Walter, 39, 40; finishing *Avenue of the Americas* film, 75, 75n; Horman's call from New York, 54
Luers, William, 198
Lutz, Augusto, 213, 265n26; González recants statements about, 226, 269n67; memorandum on Horman and Teruggi's death, 133–34, 258n71, 260n90; role in Horman-Teruggi case, 105, 113, 120–21
Lutz Herrera, Olga, 213, 259n76, 273n26

Macul Cordón, 61
Maldonado Fuentes, José, 250n5
"Manesas" (mispelling of Meneses), 124, 126, 138, 154, 180, 191, 212, 230, 251n11, 259n76, 264n22, 274n21. *See also* Meneses Pachet, Raúl
Manitzas, Elena, 221
Manitzas, Frank, 84, 145–46, 152, 165–66, 221, 225
Manuel Rodríguez Patriotic Front, 264–65n24
"Marcelo." *See* Alarcón, Fernando
Marín, Gladys, 215, 252n20
Marshall, Katherine, 138
marxism, 4, 17, 24, 25, 26, 90, 158
Marx, Karl, 22
Matta, Pedro Alejandro, 221

McNeil, (Frank) Francis, 193, 206
MCR. *See* Revolutionary Campesino Movement
Meneses Pachet, Raúl, 121, 258n72; identification of Charles Horman's body, 126, 129, 130–31; interview with Bonnefoy, 191–92, 272n24; investigation in Horman-Teruggi case, 122–25; meeting with Edmund Horman, 124, 126; about mistaken identity of Horman, 163; finds out raid at Horman's house was targeted, 158; revelation of identity, 272n20; statement on "extremist materials" in Horman's house, 160; U.S. Embassy's failure to follow up with, 210–13
Mestres, Lluis "Lucho," 37, 48, 49, 55, 75, 85, 249n103; caught out by curfew with Joyce Horman, 87; knowing about Horman's abduction, 88; Manitzas interview with, 165–66, 257n62
Meza Carvajal, Enrique, 73
Mezvinsky, Edward, 257n66
MHCHAOS Program, 188, 189
Military Intelligence Service. *See* Servicio de Inteligencia Militar (SIM)
Miller, George, 220
Miller, Henry, 22
Miller, Jeffrey, 21
MIR. *See* Movimiento Izquierda Revolucionaria
Miranda, Maga, 220
Missing (film), 5–7, 146, 147, 223–25, 267n48; ban in Chile, 176; Ed Horman's scenario based on, 173–76; Hauser's inspiration from Ed Horman's work, 118; narration of U.S. role in, 216; portrayal of Charles Horman in, 8, 11, 54; portrayal of González's appearance in, 150. *See also* Costa-Gavras
Mnookin, Robert, 240n1
Moffett, Toby, 220
Moffitt, Ronni, 7, 204
Monsalve, Raúl, 188–89
Montecino, Marcelo, 220
Morel, Enrique, 113–14, 256n57
motives, execution: arbitrary cruelty, 162–63; being foreigner and possessing leftist literature, 160–61; connection to MIR, 158–59; connection with Chile Films and Paredes, 159–60; connection with Cordones workers movement, 157–58; dossiers about activism, 161–62; González's statement, 163–64; Horman's research

motives, execution *(continued)*
into Schneider assassination, 164–66; mistaken identity of Charles Horman, 163. *See also* Horman-Teruggi case
Movement of the Revolutionary Left. *See* Movimiento Izquierda Revolucionaria (MIR)
Movimiento Izquierda Revolucionaria (MIR), 30, 32, 37, 42, 58, 64, 74, 77, 162, 261n91; actions after military rule in Chile, 61; creation of safe houses for clandestine activity, 57; preparation after Chilean coup, 61; Teruggi and Horman's connection with, 158–59
Mujica, Dolores, 251n5
Muñoz Alarcón, Juan, 263n10
Muñoz, Manuel, 190
Muñoz, Olga, 41, 42, 64, 90–91; clandestine work for MIR's Political Committee, 57–58, 159
Muskie, Edmund, 177, 270n4

NAAIC. *See* North American Anti-Imperialist Coalition
NACLA Report on the Americas magazine, 26
Napalm (documentary), 15
National Commission of Truth and Reconciliation (CNVR), 179, 216
National Liberation Army, 42
The Nation magazine, 18
Needleman, Ruth, 34n
Neruda, Pablo, *Spain in Our Hearts*, 2–3
New Left, 4, 17, 197
New York Times: early stories on Horman-Teruggi case, 143–44; "ITT Papers," 165
Nezzo, Carol, 255n46
Nixon, Richard, 3, 26, 247n81; activities against Allende, 4–5; conversation with Kissinger after Chilean coup, 96; support of new Chilean junta, 168
Non-Commissioned Officers School, 92
North American Anti-Imperialist Coalition (NAAIC), 135
North American News Source. See *Fuente de Información Norteamericana (FIN)*
Novoa, Oscar, 132
Núñez, Julio, 59, 86, 246n77, 260n84

Ochoa-Kaup, Enrique, 221
Omang, Joanne, 146, 152, 225
Operation Condor, 180–81, 268n62, 247n86
Orrego, Guillermo, 72–74, 221

Ortiz, Jaime, 121, 272n20; identification of Charles Horman's body, 126, 129, 130–31; interview with Bonnefoy, 191–92; investigating raid at Horman's house, 158; investigation in Horman-Teruggi case, 122–25; meeting with Edmund Horman, 124, 126; question to Joyce about Horman's association with *FIN*, 161; U.S. Embassy's failure to follow up with, 210–13
Osborne, Catherine, 221
Osorio, Carlos, 220
Osorio, Guillermo, 264n23
Osorio, Victoria, 85
Overbeck, Peter, 40, 41n

Page, Janis Teruggi, 24, 182, 221
Paredes, Eduardo "Coco," 41, 76–77, 129, 159–60, 265n26
Parrau, Celsa, 245n70, 264n23
Patria y Libertad, 57, 209, 246n81
Pearce, Richard, 11, 15, 21, 51–53, 221, 265n27
Pedagogy of the Oppressed (Freire), 241n13
Perán, Aldo, 221
PICH. *See* Policia de Investigaciones de Chile
Pinochet, Augusto, 56, 105, 113, 122; Ambassador Davis raises issue of disappeared Americans with, 120; leads coup against Allende, 5; military rule in Chile, 60–61, 63; Operation Condor investigation against, 179–80; relations with U.S. government, 96
The Pinochet File (Kornbluh), 97n
Pizarro Vicencio, Óscar Ernesto, 252n18
Policia de Investigaciones de Chile (PICH), 41, 132, 244n46, 254n42; investigations of Horman murder, 105–6, 116, 121, 214; role of Baeza in, 129–30. *See also* Rojas, Mario
Political Military Group. *See* Grupo Politico Militar (GPM5)
Popper, David, 137, 151, 202
Popular Unity. *See* Unidad Popular (UP)
Prats, Carlos, 44, 56, 262n5
PROA. *See* Producciones Americanas
Producciones Americanas (PROA), 66–67, 247n88
Puga, Ana Maria, 250n107
Punto Final magazine, 58
Purdy, Frederick, 79, 99–101, 173; actions to protect new Chilean junta, 155–56; confirmation of Charles Horman's death,

126; delayed notification to Teruggi family, 215; fingerprint check, 259n79; Hathaway's release into custody of, 108; interview with, 254n35; lawsuit against, 146, 177; meeting with Ed Horman, 118; receives false report on Teruggi, 107; receiving information about Horman, 261n96; role in Horman-Teruggi case, 106–7, 111, 114, 119, 132, 214; told to limit inquiries on Horman-Teruggi case, 79, 132, 206
Purdy, Gigi Mohn, 221

Que Hacer (film), 265n27
Queridos Compañeros (Dear Comrades) (film), 77

Rabinovitz, Susan, 34n
radicals, 4, 17, 197
Rapid Transit Guerrilla Communications, 25
Rastello, Isabella, 87, 88
Rauch, Rudolph "Ru," 146, 152, 263n18
The Redwoods (documentary), 15
Resistance in the Armed Forces (RITA), 27–28
Revolutionary Campesino Movement (MCR), 29
Revolutionary Students Front. *See* Frente de Estudiantes Revolucionarios (FER)
Reyes, Jorge, 39, 40, 71; finishing *Avenue of the Americas* film, 75n; post-coup meeting with Horman, 75–76
RITA. *See* Resistance in the Armed Forces
Rodríguez, Jorge, 251n10
Rojas, Carolina, 220
Rojas, Mario, 124; investigation of Horman's disappearance, 129–32, 214
Ryan, Charlotte, 34n
Ryan, Patrick J., 66, 171, 173, 257n62; lawsuit against, 177; libel suit by, 146; meeting with Horman and Simon, 68–69, 144

Saint Jean, Heliette, 88
Salas Wenzel, Hugo, 122–23, 158, 211, 264n24, 272n20
San Borja Towers, 34–35
Sandoval, Enrique, 111; information about Horman's execution, 170, 214–15; mentions dossiers on Horman, 161–62
Sandoval, Nelson, 111, 111n, 259n77, 266n41; information about Horman's execution, 170, 215

Santos Lopes, Paulo, 41–42, 61; recalling Teruggi and Horman's military ship photos, 58; searching for hideout after Chilean coup, 64–65
scenario of Edmund Horman, 168–69; appears confirmed by González's statement, 169–72; basis for Costa-Gavras's *Missing* film, 173–76; basis for *Joyce Horman et al., v. Henry Kissinger et al.*, lawsuit, 176–78; endorsed in Hauser's *The Execution of Charles Horman*, 171–73; "The View after Three Years" report, 169. *See also* Horman, Edmund (Ed); Horman-Teruggi case
Scherrer, Robert, 210, 213–14
Schesch, Adam, 114, 254n32, 255n46
Schneider, Rene, 38, 164–66; Viaux-Schnieder case, 166, 188, 243n40, 269n67
Schwaetzer, Thomas. *See* Watts, Max
SDS. *See* Students for a Democratic Society
Servicio de Inteligencia Militar (SIM), 82, 82n, 121, 122, 123, 125, 130–33, 151, 171, 180, 209
Shawcross, William, 144, 147–48, 150, 190, 226, 235, 262n4
Shemo, Diana Jean, 198
Shlaudeman, Harry, 196, 199–201, 270n6
Sikkink, Kathryn, 273n2
SIM. *See* Servicio de Inteligencia Militar
Simons, Marlise, 262n5
Simon, Terry, 49, 110, 164, 249n103; arrival to Vicuña Mackenna after coup, 74–75; conversation with American officers in Valparaiso, 66–70; and Horman's Valparaiso experience, 144–45; notes and chronology on September events, 232–33; preparation to leave Chile after coup, 84; sightseeing in Chile, 59–60
Smith, Frederick, 161, 199–201, 217, 229, 270n6
Sontag, Susan, 20
Soto Mackenney, Roberto, 132, 192, 258n75
Spacek, Sissy, 174
Spain, Spanish Civil War, 2–3, 218
Spain in Our Hearts (poem by Neruda), 2–3
Spence, Jack, 34n
Stafford, Robert T., 207
Standard Electric factory, 72
State and Revolution (Lenin), 39
State of Siege (film), 267n48
Steenland, Kyle, 34n

Steven, Robert S., 103-4, 221, 266n43; Chilean official raised Cordones factor in case, 157; examining Lutz report, 136-37; interviews regarding Horman-Teruggi case, 198, 199; writing memo regarding Horman-Teruggi case, 195-97
St. George's College, Santiago, Chile, 25, 242n20
Stone, Izzy, 223
Stout, Charles R., 226, 271n9
Students for a Democratic Society (SDS), 25
Sumar Textile factory, rain on, 57, 72, 74
The Sunday Times newspaper, 147
Sunshine Grabber animation project, 37-38, 49
Sweezy, Paul, 22

Tancazo (coup attempt in Chile), 44-47, 49, 57, 83
Terrorismo de Estadio (Bonnefoy), 191
Teruggi, Frank, 1, 11, 14, 90, 217-18; activities after Chilean coup, 61; activities before Chilean coup, 58; association with German antiwar group, 27-28; detained by Chilean soldiers, 90-92; education, 24-25, 26; evidence of execution in Chilean military custody, 127-28; false report by Chilean Embassy, 107; fingerprints identification, 107-9; family history, 24; FER, connection with, 29, 42; journey to Chile, 28-29; library of Marxist literature, 160-61; MIR, connection with, 32, 64, 158-59; Mirista housemates in Chile, 41-42; opposition to Vietnam War, 26; political associations and actions, 8; role in *FIN*, 33-34; burning documents after Chilean coup, 64-65; described as anti-American extremist, 133-37; studying economics in Chile, 32-33, 220; during Tancazo, 45-47; work in CAGLA, 26-27
Teruggi, Frank, Sr., 24
Teruggi, Johanna, 24
Teruggi, John, 24
Teruggi Bombatch, Frank Randall, 252n18
Textil Progreso factory, 72-73
Thieme, Roberto, 57
Thompson, Herbert, 102, 173, 272n20
Tipton, John, 173, 266n43
Tipton, Marian, 177
tomas, 31
Torres, Alberto, 191
Townley, Michael, 101, 208-10, 272n18
trabajo voluntario, 29

Trabucco, Sergio, 221
transportation strike in Chile (1972), 43-44
trial in Chile, 179; Bonnefoy and Kornbluh's role in, 191-93; compensatory damages to Horman and Teruggi families, 183; discussion with Judge Mario Carroza, 185-86; flawed use of evidence, 186-90; Guzmán's investigations, 180-81; statements of family lawyer Fabiola Letelier, 184-85; proceedings to extradite Davis, 183; Zepeda's investigations, 181-83, 184, 186-87, 189-90. *See also* Horman-Teruggi case
Trotsky, Leon, 22
Tupamaro exiles, 42

UNCTAD. *See* United Nations Conference on Trade and Development
Unidad Popular (UP), 21, 32
UNITAS, 58, 60, 68
United Nations Conference on Trade and Development (UNCTAD), 35
United States (U.S.): Allende, covert actions against, 95-96, 96-97n, 168; involvement in Vietnam War, 3-4, 15; Kent State killings, 4; South American countries, covert actions in, 216
United States (U.S.) Embassy: charge of coverup by, 8, 202, 208; Davidow's statement, 202-4; concealing Kessler's information by, 214-15; failure to conduct authentic investigation, 155; failure to protect American citizens during Chilean coup, 100-104; inquiries on Horman-Teruggi case, 110-11, 115-16, 205-6; internal investigation, 207-8; lackluster approach to Horman-Teruggi cases, 102-3, 105; pressure from U.S. press about detained American citizens, 99-100; report of Horman and Teruggi's detentions, 97-99
United States (U.S.) alleged involvement/role in execution: Fimbres-Driscoll memo about, 195-202; González accusation, 145-47, 167, 195, 224; Hauser's accusation, 6; theory of, 225. *See also* Horman-Teruggi case; trial in Chile
UP. *See* Unidad Popular
Urrutia, Carlos, 96-97, 101, 113, 256n57

Valenzuela, Camilo, 38, 112, 159
Vallejos Ferdinand, Guillermo Osvaldo, 252n18

INDEX

Valparaiso, 58, 60, 66–70, 143–47, 164, 228, 249n102
Van Lancker, Andre, 94, 215
Vásquez Godoy, Ernesto, 252n18
Vecchi, Ariela, 59
Velastín Rodriguez, Victor Eduardo, 215, 94, 253n21
Viaux, Roberto, 38, 166, 188; Viaux-Schnieder case, 166, 188, 243n40, 269n67
Vidal, Paulina, 30, 61
Vietnam War (1954–1975) 4, 26; U.S. involvement in, 3–4, 15
Volk, Dinah, 34
Volk, Steven, 34, 34n, 219, 220–21, 249n103, 252n16, 256n60; failed search in morgue for Horman's body, 119, 260n88; identification of Teruggi's body, 108; reporting detention of Teruggi and Hathaway, 107; statement on what Horman may have learned in Valparaiso, 144; suggestion of dependency theory, 40
Vuskovic, Pedro, 30–31

Wallem, Mark, 239n1
Warlow, Henry, 114
Watts, Max, 27, 242n24
Wine, Linda, 220
WOLA, 219
Wool, Julius, 255n46

Z (film), 37, 39
Zepeda Arancibia, Jorge, 153, 184, 214, 228, 258n75, 261n91, 268n59; citing CIA's CHAOS program, 189; failure to follow up with Meneses and Ortiz, 212–13; ignoring González retraction in verdict, 228; indictment on Pedro Espinóza, 182–83; investigation of Horman-Teruggi case, 181, 186–87; reliance on González's testimony, 190

Founded in 1893,
UNIVERSITY OF CALIFORNIA PRESS
publishes bold, progressive books and journals
on topics in the arts, humanities, social sciences,
and natural sciences—with a focus on social
justice issues—that inspire thought and action
among readers worldwide.

The UC PRESS FOUNDATION
raises funds to uphold the press's vital role
as an independent, nonprofit publisher, and
receives philanthropic support from a wide
range of individuals and institutions—and from
committed readers like you. To learn more, visit
ucpress.edu/supportus.

www.ingramcontent.com/pod-product-compliance
Lightning Source LLC
Jackson TN
JSHW081653230325
81254JS00001B/2